PRIMA OFFICIAL GAME GUIDE

Written by:

Fernando Bueno

Senior Product Marketing Manager: Donato Tica
Design & Layout: Bryan Neff, Jody Seltzer
Copyeditor: Carrie Andrews
Next-Gen Maps: David Bueno
Manufacturing: Stephanie Sanchez & Suzanne Goodwin

This guide would have not been possible without the support of Bertrand Estrallado, Johnny Szary, Mark Friesen, Devin Hitch, Vince Kudirka, Dan Wasson, Stephen Ervin, Katy Walden, Chong Kai, Jeff Sangalli, Jia Tan, Amy Beth Christenson, Stephen Chang, Gregory Harsh, Gavin Leung, Katya Alexandra King, and Anne Marie Hawkins.

Important:
Prima Games has made every effort to determine that the information contained in this book is accurate. However, the publisher makes no warranty, either expressed or implied, as to the accuracy, effectiveness, or completeness of the material in this book; nor does the publisher assume liability for damages, either incidental or consequential, that may result from using the information in this book. The publisher cannot provide any additional information or support regarding gameplay, hints and strategies, or problems with hardware or software. Such questions should be directed to the support numbers provided by the game and/or device manufacturers as set forth in their documentation. Some game tricks require precise timing and may require repeated attempts before the desired result is achieved.

ISBN: 978-0-307-46909-0
Library of Congress Catalog Card Number: 2010936720
Printed in the United States of America

10 11 12 13 LL 10 9 8 7 6 5 4 3 2 1

Prima Games
An Imprint of Random House, Inc.
3000 Lava Ridge Court, Suite 100
Roseville, CA 95661
www.primagames.com

CONTENTS

INTRODUCTION

Acknowledgements

There was no better way for me to revisit the world of *Star Wars: The Force Unleashed* than by entering another world I love just as much—the Prima Games offices. After spending nearly a month with them, I was reminded of just how much fun that entire office can be.

Thanks to Don "Vader" Tica for everything. He's a great product manager, an amazing coworker, and a best friend. Thanks to Carrie Andrews and Jody Seltzer; you guys are my favorite team. Muchas gracias to the great folks at LucasArts. Had it not been for Bertrand Estrellado, Johnny Szary, Mark Friesen, Devin Hitch, Vince Kudirka, and the rest of the LucasArts crew, this guide would not have gotten done. Best of all, they're great guys too! Thanks for being so accommodating on my all-too-brief visit.

Previously on *Star Wars: The Force Unleashed...*

When Anakin Skywalker turned to the dark side, he became Lord Vader. In the wake of Order 66, the Dark Lord began to hunt down the remaining Jedi. When he encountered a Jedi on the planet of Kashyyyk, he got more than he bargained for. The Jedi was no more powerful than any other Jedi that Vader had already defeated, but there was something present that was far more connected to the Force than the rogue Jedi—his son.

Though barely a toddler, the Jedi's son was highly skilled in the ways of the Force. After striking down the rogue Jedi, Vader saved the boy and raised him in secret. The child's power grew just as he did.

When it was time, Vader unleashed his secret apprentice, code-named Starkiller, on the remaining Jedi in the galaxy. But while Starkiller hunted and destroyed the last of the Jedi, there was a darker plot brewing.

While Starkiller thought that ridding the galaxy of Jedi was his destiny, it was actually Vader's plan to train Starkiller and use him to overthrow the Emperor.

While Starkiller traversed the galaxy hunting Jedi after Jedi, trouble was brewing in the Galactic Empire. The Emperor was no fool; he sniffed out Vader's betrayal! To prove to the Emperor that he was loyal, Vader turned on his secret apprentice and ran his lightsaber through him.

The Emperor was satisfied with Vader's show of loyalty and returned to his ship as Starkiller's lifeless body drifted deep into space.

But Vader was not done with his secret apprentice. He salvaged Starkiller's body and created a new plot to overthrow the Emperor. Starkiller was to secretly locate the remaining Jedi, join them, and create a Rebel Alliance to distract the Emperor. While the Emperor was distracted by the Rebel Alliance's uprising, Vader and Starkiller would strike!

The Dark Lord's plan worked. Starkiller united the remaining Jedi with the help of his first victim, Master Rahm Kota. The pair traveled the galaxy uniting the Rebels in their common cause until Starkiller was once again betrayed by his master.

This was the final straw. Having been betrayed twice by his master and swayed by his love for Juno Eclipse—the captain assigned to his ship, the *Rogue Shadow*—Starkiller finally turned to the side of light.

He hunted down his master, Lord Vader, and confronted him. As Vader nearly fell to Starkiller's lightsaber, Starkiller was faced with a choice: destroy Vader and join the Emperor, or strike down the Emperor and free the Rebel leaders.

His decision made, Starkiller attacked the Emperor and allowed the Rebel leaders to escape. However, the Emperor was too strong. He defeated Starkiller but was unable to destroy the Rebels too.

The Rebel Alliance would meet in secret, just as Starkiller intended, and would rally around their martyred leader. The Rebel Alliance was born, but what happened to Starkiller's body?

NEIMOIDIAN NOTES

All screens in this chapter were taken from *Star Wars: The Force Unleashed: Ultimate Sith Edition*. You may know the story, but why not go back and experience it? Pick up the game and *be* Starkiller!

How to Use This Book

This book covers many versions of *Star Wars: The Force Unleashed II*. In order to provide you thorough walkthroughs of the Xbox 360, PlayStation 3, and Wii versions of the game, we've split the walkthrough into two parts. Jump to the corresponding section of the walkthrough for the version of the game that you purchased.

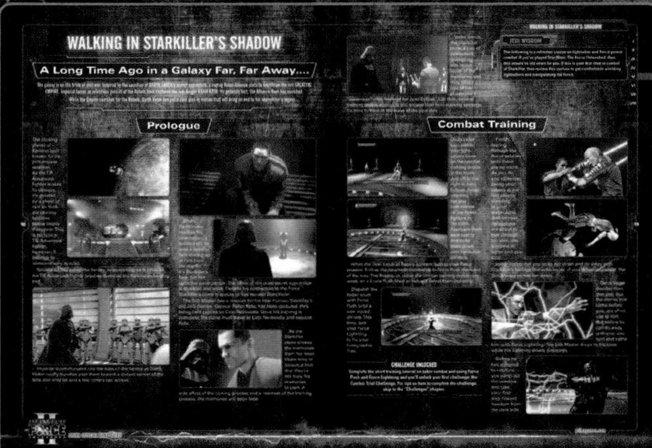

Xbox 360 and PlayStation 3

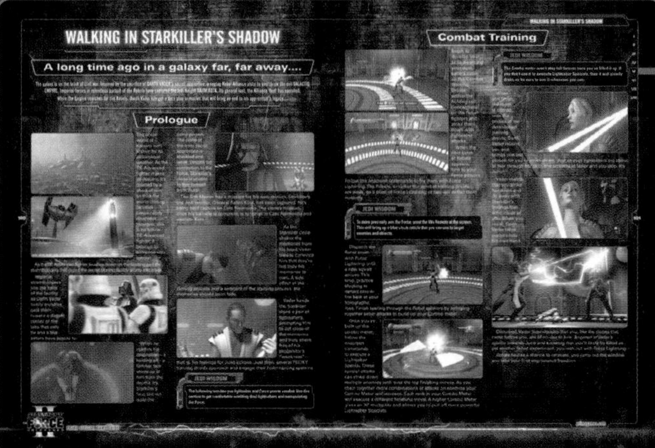

Wii

NEIMOIDIAN NOTES, CLONER'S CAUTION, AND JEDI WISDOM BOXES

Scattered across this book are several different boxes full of useful information.

JEDI WISDOM

The Jedi Wisdom boxes are specifically designed to make you a stronger opponent of the dark side. These boxes will often bring to light a stronger approach, make you a stronger combatant, or even help you increase your skill.

CLONER'S CAUTION

Cloner's Caution boxes have one purpose: to keep you alive. The cloners of Kamino have not stayed in business this long without having strong survival skills. The oceanic planet of Kamino can be harsh. If you're going to trust anything to keep you alive, trust the Cloner's Caution boxes!

NEIMOIDIAN NOTES

The Neimodian Notes boxes don't help keep you alive or improve your skills as a fighter, but they do share tidbits of info about the game, the world of *Star Wars: The Force Unleashed*, and this book. Feel free to ignore these if you'd like, but it certainly couldn't hurt to check them out!

CONSOLE-SPECIFIC BOXES

While all versions of the game have holocron boxes, there are a few other box-outs that are specific to each version of the game. The Xbox 360/PlayStation 3 version has Achievement and Trophy Unlocked Boxes. Meanwhile, the Wii version has Item Found boxes that do not appear in the Xbox 360/PlayStation 3 walkthrough. Read on for more information on all the different box-outs that appear in the walkthrough!

HOLOCRON

Holocron boxes appear in both sections of the walkthrough. They reveal the location of all the holocrons available throughout your adventure. Pick them up to unlock everything from saber crystals in the Xbox 360/PlayStation 3 version to experience points in the Wii version!

ACHIEVEMENT/TROPHY UNLOCKED

This box appears only in the Xbox 360/PlayStation 3 section of the walkthrough. These boxes will tell you how to unlock special achievements or trophies that appear only in these two versions of the game.

CHALLENGE UNLOCKED

The Xbox 360/PlayStation 3 versions also have special challenges that you can unlock throughout your single-player adventure. These boxes will highlight every location where you can unlock a new challenge. There are 10 challenges total.

ITEM FOUND

Item Found boxes appear only in the Wii walkthrough. Even though the Xbox 360/PlayStation 3 version also has saber crystal and bacta tank upgrades to unlock, you unlock these by finding holocrons. In the Wii version, you must find the actual item to unlock. For example, in order to unlock a green color crystal, you must actually find the green color crystal in the game. Keep an eye out for these to find everything from power crystals to Force Energy Tanks!

THE CAST

Playable Characters

STARKILLER'S CLONE

Darth Vader's secret apprentice, Starkiller, may have perished, but that didn't stop the Dark Lord from creating an army of Starkiller clones. After several failed attempts, Vader is confident that this clone is exactly what he needs—a new puppet to control, a powerful Force wielder who can succeed where Starkiller failed...a clone that will fulfill Starkiller's destiny.

When he escapes, however, Starkiller's clone proves that even though he may have Starkiller's powers, memories, and master, he still has the power to choose his own destiny.

Nonplayable Characters

JUNO ECLIPSE

Juno Eclipse is a talented pilot who was once employed by the Galactic Empire. Hand-chosen by Darth Vader, Juno became Starkiller's private pilot while he hunted the rogue Jedi across the galaxy. Over time, however, Juno and Starkiller fell in love. When it came time for Starkiller to make his final decision, his choice was guided by a single, peaceful thought: Juno.

In the wake of Starkiller's death, Juno joined the Rebel Alliance and became an integral part of the Rebellion. But when Starkiller's clone escaped from Kamino, Juno's destiny became intertwined with the clone's. Now she's become a pawn in Vader's game of control over Starkiller's clone.

BOBA FETT

Boba Fett is a galaxy-class bounty hunter. With no job too big, Boba Fett is always busy chasing after a bounty. Boba Fett comes from a long line of Mandalorian mercenaries; he was cloned and raised by none other than Jango Fett, the prototype soldier for the Galactic Empire's clone army.

Now that Starkiller's clone is on the loose, Darth Vader hires the bounty hunter to capture his rogue clone. Accompanied by a squad of Vader's terror troopers, Boba Fett terrorizes the galaxy on his quest to recover the clone.

GENERAL RAHM KOTA

Master Kota is one of the few remaining Jedi in the galaxy. When he first encountered Starkiller, he almost became the apprentice's first victim. By a stroke of luck (or fate?), Kota survived Starkiller's attack and eventually became his Jedi mentor.

When Starkiller fell, however, the general took Starkiller's charge and became one of the Rebel Alliance's fearless leaders—that is, until he was captured by Baron Tarko. Now that he's under Tarko's thumb, Kota struggles daily in the Tarko-se arena.

MASTER YODA

Few Jedi have the connection to the Force as powerful as Master Yoda's. Master Yoda is one of the last remaining Jedi, and his wisdom is still a great well for others to draw from. Unbeknownst to the Galactic Empire, Master Yoda now makes the swampy planet of Dagobah his home.

PROXY

PROXY, Starkiller's prototype holodroid, once helped the secret apprentice hone his combat skills, but when his master was destroyed, PROXY continued the fight alongside Juno. Eventually PROXY was scrapped, then saved, and now he works alongside Captain Eclipse.

BARON TARKO

Baron Tarko is a powerful man. The tyrant presides over his own private city, Tarko-se, where he runs a battle arena. As a member of the Galactic Empire, the baron works with Darth Vader to keep a firm grip on Tarko-se City. Rumor has it that Baron Tarko has a very special pet hidden under the arena.

Enemies

IMPERIAL SOLDIERS

Imperial Stormtroopers and Stormtrooper Commanders

The Imperial stormtrooper is on the lowest rung of the Galactic Empire's ladder. However, just because they're among the weakest of the clone army doesn't mean they're not dangerous. The Imperial stormtrooper never travels alone and is always equipped with a blaster rifle.

The stormtrooper commanders are a bit tougher than their lesser counterparts. In addition to blaster rifles, the commanders also carry thermal detonators. Eliminate stormtroopers and their commanders easily with Force power attacks or simple saber combos.

NEIMOIDIAN NOTES

Stormtrooper commanders appear only in the Wii version of the game. Though the commander looks almost identical to the regular stormtrooper, he can be identified by the pad on his right shoulder.

Imperial Jumptrooper

Like stormtroopers, jumptroopers are Imperial soldiers equipped with blaster rifles. However, these soldiers are also equipped with jet packs, allowing them to fly and hover. The jumptrooper's ability to fly makes him difficult to reach with saber attacks. To eliminate this pesky foe, you must first clip his wings with Force Lightning.

Zap jumptroopers to short their jet packs and bring them back to ground level. Once they're back on the ground, strike them down with saber combos or finish them off with other Force power attacks.

NEIMOIDIAN NOTES

In the Xbox 360 and PS3 versions of the game, just fry their jet packs with Lightning. They'll short out and go down with one blast; there's no need to follow up with other attacks.

Imperial Scout Troopers

Unlike stormtroopers and commanders, scout troopers aren't equipped with regular blasters. They carry high-powered blaster rifles capable of blasting you from across great distances. Rarely do scout troopers travel alone, making them even more dangerous. Once a scout trooper locks in on you, he'll track you until he's got a clean shot. One blast of the scout trooper's sniper rifle will knock you off your feet long enough for his comrades to fire their rifles as well.

Whenever you enter a new area, look for the red targeting beam to reveal the presence of a scout trooper. If you see a red laser beam honing in on you, zigzag away from it so the scout trooper can't lock on and fire. Follow the laser beam to its source and eliminate the scout trooper just as you would a stormtrooper.

JEDI WISDOM

Mind Tricking scout troopers into becoming allies is a great tactic to use in large rooms. Not only will they turn on other Imperials, but also they'll typically be out of reach of retaliation.

Proxy

Baron Tarko

Imperial Stormtrooper

Imperial Jumptrooper

Imperial Scout Trooper

Imperial Riot Trooper

The riot trooper is one of the few primary melee combatants. Armed with an electrostaff, these melee specialists are highly skilled combatants capable of holding their own even against talented Jedi. Rather than attack these warriors with saber combos, attack them first with Force powers such as Lightning. Once stunned, the riot trooper is vulnerable to saber combos, so follow up with your lightsabers or wipe them out with more Force power attacks.

TERROR SOLDIERS

Terror Trooper

The terror trooper is one of the most insidious enemies in the game. Rather than face you head-on, terror troopers employ hit-and-run tactics while cloaked. Though they don't carry any weapons, they are very skilled hand-to-hand combatants. Combined with their ability to disappear, the terror troopers truly live up to their name as they terrorize targets, slashing at them from every angle while invisible. Some terror troopers can also generate electrical and flame projectiles, making them even deadlier.

To eliminate these foes, you must first make them visible, or rather force them to stay visible. When they appear, either stun them with Force Lightning or Mind Trick, then strike them down with saber combos while they're unable to disappear again.

JEDI WISDOM

In the Wii version of the game, you can use Force Vision to reveal the terror troopers' locations. While Force Vision is active, terror troopers will appear as bright blue silhouettes while invisible.

Terror Spider Droids

The terror spider droid is a small, spiderlike droid that attaches itself to its target and attacks with fierceness. These mechanical critters never appear alone and will swarm around their target in great numbers, attacking from all sides. If left unchecked, terror spider droids can quickly overwhelm their victim before they can even see them coming.

Whenever these spider droids attack, use Force Repulse to repel them. If the Force shock wave doesn't destroy them, it will at least temporarily repel them. Once upgraded, Force Repulse can destroy several terror spider droids with just one blast.

Terror Giant

Terror giants are large, hulking droids capable of slashing through even the toughest Jedi. Their massive arms are razor-sharp and, coupled with the giant's extraordinary speed, is extremely lethal from a distance. Terror giants dash toward their prey with great speed and stab their enemy with deadly precision.

If they miss, terror giants typically get stuck in the ground as their giant spikelike arms pierce the ground. Seize the opportunity and attack while they're stuck in the ground. Use Force Lightning and saber attacks to dish out damage, then follow the onscreen commands to finish them off.

NEIMOIDIAN NOTES

Terror giants appear only in the Xbox 360 and PS3 versions of the game.

SITH SOLDIERS

Saber Guard

Saber guards are tough enemies that have been trained in the dual-lightsaber arts. Like the riot trooper, these combatants are skilled in weapons combat, so attack them with Force powers first before launching into saber combat. If you attack the saber guard with saber attacks right away, be sure to use well-timed blocks to keep them off balance.

A combination of Force powers and saber combat is the best way to dispose of a saber guard. Of course, saber guards rarely attack alone, so practice moving from enemy to enemy as you string your saber attacks together into combos. If you focus on one saber guard while others are around, you're asking to be slashed to ribbons.

Imperial Riot Trooper

Terror Trooper

Terror Giant

Saber Guard

Terror Spider Droid

Sith Acolyte

The Sith acolyte is a powerful Force wielder. He's so powerful, in fact, that he doesn't require weapons of any kind. Acolytes typically attack using Force projectiles, Repulse-like attacks, and hand-to-hand combat. Because they are Force wielders, they are also Force-resistant. Force attacks such as Push, Lightning, and Mind Trick have no effect on them at first.

The only way to make them vulnerable to Force attacks is to weaken them first with saber combos. Do not approach an acolyte and attack with Force powers right away. Primarily use saber attacks against these warriors.

NEIMOIDIAN NOTES

Sith acolytes appear only in the Xbox 360 and PS3 versions of the game.

Dark Clone

You are not the only animated clone that exists. In fact, in his attempt to create the perfect Starkiller clone, Vader created an army of them. Only a few were able to survive long enough to move on to training; many others were failed experiments that resulted in mutant aberrations. Still, Vader has his uses for these monstrosities. Many of the dark clones have an innate ability to wield the Force and are capable of creating Force Lightning projectiles. Others can fire powerful flame attacks.

Because they are nothing more than animated flesh, these zombielike clones can be easily turned with Mind Trick. Whenever you encounter a dark clone, either dispatch them with attacks of your choice or turn them into allies with Mind Trick.

MECHANICAL MENACES

War Droids

War droids are large mechanical menaces that come in two variations: carbonite and incinerator. Both types of war droids carry massive shields that protect them from attacks, so your first step in taking one down is to rip away its shield using Force Grip. Once it's unprotected, use the Force to grip their fireball or carbonite projectiles in midair, then fire them back at the clunkers.

Whittle them down with Force Lightning as you avoid their attacks by dashing away. Mix in a few Lightning-infused saber combos, then finish them off.

AT-ST

The All Terrain Scout Transport, or AT-ST, is an integral part of the Imperial army. Standing several feet tall, these walkers are intimidating foes. Not only are they highly maneuverable, but also their blaster turrets and thermal detonators make them deadly stalkers. There's no way to minimize their blaster fire—blocking does little to nothing—so dash away from their blaster fire and use their thermal detonators against them when they hurl them at you.

AT-MP

Don't mistake these compact walkers for weaker versions of the AT-ST. In fact, the AT-MP is far more dangerous than its larger cousin. Even though it's smaller, it's quicker, and instead of using thermal detonators that simply lay on the ground once fired, the AT-MP uses highly accurate heat-seeking missiles to hunt you down and blast you to bits. If two AT-MPs gang up on you, they can easily pepper you with missiles and keep you grounded until you rejoin the Force.

Use the AT-MP's most powerful weapon against it. Either Force Grip the missile in midair and send it back, or time your blocks just as the missiles are about to hit you to reflect them back at the walker. A healthy dose of Force Lightning also helps bring down these walkers with ease.

NEIMOIDIAN NOTES

You can not deflect or Force Grip an AT-MP's missiles in the Wii version.

Sith Acolyte

Dark Clone

Carbonite War Droid

AT-ST

AT-MP

TIE Fighter

TIE fighters are small, agile starfighters. These single pilot ships can't travel long distances alone—they require a host ship nearby and rely on large numbers to overwhelm their enemies. Despite their short range, TIE fighters are the most relied-upon vehicles in the Galactic Empire. Use Force Grip to grab these enemies out of the sky and crush them in midair.

NEIMOIDIAN NOTES

These enemies appear only in the Xbox 360 and PS3 versions of the game.

OTHER ENEMIES

Ugnaughts

Ughnaughts are small, mysterious creatures. They are the working force of Baron Tarko's city. They're not particularly tough, so when angered, they attack in packs. Dispatch them using Force Repulse and saber combos.

BOSS ENEMIES

Bosses are unique enemies. Each boss requires a very specific approach to defeat it, depending on the version of the game you're playing. To find out how, skip to their respective chapters in the walkthrough.

Gorog

The Gorog is a massive creature made of 90 percent muscle, nine percent rage, and one percent brain. It's a beast and nothing more. Now the Gorog lives under the baron's arena. Were it not for the shackle supports the baron installed in the arena, he'd have no way to control the monster.

Terror Walker

The terror walker is a droid boss much like terror spider droids, only they are much, much bigger. It's an arachnid-like droid equipped with lasers and a protective shield. The only way to make it vulnerable to attack is to remove its shield first.

Darth Vader

Darth Vader is the embodiment of all evil. Under the guidance of Emperor Palpatine—aka Darth Sidious—Lord Vader controls the Galactic Empire with an iron fist. He's an unparalleled lightsaber combatant and an even more capable Force wielder. Behind every dark occurrence in the galaxy, you can be sure to find Darth Vader's cybernetic hand at work.

TIE Fighter

Gorog

Terror Walker

Darth Vader

Ugnaughts

I
II
III
IV
V
VI
VII
VIII

A FRESH START

Just because you're Starkiller's clone doesn't mean that everything will come easy to you. Even Starkiller struggled to get a grip on his powers at first. This chapter will show you how to take control of your own destiny.

NEIMOIDIAN NOTES

This section of the book covers the Xbox 360 and PlayStation 3 only. For Wii-specific information, skip to the "Welcome to the Wii" chapter to learn more!

Controls

HEADS-UP DISPLAY (HUD)

1. **Health bar:** This displays your current health. Don't allow it to deplete completely or you'll join the Force...permanently.
2. **Force Energy meter:** This displays how much Force Energy you currently have. You use Force Energy to execute Force attacks. Once depleted, the Force Energy replenishes on its own.
3. **Force points counter:** This shows you how many Force points you gain by defeating enemies. The more creatively you dispatch your foes, the more you build up your Force points multiplier.
4. **Force Fury meter:** This meter fills up over time as you combat enemies. Once it's full, you can unleash your Force Fury.

NEIMOIDIAN NOTES

Since many of you are returning to the world of *Star Wars: The Force Unleashed* for a heaping second serving of galactic adventure, we're going to keep the basics brief. For advanced combat tactics, skip to the "Becoming the Starkiller" chapter. If you're new to *Star Wars: The Force Unleashed*, make the most of the following pages.

BASIC MOVEMENT

Walking and Running

Action	Xbox 360	PS3
Walk	Press Ⓛ lightly	Press left thumbstick lightly
Run	Press Ⓛ firmly	Press left thumbstick firmly

Movement is simple. Simply press the movement thumbstick in the direction you want to go. To walk, press it lightly. To run, press it firmly. The main difference between walking and running (besides getting to your destination more quickly when running) is that walking allows you to deflect blaster fire more efficiently.

Jump and Double-Jump

Action	Xbox 360	PS3
Jump	Ⓐ	×
Double-jump	Ⓐ, Ⓐ	×, ×

Jumping and double-jumping are basic skills that you will use often throughout your adventure. While navigating platforms, be careful not to double-jump past your target. You can usually time the second jump in your double-jump so that you can reach landing targets near or far. Practice this ability frequently so you don't wipe yourself out down the line.

In battle, use your jumping ability to get a better vantage point on your enemies. Leap over their heads and come down on them with devastating attacks.

JEDI WISDOM

Pair your double-jump with Force Dash to execute a double-jump dash. This maneuver can help you reach distant areas and enemies!

Lightsaber Block

Action	Xbox 360	PS3
Lightsaber Block	LT	L2

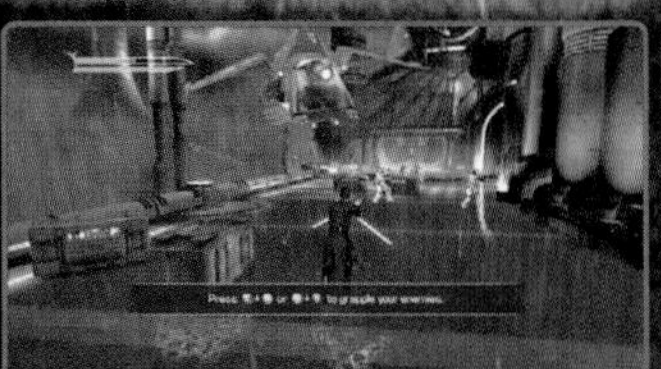

Just because you're now an ultrapowerful clone strong in the ways of the Force doesn't mean you can rampage through everything. You must still block enemy attacks! Blocking allows you to deflect enemy blaster fire as well as hand-weapon attacks. While engaged in weapon combat, time your blocks properly to execute a quick counterattack that temporarily knocks your enemy back!

Lock On

Action	Xbox 360	PS3
Lock On	Press and hold RB	Press and hold R1

Lock On is a helpful ability in combat. Use it when you're trying to focus on only one enemy, such as a war droid or a boss. If you attempt to use this on groups of foes, you may end up targeting the wrong enemy. Your movement will also be altered while locked on to an enemy: You will no longer move in a straight line, but rather will strafe left and right around your target. This also applies to dashing left and right while locked on.

Camera Control

Action	Xbox 360	PS3
Look around	R	Right thumbstick
Center camera	Click R	Click right thumbstick

Camera control is essential for navigating the complicated locales you'll traverse. Move the camera around to get a better view of your area. You can use this to spot hidden holocrons, look around corners, and peer below you while standing on high platforms.

Force Powers

You have the same Force powers as the original Starkiller. In fact, you even have Force powers that he didn't! Read on to learn more about all of your Force powers and how to use them more effectively.

FORCE DASH

Action	Xbox 360	PS3
Dash	LB	L1

Force Dash isn't a typical attack. In fact, it doesn't have to be used as an attack—it's also a very handy way of covering a lot of distance in a short time. However, you can use Force Dash to barrel through small groups of enemies!

FORCE LIGHTNING

Action	Xbox 360	PS3
Force Lightning	Y	▲

This is one of your most powerful Force powers. You use Force Lightning to power many other attacks, such as infusing saber strikes, creating Lightning projectiles, and charging objects to create explosives. It's also a very powerful weapon. At lower levels, it can stun most enemies and electrocute weaker storm-troopers. When upgraded, it can bring down even large war droids with sustained Lightning blasts.

FORCE PUSH

Action	Xbox 360	PS3
Force Push	Ⓑ	●

Force Push is one of the most effective powers against all enemies. Use Force Push to bully foes around and shove them off ledges and high platforms. You can also add Force Push to the end of saber combos to blast enemies away. In addition, Force Push is necessary for bringing down large obstacles, blowing down doors, and moving objects out of the way quickly.

FORCE GRIP

Action	Xbox 360	PS3
Force Grip	(RT)	R2
Move gripped object	Left and right thumbsticks	Left and right thumbsticks
Throw	Hold (RT), move object toward target, then release	Hold R2, move object toward target, then release

Very few enemies have a suitable defense against Force Grip. Once they're in your grip, they are helpless and at your mercy. You can move enemies and items around or even toss them aside. Force Grip enemies and hurl them over ledges or into lethal objects such as flame jets, fans, and explosive objects. Force Grip is also useful in moving objects, opening doors, and grabbing enemy vehicles like TIE fighters.

JEDI WISDOM

You can electrocute and impale enemies while they're in your Force Grip. To do so, press the Force Lightning and Attack button, respectively, while holding an enemy with Force Grip.

SABER THROW

Action	Xbox 360	PS3
Saber Throw	Hold (LT), then press Ⓧ	Hold L2, then press ■

Saber Throw is a great power that can dish out decent damage from afar. Many enemies, such as war droids, are far too dangerous to take on hand-to-hand. When in combat with these large clunkers, keep your distance and use Saber Throw to slice them from afar. Saber Throw is a great ranged attack, but keep in mind that while your lightsabers are in the air, you are defenseless to blaster fire and other enemy attacks. You can also use Saber Throw to solve environmental puzzles and chop down structures.

FORCE REPULSE

Action	Xbox 360	PS3
Repulse	Hold (RT), then press Ⓑ	Hold L2, then press ●

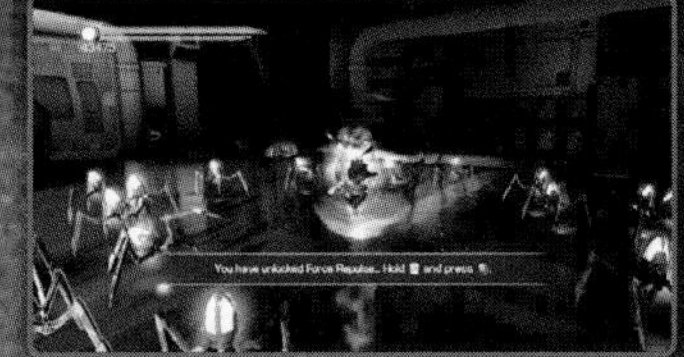
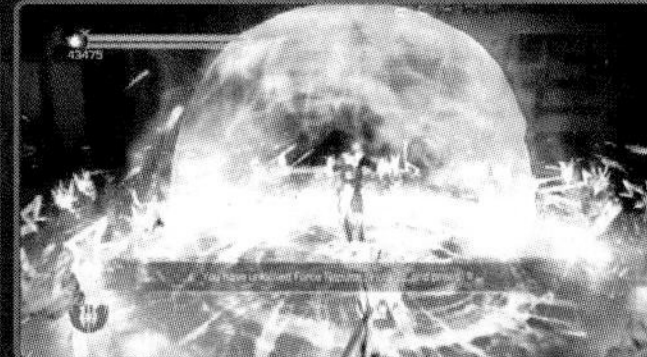

Force Repulse isn't just another Force attack—it can also be used as a defensive maneuver against enemies. Charge Force Repulse to gather your Force Energy around you like a bubble, then release it to cause a Force explosion that radiates 360 degrees around you. While it may not immediately destroy most enemies (though it is very effective against lower-level enemies like terror spider droids), it is very useful in repelling foes as they surround you.

MIND TRICK

Action	Xbox 360	PS3
Mind Trick	Hold (LT), then press Ⓨ	Hold ⇨, then press ▲

Mind Trick is one of your sneakiest skills. It allows you to fool your enemies into thinking what you what them to think. In some cases you can convince them that life is not worth living so they'll throw themselves over a ledge. In other cases you can convince enemies to turn on their comrades, turning them into temporary allies. This skill is especially useful when facing several different types of foes at once. Use it to turn a few strong enemies on weaker ones, or use it to turn many weak enemies on a few stronger ones.

Combat Controls

SABER AND FORCE COMBOS

More often than not, you will dispose of enemies with your lightsabers rather than your Force powers. You will undoubtedly develop your own combat style. For example, you may prefer to lead with your Force powers but finish a fight with a saber strike or two. Or you may like to lead with saber combos and finish enemies off with Force power attacks. Regardless, you should incorporate saber combos into nearly all attacks. The following table lists all available saber and Force combos.

Combo	Xbox 360	PS3
Lightsaber Combo 1	X, X	■, ■
Lightsaber Combo 2	X, X, X	■, ■, ■
Lightsaber Combo 3	X, X, X, X	■, ■, ■, ■
Lightsaber Combo 4	X, X, X, X, X	■, ■, ■, ■, ■
Lightsaber Combo 5	X, X (pause) X, X	■, ■ (pause) ■, ■
Lightsaber Combo 6	X, X, X (pause) X, X, X	■, ■, ■ (pause) ■, ■, ■
Lightsaber Combo 7	X, X, X, X (pause) X, X, X, X	■, ■, ■, ■ (pause) ■, ■, ■, ■
Saber Flurry	X (pause), X (pause), X (pause), X	■ (pause), ■ (pause), ■ (pause), ■
Saber Blast	X, B	■, ●
Saber Sling	X, X, B	■, ■, ●
Saber Slam 1	X, X, X, B	■, ■, ■, ●
Saber Slam 2	X, X, X, X, B	■, ■, ■, ■, ●
Saber Slash	X, Y, Y	■, ▲, ▲
Saber Smash 1	X, X, Y	■, ■, ▲
Saber Smash 2	X, X, X, Y	■, ■, ■, ▲
Saber Smash 3	X, X, X, X, Y	■, ■, ■, ■, ▲
Dashing Blast	LB, B	L1, ●
Dashing Slash	LB, X	L1, ■
Dashing Shock	LB, Y	L1, ▲
Cannonball	RT, B	R1, ●
Lightning Grenade	RT, Y	R1, ▲
Lightning Strike	X, Y	■, ▲
Leaping Slash 1	A, X	×, ■
Leaping Slash 2	A, X, X	×, ■, ■
Leaping Slash 3	A, X, X, X	×, ■, ■, ■
Leaping Slam 1	A, X (hold)	×, ■ (hold)
Leaping Slam 2	A, X, X (hold)	×, ■, ■ (hold)
Leaping Slam 3	A, X, X, X (hold)	×, ■, ■, ■ (hold)

Combo	Xbox 360	PS3
Aerial Ambush 1	X, X, X, B (hold)	■, ■, ■, ● (hold)
Aerial Ambush 2	X, X, X, X, B (hold)	■, ■, ■, ■, ● (hold)
Aerial Ambush Flurry 1	X, X, X, B (hold) X, X, X	■, ■, ■, ● (hold) ■, ■, ■
Aerial Ambush Flurry 2	X, X, X, X, B (hold) X, X, X	■, ■, ■, ■, ● (hold) ■, ■, ■
Aerial Ambush Flurry 3	X, X, X, X, B (hold) X, B	■, ■, ■, ■, ● (hold) ■, ●
Aerial Ambush Flurry 4	X, X, X, X, B (hold) X, Y	■, ■, ■, ■, ● (hold) ■, ▲
Aerial Ambush Flurry 5	X, X, X, X, B (hold) X, X, B	■, ■, ■, ■, ● (hold) ■, ■, ●
Aerial Ambush Flurry 6	X, X, X, X, B (hold) X, X, Y	■, ■, ■, ■, ● (hold) ■, ■, ▲
Aerial Assault 1	X, X, X, B (hold), X	■, ■, ■, ● (hold), ■
Aerial Assault 2	X, X, X, B (hold), X, X	■, ■, ■, ● (hold), ■, ■
Aerial Assault 3	X, X, X, B (hold), X, X, B	■, ■, ■, ● (hold), ■, ■, ●
Aerial Assault 4	X, X, X, B (hold), X, X, Y	■, ■, ■, ● (hold), ■, ■, ▲
Aerial Blast 1	X, X, X, B (hold), B	■, ■, ■, ● (hold), ●
Aerial Blast 2	X, X, X, B (hold), X, B	■, ■, ■, ● (hold), ■, ●
Aerial Shock 1	X, X, X, B (hold), Y	■, ■, ■, ● (hold), ▲
Aerial Shock 2	X, X, X, B (hold), X, Y	■, ■, ■, ● (hold), ■, ▲
Aerial Throw 1	X, X, X, B (hold), [X + A]	■, ■, ■, ● (hold), [■ + ×]
Aerial Throw 2	X, X, X, B (hold), [Y + B]	■, ■, ■, ● (hold), [▲ + ●]

GRAPPLE ATTACKS

Action	Xbox 360	PS3
Grapple Attack 1	A + X	▲ + ●
Grapple Attack 2	B + Y	× + ■

Throughout your adventure, enemies will often surround you quickly. Use grapple attacks to pull close enemies in closer and savagely attack them in close-quarter combat. After pulling them in for the attack, you'll either strike them with their own weapon, impale them with yours, or toss them into the air before finishing them off with a saber strike—depending on the enemy and the grapple attack you execute. Regardless of what the attack looks like, the outcome is always the same: one less enemy to worry about.

ACHIEVEMENT/TROPHY UNLOCKED

To unlock the "Aww Yeah..." Achievement or Trophy, execute all of the above listed moves and combos throughout your adventure. This also includes moves executed in challenges.

JEDI WISDOM

Get yourself more familiar with many of the combos listed above by playing the "Combat Trial" challenge as soon as you unlock it!

BECOMING STARKILLER

Advanced Combat Training

Now that you've mastered basic combat and Force powers, you must learn how to put it all together into a solid fighting repertoire. This chapter details advanced combat tactics. After all, what good is knowing a combo if you're using it at the wrong time or against the wrong enemy?

JEDI SKILLS

Whenever you encounter more than one enemy, you must first decide which enemy to attack first. While there are several different approaches for this, the answer will almost always change from encounter to encounter. That doesn't mean there isn't a good rule of thumb to follow when ambushed by large groups.

Whenever you approach a group of enemies, always take out the biggest threat first. That doesn't necessarily mean that the biggest enemy is the biggest threat. If you are in a large room with a war droid but several scout troopers have you pinned from afar, you will have a harder time defeating the war droid near you because of the scout troopers' precision. They are the bigger threat. By that same token, if you find yourself in a small room with a large enemy like a terror giant, then there will be nowhere to run from its attacks; therefore, take it out first, leaving other enemies like terror troopers for last.

ALWAYS CREATE ELBOW ROOM

You will rarely face enemies one-on-one, so don't allow yourself to get surrounded. If you do, you can easily find yourself on the ground with little chance of getting up. Your foes are fierce, so if they knock you down, you risk being knocked down again when trying to rise.

To keep from getting surrounded, use Force Repulse to create some breathing room or use Dash to bully through enemies. Once you've made some room, use wide-sweeping attacks or use Force Push to keep enemies at a distance.

WATCH FOR PROJECTILES

Be mindful of scout troopers and AT-MPs; they can pick you off from afar and keep you grounded. These foes can often be your most dangerous enemies; not because they are extremely powerful or because they inflict major damage—though AT-MPs typically do—but because they can knock you off your feet and keep you on the floor.

Once you're off your feet, other nearby enemies can pounce and capitalize on their comrade's precision shooting. If possible, always eliminate enemies with projectiles first (they are often the biggest threat).

MATCH THE ATTACK TO THE ENEMY

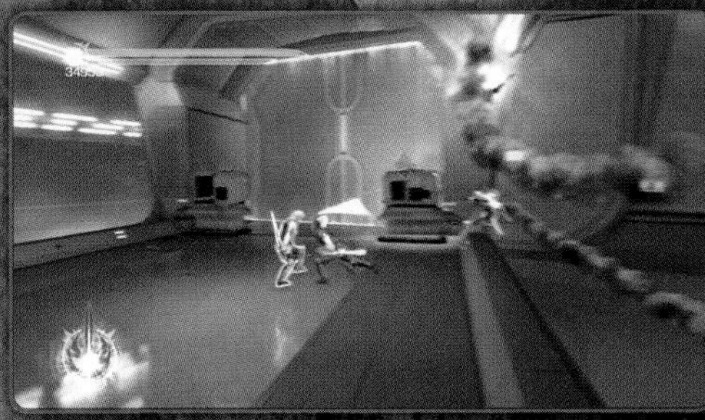

Not all enemies are created equal. While some will go down with a simple saber combo, others require more persuasive means to dispatch. For example, riot troopers are resistant to saber combos but are weak against Force powers. Similarly, Sith acolytes are resistant to Force powers but are weak against saber combos.

If you don't use the right attacks against enemies, you'll merely tread water in combat. The trick to staying alive is to dispatch enemies as quickly as possible; the best way to do so is to always match the attack to the enemy.

MAKE FRIENDS

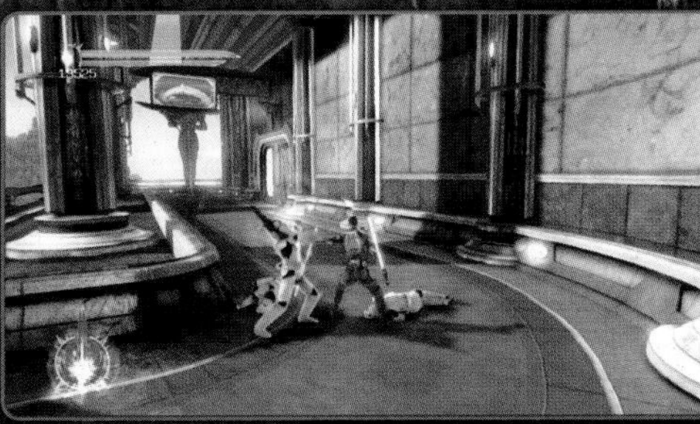

There is safety in numbers. Whether you like it or not, you may sometimes need a helping hand in combat. Recruit your enemies with Mind Trick and turn them into allies. Whenever you encounter a group of mixed enemies—for example, riot troopers, guards, and stormtroopers—use Mind Trick to turn the more powerful enemies into allies. Not only will you eliminate the strongest enemy in the group (by aligning them with you), but also you'll turn them on their own comrades.

NEIMOIDIAN NOTES

Not all enemies will turn on their comrades when you use Mind Trick. In some cases, they'll just eliminate themselves, which can be just as helpful.

THERE IS POWER IN POWER CRYSTALS

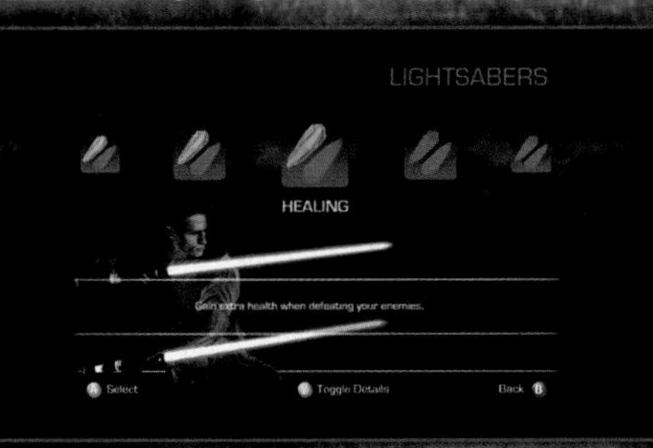

There's no use collecting all of the power crystals if you don't use them. Each one has its own special effect that can make the difference in a fight...when equipped. Try mixing and matching power-crystal combinations to find a desired effect that suits your combat style.

If you prefer to rely mostly on lightsaber combat, then equip in your primary lightsaber a power crystal that augments lightsaber damage. If Force Lightning is your best weapon, then equip in your primary lightsaber a power crystal that increases Lightning damage. For more information on power-crystal effects, see the following table.

Xbox 360/PS3 Power Crystals

Power Crystal	Effect	Tip
Crimson	None	Replace this crystal as soon as you acquire a new one.
Chaos	Gain extra Force points for destroying your environment	Equip this crystal if you prefer to frequently use Force powers such as Force Repulse, Force Push, and other destructive Force powers.
Meditation	Replenishes your Force Energy with each strike	This crystal is best used if you rely on Force power attacks before launching into lightsaber combos.
Protection	Increases your defensive skills	If you're a reckless fighter who likes to rush into combat, equip this crystal to give you a defensive edge.
Fury	Increases your Force Fury meter with each enemy defeated	This is one of the most useful power crystals in the game. Equip it to give you an instant edge against nearly every enemy in the game. It will grant you more one-hit-kill opportunities.
Healing	Gain extra health when defeating your enemies	This crystal is extremely useful. It complements nearly every other crystal combination.
Corrosion	Grants a chance to do corrosive damage to your enemies	This crystal is useful when you know you're going to face large enemies with lots of health.
Life Drain	Grants a chance to drain your enemies' health	When equipped with the Healing crystal, this is a powerful life-sustaining crystal combination.
Focus	Your Force powers consume less energy.	If you rely heavily on Force powers, this is a great crystal to keep you from running on empty.
Regeneration	Improves your health regeneration	Like the other two crystals that affect health, this one is best used to keep your health replenished at a better rate. This is especially useful when playing at higher difficulty settings.
Wisdom	Gain extra Force points when defeating your enemies	This crystal is helpful in maximizing your Force power upgrades. Equip it to gain extra Force points, then apply those points toward upgrades.
Incineration	Grants a chance to set your enemies on fire	Like the Corrosion crystal, this helps cause damage over time.
Shock	Grants a chance to deal additional Lightning damage	This crystal is helpful in stunning enemies such as riot troopers, acolytes, and AT-MPs with lightsaber strikes.
Disintegration	Grants a chance to disintegrate your enemies	Equipping this crystal grants you the opportunity to dish out one-hit-kill attacks.

Wii Power Crystals

Power Crystal	Effect	Tip
Ilum	None	Replace this crystal as soon as you acquire a new one.
Rubat	Increases damage with the lightsaber	Equip this if you prefer to use lightsaber combat more than Force powers.
Lorrdian	Improves accuracy for Force-reflected projectiles	This crystal is great for defensive fighters.
Opila	Execute more powerful Saber Throws	If you like to attack enemies from afar, this crystal is for you.
Kaiburr	Force Push and Force Repulse will intensify, causing damage increase	Equip this crystal if you prefer to frequently use Force powers such as Force Repulse, Force Push, and other destructive Force powers.
Velmorite	Increases rate at which the Combo meter builds up	This is one of the most useful crystals in the game. Equip it to gain a hearty advantage by always having a Lightsaber Special in your pocket.
Sigil	Deal more damage with Force Lightning	Like the Opila crystal, this is best suited for fighters who like to keep enemies at a distance. It is also best for fighters who aren't afraid of taking on multiple enemies at once.
Katak	Lightsaber attacks drain a portion of an enemy's health and apply it to yours.	When equipped, this crystal is great for keeping you healthy and keeping enemies at a disadvantage.
Mephite	Increases the rate at which the user earns Force Rage	This is one of the most useful power crystals in the game. Equip it to give you an instant edge against nearly every enemy in the game. It will grant you more one-hit-kill opportunities.
Bondar	Deal more punishing blows, occasionally breaking an opponent's block or knocking them down	Equip this crystal if you rely heavily on lightsaber combat.
Qixoni	Enables the user to regenerate Force Energy at a faster rate	Equip this crystal if you rely on Force powers more than lightsaber combat.
Ruusan	Allows wielder to better focus the Force; all Force powers cost less Force Energy.	Equip this crystal if you rely on Force powers more than lightsaber combat.

RETREAT AND RECOVER

There is no shame in backing off to regain health. You will not always have the upper hand in battle and will often find yourself on the wrong end of an ambush. When you do, back away from the battle to allow your health to regenerate.

The key to this is finding a safe place to retreat to. When you see that your health is about to deplete, Force Dash to an area with no enemies and wait for your health to replenish before returning to combat.

BE MINDFUL OF THE FORCE

This bit of Jedi wisdom is as old as Master Yoda himself, probably older. Always be mindful of your Force Energy. Even if you don't rely heavily on your Force powers, your Force Energy will still deplete. Keep an eye on it as you fight to make sure that you always have enough Force Energy to dash away or use Force Repulse in a last-ditch effort to escape. The last thing you want in battle is to run out of Force Energy when you need it most.

SAFETY OVER STYLE

When it comes to your safety, there's no room for style. So if you find yourself in a predicament, rather than go for extra experience points by stringing together a creative combo, go straight for the easy way out with something simple and quick.

Use Force Push or Force Repulse to quickly eliminate enemies to get yourself out of danger quickly instead of going for the extra Force points. Flourish has its place, but not in a life-or-death situation.

BE MINDFUL OF YOUR ENVIRONMENT

Just as you must be mindful of the Force, you must also be mindful of the area around you. Use the space as a defensive measure: for example, utilize walls, obstacles, and other things in the environment as barriers between you and your opponent, or use them as safe havens to escape into and recover health.

The environment can also be a weapon or provide weapons. Look around whenever you enter a new area; you can frequently find objects to use as projectiles or can find environmental hazards to throw enemies into.

LET FORCE VISION GUIDE YOU (WII ONLY)

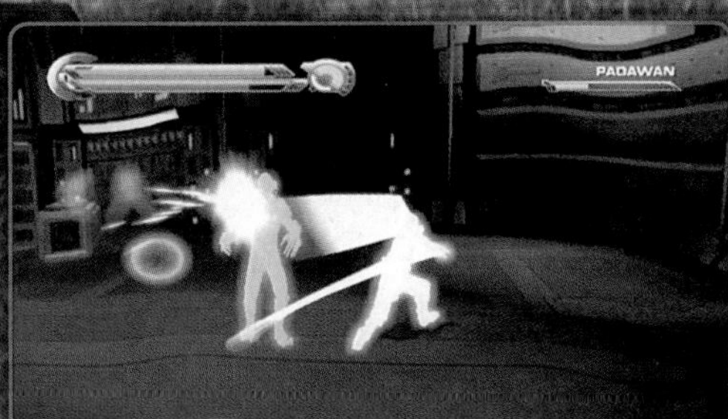

Force Vision isn't just useful for picking door locks and spotting cloaked terror troopers. You can also use it to locate hidden items such as holocrons, bacta tanks, and saber crystals through walls and other barriers!

Aside from items, you can also spot other enemies through walls and barriers. This is especially handy when you're traversing a new area, exploring winding hallways, and keeping an eye out for ambushes.

NEIMOIDIAN NOTES

Force Vision is available only in the Wii version of the game.

UPGRADE YOUR POWERS

Just like you must make use of your power crystals, you must also make use of your experience points. As you defeat enemies and gain experience points, you can upgrade your Force powers. While you don't have to upgrade all Force powers, always upgrade the ones you rely on the most. They're as integral a part of your fighting repertoire as your lightsabers. If you make heavy use of Force Lightning, upgrade that Force power to make you a more efficient wielder of it.

WALKING IN STARKILLER'S SHADOW

A long time ago in a galaxy far, far away....

The galaxy is on the brink of civil war. Inspired by the sacrifice of DARTH VADER's secret apprentice, a ragtag Rebel Alliance plots to overthrow the evil GALACTIC EMPIRE. Imperial forces in relentless pursuit of the Rebels have captured the Jedi Knight RAHM KOTA. Its general lost, the Alliance fleet has vanished.

While the Empire searches for the Rebels, Darth Vader has put a dark plan in motion that will bring an end to his apprentice's legacy....

Prologue

The cloning planet of Kamino isn't known for its picturesque weather. As the TIE Advanced fighter makes its descent, it's greeted by a sheet of rain so thick the cloning facilities below nearly disappear. This is no typical TIE Advanced fighter, however; it belongs to someone very special.

Several AT-STs patrol the facility, crisscrossing each other as the TIE Advanced fighter touches down on the Kaminoan landing pad.

Imperial stormtroopers line the halls of the facility as Darth Vader coolly trundles past them toward a distant corner of the labs that only he and a few others can access.

When Darth Vader reaches his destination, a holding pit, he sees a familiar face staring up at him from the depths. It's Starkiller's face, but not quite the same person. The clone of the once-secret apprentice is shackled and weak. Despite his connection to the Force, Starkiller's clone is unable to free himself from Vader.

Darth Vader has a mission for his new minion. Starkiller's old Jedi mentor, General Rahm Kota, has been captured. He's being held captive on Cato Neimoidia. Once his training is complete, the clone must travel to Cato Neimoidia and execute Kota.

As the Starkiller clone shakes the memories from his head, Vader tries to convince him that they're not truly his memories to own. A side effect of the cloning process and a remnant of the training process, the memories will soon fade.

Vader hands the Starkiller clone a pair of lightsabers, prompting him to cut loose of the memories and truly shake free of his progenitor's "weakness"—his feelings for Juno Eclipse. Just then, several training droids approach and engage their holo-training systems. It's time to train in the ways of the dark side.

JEDI WISDOM

The following is a refresher course on lightsaber and Force power combat. If you've played Star Wars: The Force Unleashed, then this should be old news for you. If this is your first time in control of Starkiller, then review this section to get comfortable wielding lightsabers and manipulating the Force.

Combat Training

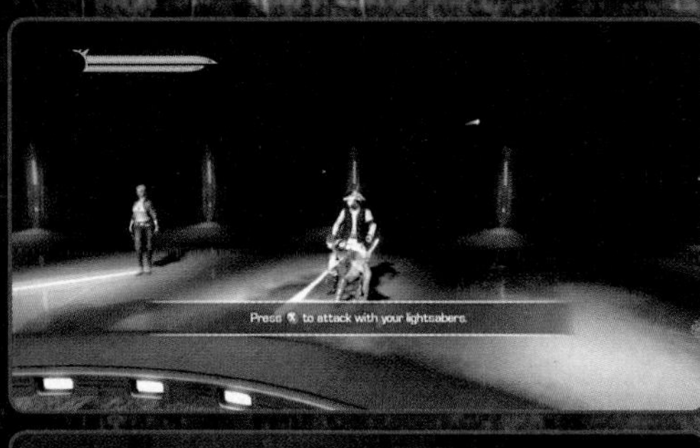

Do as Vader says and let your lightsabers loose on the combat training droids in the room. Just off to the right is Juno Eclipse. Avoid attacking her and concentrate on the Rebel fighters in the room. Approach them each calmly and strike them down with lightsaber combos.

When the next batch of Rebels appears, turn to your Force powers. Follow the onscreen commands to Force Push them out of the way. The Rebels, or rather the combat training droids, are weak, so a Force Push blast or two will defeat them instantly.

Dispatch the Rebel scum with Force Push until a new squad arrives. This time, use your Force Lightning to fry your holographic foes.

CHALLENGE UNLOCKED

Complete the short training tutorial on saber combat and using Force Push and Force Lightning and you'll unlock your first challenge: the Combat Trial Challenge. For tips on how to complete the challenge, skip to the "Challenges" chapter.

Finish tearing through the Rebel soldiers until there are no more. As you do, you violently swing your sabers at the last person standing in your way—Juno. Just as your lightsabers are about to tear through her skin, she screams in terror and you stop.

Vader insists that you strike her down and do away with Starkiller's feelings that echo inside of you. When you resist, Vader strikes her down.

Darth Vader decides then that you, like the clones that came before you, are of no use to him. But before he can do away with you, you turn and bathe him with Force Lightning! The Sith Master drops to his knee while the lightning slowly dissipates.

Before he has a chance to retaliate, you jump out the window and take your first step toward freedom from the dark side.

The Escape

1
START
2
3
4
5
6
7
8
9
10
11
12

MISSION DETAILS

OBJECTIVE

After being held captive in a pit for 13 days, you manage to escape from Darth Vader's clutches. You must now escape the Kaminoan cloning facility.

ENEMIES ENCOUNTERED

- Imperial stormtrooper
- Imperial riot trooper
- Imperial jumptrooper
- TIE fighter
- Carbonite droid
- AT-ST

HOLOCRONS FOUND

- 2 holocrons
- 1 Health Bacta holocron
- 1 Energy Bacta holocron
- Meditation saber crystal (blue)
- Chaos saber crystal (orange)

LEGEND

- # Waypoints (see corresponding images)
- Saber Crystal Holocron
- Green Bacta Holocron
- Experience Points Holocron
- Force Energy Holocron

Free...for Now

ACHIEVEMENT/TROPHY UNLOCKED

The Stakross Medal of Excellence Achievement or Trophy can be unlocked here. To do so, use Force Lightning to destroy the passing TIE fighters before you reach the base of the facility. You don't need to destroy the swarm of TIE fighters before the glass dome, but rather the TIE fighters zipping left and right as you dodge the platforms on the way down.

Though brave and bold, your escape is also hasty and extremely dangerous. You've managed to get away from Darth Vader, but you're now free-falling headfirst down the side of the Kaminoan facility, past spires, and enemy-infested platforms.

Focus on the obstacles in your way, and carefully glide left and right past the thin obstructions. Save your Force Energy to push through large obstacles such as platforms.

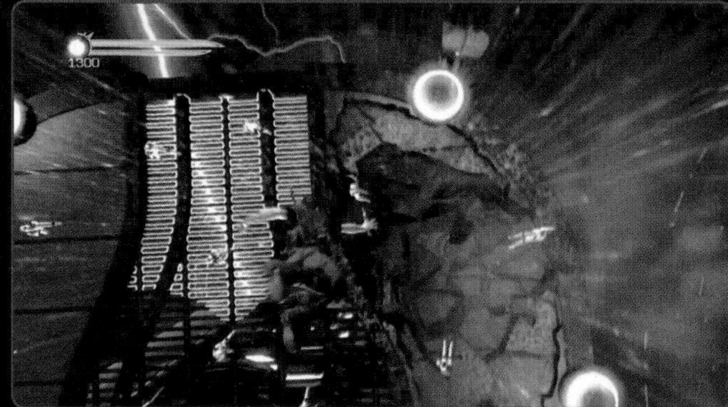

As you approach the platforms, fire a Force Push blast ahead of you to create a hole, then glide through the hole to pass through undamaged.

When you reach the base of the tower, a swarm of TIE fighters rushes up at you. Carefully Force Push through the swarm.

JEDI WISDOM

One Force Push blast can destroy a TIE fighter, so choose each blast carefully. Don't use up all of your Force Energy by rapidly mashing on the Force Push button. If you do, you may find yourself out of Force Energy when you need it most.

①

After surviving the onslaught of TIE fighters, you come crashing down through a large glass dome. The Imperial stormtroopers in the room are crushed by the sheer force of your impact.

Turn and greet the stormtrooper battalion that rushes through the door on the right. Follow the onscreen commands and execute saber combos to put the enemies down. After you wipe out the battalion, the door's force field drops, allowing you passage outside.

Exit the domed room and bully your way past the stormtroopers in your way. Double-jump over the small gap in the walkway where a small batch of stormtroopers will meet you.

Upon your landing on the other side, a small transport swoops by and drops off another battalion of Imperial stormtroopers. Practice your grappling skills on the hapless foes, then rush past their fallen bodies toward the next door.

ACHIEVEMENT/TROPHY UNLOCKED

With all of the explosive consoles around, this is an excellent area to unlock the Poor Bob Achievement or Trophy. Just be sure to Force Grip an untouched stormtrooper before you stick him, zap him, and slam him.

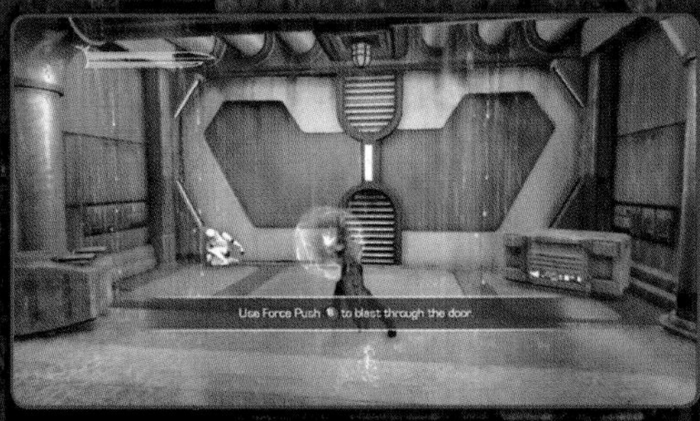

Make short work of the Imperial stormtroopers that rush out of the door; then use Force Push to blast through the door. After you pass through the door, several more stormtroopers rush out of small compartments lining the walkway.

Grab the stormtroopers with Force Grip and practice tossing them at distant enemies. Otherwise, send foes flying by flinging them from afar with Force Push. Double-jump onto the large circular walkway and follow it around to the other side of the platform.

JEDI WISDOM

This large circular walkway is a good place to practice your Force Gripping skills. Wait for the TIE fighters to zoom by on the left and grab them with the Force. Crush them, then toss them at the other TIE fighters that pass by. Not only will you be able to hone your Force Gripping skills, but you'll also rack up some decent Force points in the process.

On the other side of the circular walkway is a small gap. Look right and locate a platform hidden inside the right wall. Use the Force to yank it out, then double-jump across to the other side of the walkway.

HOLOCRON

There is a saber holocron sitting on the other side of the gap. After double-jumping across the new platform, grab it. It's the Chaos saber crystal holocron!

JEDI WISDOM

Since your current red saber crystals don't have any extra effects, now is a good time to equip your new saber crystal. You will gain extra Force points for destroying the environment.

Drop down onto the other side, then double-jump dash over the next wide gap. Immediately upon landing, run your lightsabers through the pair of Imperial riot troopers that rush out of the door at the far end.

Block their incoming attacks, then focus on one enemy at a time. Use lightning-infused saber attacks to stun them, then finish them off with lightsaber combos.

JEDI WISDOM

The Imperial riot trooper is one of the most technical fighters you'll encounter. However, you can quickly rob him of his weapon by using throws: You'll rip his staff out of his hand, slap him with it, and knock him to the floor. Once he's grounded, rush the fallen trooper and run both sabers through his torso.

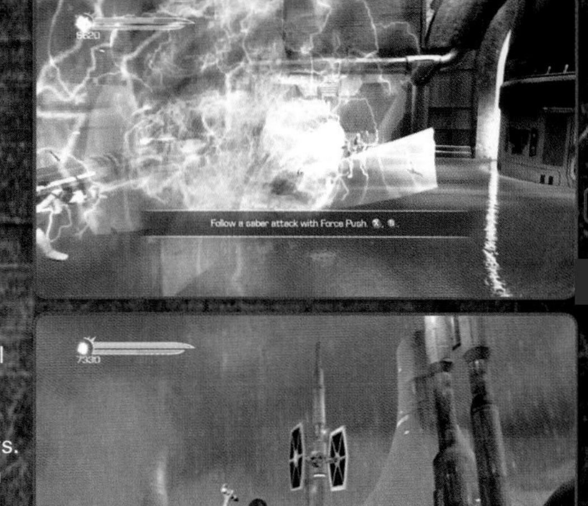

After dispatching the first two Imperial riot troopers, another pair rushes out of the door ahead of you. This time, they've brought help—a small complement of Imperial stormtroopers. Slice through the weaker stormtroopers first, then turn to the stronger, better-equipped riot troopers. After you destroy the Imperials, the door behind them unlocks. Pass through to the next area.

Immediately after you pass through the door, a group of TIE fighters zooms toward you from the left! Turn toward them and use the Force to grip them in midair. Hold them in place with the Force and crush them! Turn several TIE fighters into heaping scraps of debris, and the next door slides open.

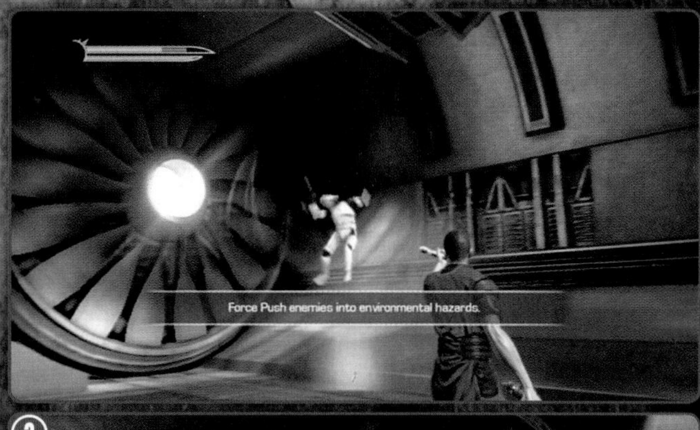

Inside the door are several more stormtroopers. Unfortunately for them, they've taken station just right of a ventilation fan. Use Force Grip to pick them up and hurl them into the fan.

Next, pick up one of the crates and hurl it down the hall to the right. You cannot see them yet, but there is a small group of stormtroopers waiting to ambush you as you enter the hall. Toss the crate at them as you enter to spread them apart and make them easier to pick off with your sabers or Force Lightning.

Wipe out the rest of the Imperial stormtroopers in this hall, either by conventional means or by more creative methods like Force Gripping them over the flame hazards nearby.

Dash past the flame hazards when they stop firing, and reach the end of the hall. There are two more Imperials waiting there. Run your sabers through them before they get a chance to open fire.

HOLOCRON

There's another holocron at the end of this hall, just past the flame hazards. Pick it up to find the blue Meditation saber crystal.

JEDI WISDOM

Since you can equip two saber crystals at the same time, replace your second crystal with this one to create your first saber crystal combo.

Turn left at the hall's end and locate another group of enemies. Use a Force Push blast to send the troopers flying into the fan behind them. This will give you clear passage out of the hall and back into the rainy Kaminoan landscape.

Another group of Imperials stands their ground outside. Dash past the riot trooper and take out the stormtroopers first. Turn on the riot trooper next and cut him down.

More TIE fighters zoom by overhead. As you trek farther along the outside of the Kaminoan facility, Force Grip the TIE fighters and turn them into weapons to use against the enemies ahead of you. It may take some practice, but nothing beats dropping a large metal chunk on a stormtrooper's head. Follow the circular walkway left as it leads around to the walkway's other side.

HOLOCRON

There's a green Bacta Tank holocron sitting on the far end of a support about halfway down the circular walkway. Carefully jump out onto the long, narrow walkway and go out to its end to grab the holocron.

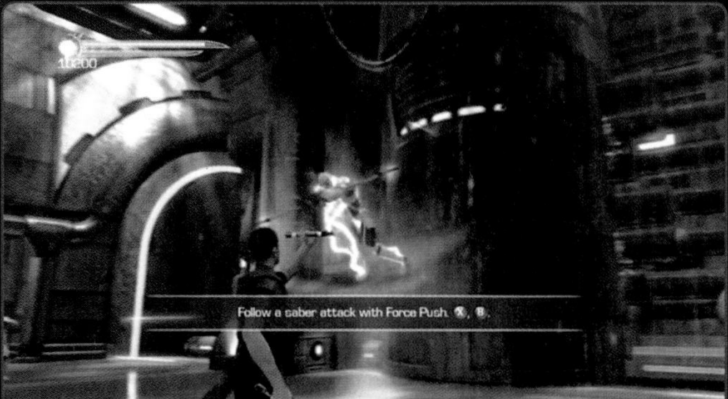

Continue fighting your way down the walkway, tearing through Imperials as you go, until you reach another sealed door. This time, use a Force Push blast to blow the door open. Dash through the dented doorway and deal with a small group of enemies.

Double-jump onto the raised area on the door's other side and Force Push enemies off the platform. As they go flying off into the Kaminoan depths, rush around the platform to the next walkway below.

5

Drop onto the walkway and battle past the Imperials between you and the next door. Let your lightsabers guide the way as you slice through your enemies. If a riot trooper approaches you, use lightning-infused saber combos to stun all of the enemies in your way. While they are stunned, finish them off with saber combos.

Once you've destroyed all the enemies in your way, Force Push through the next door, revealing a path back into the facility's interior. However, the path is blocked by large fans.

ACHIEVEMENT/TROPHY UNLOCKED

To unlock the Kamfetti Achievement or Trophy, you must first open the doors to the facility interior without killing all of the enemies. To do so, rush past the first five enemies and approach the group of stormtroopers nearest to the sealed door. Destroy them and the door will open. Now turn around and Force Grip each of the remaining stormtroopers—at least five—and hurl them into the large spinning fan.

CLONER'S CAUTION

Don't attempt to rush past the spinning blades! If you do, you'll only incur damage and get knocked back.

6

Use Force Grip to stop the blades from spinning, then crush the last batch of stormtroopers in your way. At the hall's far end, past the two spinning fans, is a large tube leading down into the cloning facility. Hop down.

You land in a room sealed off by a force field. Approach it and Force Grip the crates just beyond the field; hurl them at the control consoles nearby. When the consoles explode, the force field shuts off, granting you access deeper into the cloning facility.

Use the crates nearby as projectiles against the small squad of stormtroopers that rush out of the hall's far end. Dash past the fallen troopers into a large circular room with a console at the center.

HOLOCRON

There's a holocron in this room. Hop onto the center console to grab it.

Pass through the next door and enter a short hallway guarded by a single Imperial stormtrooper. Sneak up behind the weak-minded foe and use your Force powers to confuse him. Follow the onscreen commands to use your Mind Trick ability on him. When you do, the trooper jumps out of the nearest window to his death.

Unfortunately, this also gets the attention of the turbo laser turrets just outside the passage. The turrets begin firing on the hall, tearing through the glass as it works its way toward you. Dash out of the window the stormtrooper leaped out of, and hop down to the area below.

The area below is a labyrinthine series of deadly red force fields! In order to bring each force field down, you must destroy the enemies in your way. Begin with the stormtroopers on the far right. Cut them down, then turn left, toward the first red field.

ACHIEVEMENT/TROPHY UNLOCKED

This is a perfect place to unlock the It Burns! Achievement or Trophy. As you work your way past each of the red force fields, use Force Grip to toss enemies into the fields and disintegrate them. Zap 10 enemies and the achievement or trophy will unlock!

You could also get to work on the No Match for a Blaster... accolade. Lure your enemies into the fire of the turboblasters above to get started on it. You'll most likely need to revisit this area a second time to unlock it.

As you battle the enemies, lure them toward the glowing red power nodes. Zap the power nodes with Force Lightning to send out powerful electromagnetic pulses. The pulses can cause major damage on nearby enemies, so be sure to get as many foes near them as possible.

When riot troopers rush out of the nearby door, use your Mind Trick to turn them into allies. Let them turn on the stormtroopers while you pick off the rest of the enemies. Work your way past the batches of enemies, bringing down each red force field as you go, until you reach the area's center.

JEDI WISDOM

There are so many different ways to eradicate enemies inside the force-field labyrinth. Aside from conventional means—lightsaber and Force powers—you can also do the following:

- **Toss them into red force fields**
- **Detonate the red power nodes**
- **Lure enemies into the large turret's line of fire**
- **Use your Mind Trick to turn more powerful enemies on the weaker ones**

CARBONITE WAR DROID BATTLE

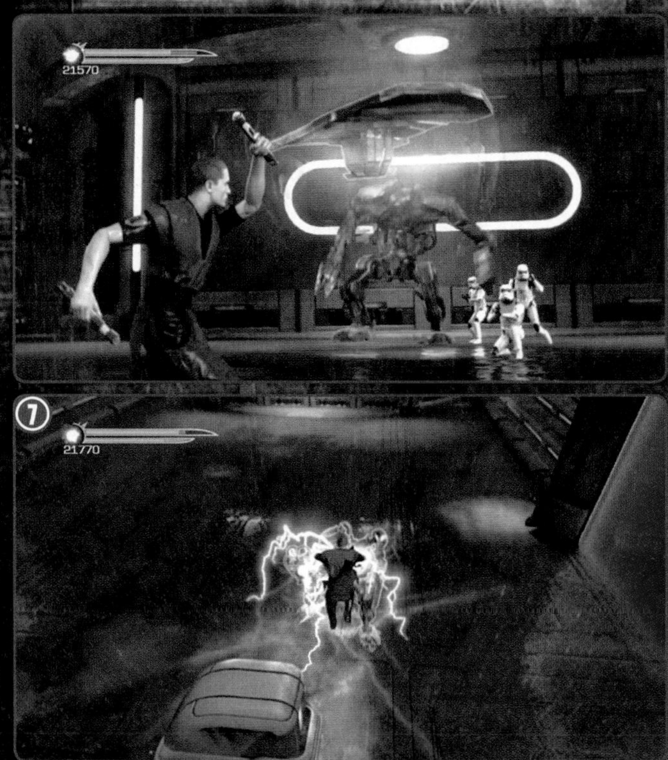

When you reach the center of the red maze, a large, hulking carbonite droid comes stomping out of the nearby gate. It carries a massive shield and is accompanied by several Imperial stormtroopers. Use your Mind Trick on the stormtroopers first. This will distract the Carbonite War Droid temporarily, allowing you to grab its shield with Force Grip and rip it from its hand.

Dodge the carbonite droid's dashing attack by sidestepping it when it approaches you. Lock on to the clanking beast as it stomps around, and dash around it, keeping it at a safe distance. If it fires carbonite at you, follow the onscreen commands to shake it off, then zap the droid with Force Lightning.

Continue strafing around the droid, zapping it with Force Lightning as you go, and use the large protrusions in the area as obstacles for your foe. Position the protrusions between yourself and the clanker while you zap it repeatedly. Eventually, the menace will weaken and drop its guard.

When it does, rush it and follow the onscreen commands to destroy it. When you do, the nearby gate opens up. Go through the gate to the next area.

CLONER'S CAUTION

You can also defeat the carbonite droid with lightsaber combos, but that will require you to get up close and personal where the droid can swat you away with its large hand. This can slap huge chunks of energy from your Health bar.

CHALLENGE UNLOCKED

When you beat the carbonite droid, you unlock a the Kamino Drill Grounds Trial Challenge!

INTO THE COLD

Trek deeper into the cloning facility until you reach another force field. Use the crates on the other side to destroy the consoles and bring the force field down. Rush the stormtroopers nearby, and slash through them on your way back out into the pouring rain.

Use the red power nodes nearby to bounce the approaching riot troopers, then Force Grip the TIE fighters flying overhead to turn them into oversized metal projectiles.

Continue fighting up the watery walkway until you reach a large circular platform. There you are greeted by a small transport ship that delivers several more Imperial stormtroopers.

Mind Trick the stronger riot troopers nearby, then easily cut through the weaker enemies. When a second transport arrives, greet the new soldiers with Force Push and knock them off the platform all the way down to the water below.

ACHIEVEMENT/TROPHY UNLOCKED

This is a great place to unlock the Pied Piper Achievement or Trophy. Use Mind Trick as much as possible to trick enemies into jumping over the side of the ledge and to their demise. When 10 weak-minded enemies leap, you'll unlock the achievement or trophy.

When you reach the walkway's end, use the Force to lift a nearby platform up and into position. Double-jump onto the platform and onto the next walkway where more enemies await.

Use Mind Trick on them as they approach, and watch them either fight each other or throw themselves over the edge. With the first wave of enemies gone, turn right and hurl crates at the next wave of stormtroopers.

Since the walkway is long and cluttered, the troopers ahead of you will often gather close to each other. Dash forward and hurl Force Lightning projectiles at them to stun them, then rush ahead and finish them off while they're incapacitated. After crushing all of the enemies nearby, approach the edge of the walkway and stop.

HOLOCRON

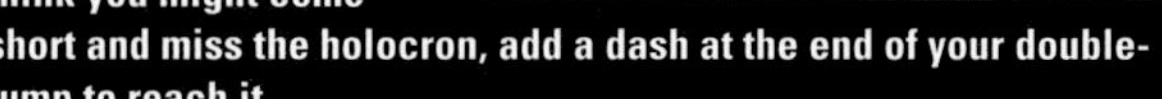

There's another holocron floating overhead between the gaps in the walkway. Time your jump carefully and snag it on the second bound of your double-jump. If you think you might come short and miss the holocron, add a dash at the end of your double-jump to reach it.

Just as you reach the walkway's end, a small squad of Imperial jumptroopers shows up. Lock on to them and zap them with Force Lightning before double-jump dashing across the gap.

Once on the other side, slash past the few stormtroopers in your way, then scorch the next wave of jumptroopers. Dash past the jumptroopers as their jet packs go haywire, and reach another large circular platform.

As you approach the walkway's end, a group of stormtroopers rushes out of the far door—followed by another carbonite droid! Mind Trick the troopers to get them out of the way, and yank the droid's shield away immediately. This time use the red power nodes as obstacles, hitting the droid with electromagnetic pulses. Once it is weakened, rush in and finish it off. With the droid out of the way, go through the far door to reenter the facility.

HOLOCRON

There's a blue Bacta Tank holocron just left of the entryway to this hall. Turn left and grab it as soon as you enter. If you turn right immediately, you risk getting sucked into the next sequence before grabbing it.

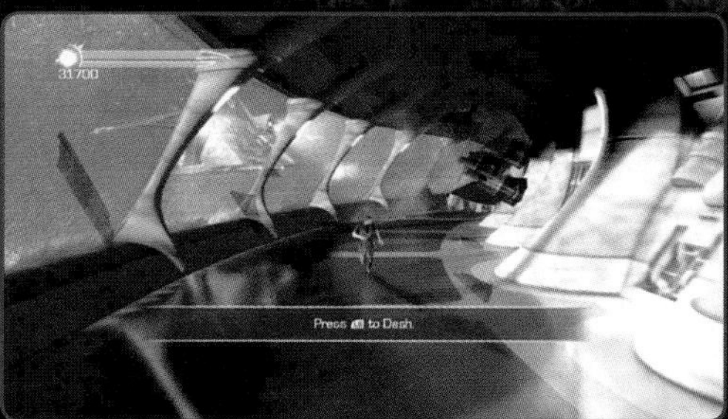

Turn right after entering the facility again and slowly creep down the hall. When you do, a nearby gunship opens fire on the hall! Quickly leap into a dash and speed down the hall, leaving the explosions behind you. If you slow down or run into an obstacle, you'll be blown to bits, so stay ahead of the explosions as you dash repeatedly down the hall.

JEDI WISDOM

As you dash down the hall, stay near the hall's center to dodge the obstacles in your way. There will be three batches of stormtroopers lining the hall's edges near stacked crates, but there is also a clear path down the center of the hall. If you run into a stormtrooper, don't fight it. Instead, dash past it on your way to the hall's end.

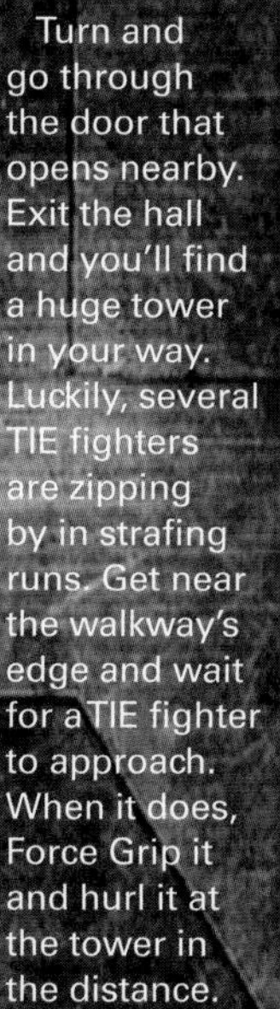

Turn and go through the door that opens nearby. Exit the hall and you'll find a huge tower in your way. Luckily, several TIE fighters are zipping by in strafing runs. Get near the walkway's edge and wait for a TIE fighter to approach. When it does, Force Grip it and hurl it at the tower in the distance. Do this three times to bring the large tower crashing down and create a bridge to Darth Vader's TIE Advanced fighter.

Once the tower has fallen, dash across the makeshift bridge to the landing pad where three AT-STs stand guard over Vader's vessel.

Immediately upon landing on the platform, follow the onscreen command to activate your Force Fury. In this crazed state, you'll be invulnerable and have infinite Force energy. Make short work of the AT-STs by either zapping them with Force Lightning or slicing through them with your lightsabers.

When a pair of transport ships arrives and drops off two squads of stormtroopers, either use Mind Trick to turn all of them against each other or fry them all at once. Once the remaining troopers are destroyed, you board Vader's TIE fighter and escape the cloning facility.

Cato Neimoidia

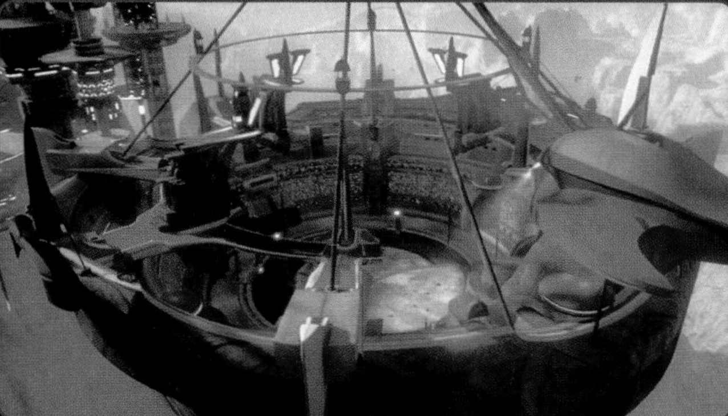

High above the planet of Cato Neimoidia hangs the city of Tarko-se. There, in the Tarko-se arena, several of the most powerful warriors put their skills to the test (often unwillingly) against the galaxy's most fearsome creatures. Today, the crowd cheers for Tarko-se's greatest champion.

As the champion slowly steps forward, a large, grizzly lizard lets out a deafening roar before leaping into a full charge! With one swift, fluid motion, the champion steps aside, swings his lightsaber, and strikes down the reptilian menace.

The warrior, General Rahm Kota, is not fazed by his opponent's size, speed, or strength. He's got the Force on his side. Just then, another opponent, this one a humanoid, rushes in for the attack...and he meets with the same fate as the leaping lizard.

Having struck down all of his opponents, Rahm Kota defiantly waves his lightsaber at the spectator stands. He challenges the baron to throw him all he's got, so the baron unleashes the Corellian slice hounds.

As the baron contemplates his next move, a Neimoidian attendant delivers some troubling news. While the baron watched over his arena battle, a TIE Advanced fighter touched down in the plaza.

The baron hastily runs off to meet the TIE Advanced fighter's pilot, but is surprised to find that it is not who he expected. Where the baron had expected to see Darth Vader, he finds instead a young but weathered boy resembling Starkiller, Vader's secret apprentice.

When the baron realizes he isn't going to face Lord Vader, he threatens Starkiller's clone to reveal the security codes to this sector. He knew that capturing Rahm Kota would draw Vader to him, but he'd never expected to see Starkiller...or his clone.

The devious despot eventually realizes he isn't going to get what he wants from the clone, so he orders his stormtrooper squad to open fire and retreats like the coward that he is. The Baron makes a narrow escape just as his drawbridge retracts, leaving the Starkiller clone alone with the troopers.

The Eastern Arch

LEGEND

- Waypoints (see corresponding images)
- Saber Crystal Holocron
- Green Bacta Holocron
- Experience Points Holocron
- Force Energy Holocron

START

ARENA BOUND

The baron's first line of offense are Imperial stormtroopers. They can be removed easily enough. Mind Trick the nearest troopers, then cook the other, more distant foes with Force Lightning. If the stormtroopers are beyond the reach of your Force Lightning, then use Force Push to knock them off the platform quickly.

After you've destroyed the nearby stormtroopers, an AT-MP comes clanking out on the platform opposite yours. The cowardly clanker immediately begins firing missiles at you from afar. With no way to reach it across the long gap, use its projectiles against it by bouncing them back. Block the missile just as it reaches you, and the projectile will bounce back at the Imperial walker. After three hits, the AT-MP is destroyed and a bridge extends, connecting both platforms.

MISSION DETAILS

OBJECTIVE

Cross the city of Tarko-se and reach the baron's arena.

ENEMIES ENCOUNTERED

- Imperial stormtrooper
- Imperial riot trooper
- Jumptrooper
- Sith Acolyte
- AT-MP
- TIE fighter
- Gunship

HOLOCRONS FOUND

- 2 holocrons
- 1 Health Bacta holocron
- 1 Energy Bacta holocron
- Fury saber crystal (Magenta)
- Protection saber crystal (Purple)
- Healing saber crystal (Dark Green)
- Costume holocron

JEDI WISDOM

If you have at least 22,500 Force points, now is a good time to upgrade Mind Trick. The city of Tarko-se hangs high above the Cato Neimoidian landscape, so you'll have plenty of opportunities to coerce enemies into throwing themselves over a ledge.

ACHIEVEMENT/TROPHY UNLOCKED

Not a fan of Darth Vader? Why not show him how much you like him by destroying his personal TIE Advanced fighter? Better yet, Force Grip the vehicle and toss it at the AT-MP that comes stumbling across the gap to unlock the Valet Achievement or Trophy.

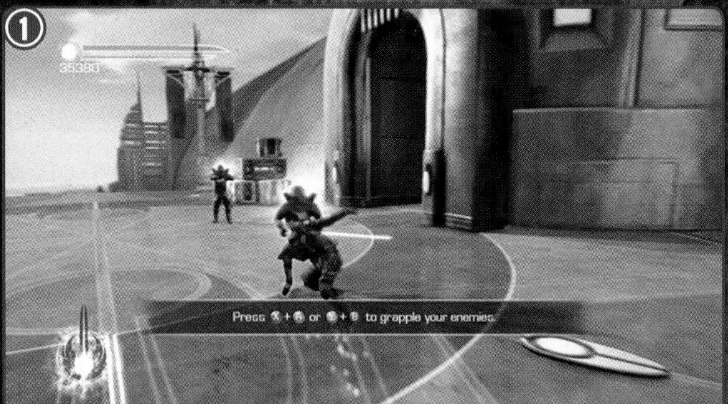

Dash across the bridge to meet with two Sith acolytes. These Force-resistant fighters are highly skilled in the ways of the dark side and can resist many of your Force attacks. Don't bother using Force Push or Lightning; instead use swift saber combos to shred them to pieces.

CLONER'S CAUTION

Be careful of the Sith acolyte's Force projectile attack. They can create a tangible sphere made of the Force and hurl it at you with great precision. If get hit, the sphere can knock you back and shock you, causing great damage.

HOLOCRON

There's a hidden saber crystal holocron—the purple Protection crystal—on the platform just left before you hop onto the elevator. Dash out to the circular part of the platform and remove the stacked crates at the end. The holocron is tucked behind the crates.

When you're ready, make a right and step on the circular elevator platform to follow the cowardly baron.

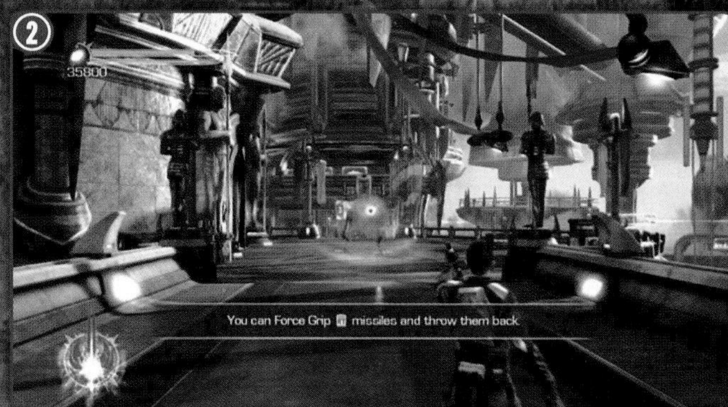

The elevator drops you onto a lower level of the city where another AT-MP waits with its missiles ready. As soon as it fires a missile at you, Force Grip the projectile and throw it back at the walker. Keep a safe distance as you pelt the pest with its own projectiles and bring it down before crossing the long walkway.

ACHIEVEMENT/TROPHY UNLOCKED

If you Force Grip all of the missiles and hurl them back at the AT-MP to destroy it, you'll unlock the Return to Sender Achievement or Trophy.

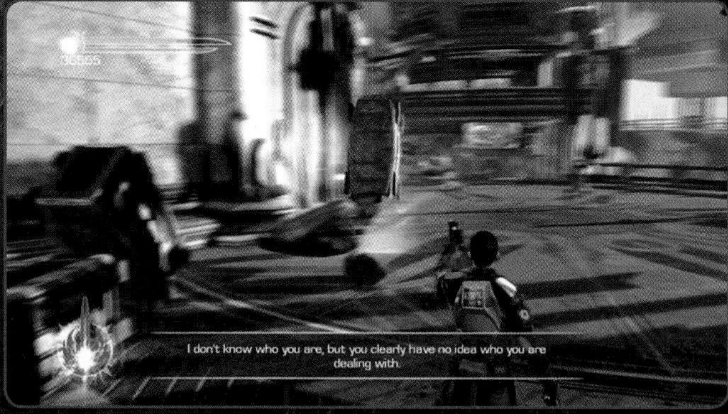

With the walker out of commission, use the nearby boxes as weapons against the stormtroopers that challenge you. Force Grip them, then zap them with Lightning to turn them into charged explosives! Once charged, hurl them at the enemy. Rush down the walkway on the other end of the circular platform, and use powerful Force Push blasts to demolish the enemies in your way.

Turn right down the attached walkway to reach the baron as he flees on his transport. Just as you reach his transport, the unit takes off like a rocket. The baron has managed to escape, for now.

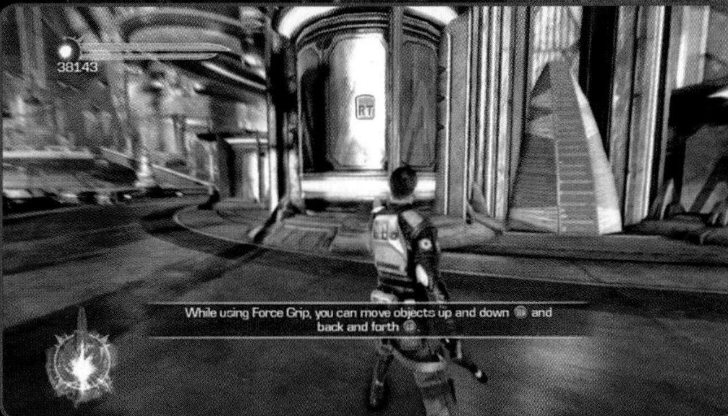

Turn back around and return the way you came. As you go up the walkway, several Imperials rush down to attack. Fry your frantic foes as they approach and get rid of them quickly.

If more enemies show up, either slice through them or use Mind Trick to turn them against each other. Once they're out of the way, turn toward the three sliding elevators attached to the building. Use Force Grip to move the two on the right up. Move the elevator on the farthest right all the way up.

Shift the center elevator up just enough to create a step between the left and right lifts. Hop up the elevators until you reach a platform high atop the building.

HOLOCRON

The next holocron is on the edge of the platform, just as you reach it. Grab it to score some experience points!

Dash down the walkway, scorching troopers as you go, until you reach a large, wide-open area on the right. Just across the ledge on the right is a large platform suspended by a mechanical arm.

Target the arm and use your new Saber Throw ability to disable it. When you do, the platform falls and several stormtroopers fall to their demise.

Double-jump onto the fallen platform and locate another nearby ledge supported by a mechanical arm. Once again, use Saber Throw to slice through the arm's support and bring the platform plunging down.

This time, double-jump dash across the next two platforms until you reach the next entry into the baron's palace. As you dash over to the entryway, finish with a downward smash of your lightsaber to knock the enemies off the ledge.

Enter the palace and Force Grip the large spherical statue at the room's center. Hurl it right, down the long hallway and bowl over the Imperial stormtroopers waiting to blast holes through you.

ACHIEVEMENT/TROPHY UNLOCKED

Bowl over three enemies with one toss of the sphere, and you'll get the Strike! Achievement or Trophy.

Turn right and storm down the hall toward the scout troopers at the far end. If the sphere is nearby, hurl it at them too. If not, there is plenty of other debris around the hall to throw.

Exit the hall through a door on the left and follow the walkway right. As you do, two Sith acolytes will appear out of thin air. They're resistant to Force powers, so use strong lightsaber combos to dispatch them quickly.

The path ahead is blocked by a large red force field. Use Force Grip to tear it down, then dash deeper into the baron's palace.

The next area is another circular walkway with a small structure at the center. Follow the walkway to the right, crushing enemies as you go, and reach the entry to the next corridor. Use Force Push to blast the door open; then dash into the next area.

Several Imperials litter the hallways. Turn them into piles of stormtrooper armor and fight your way to the Imperial riot troopers at the far end. Destroy them and turn right down the hall.

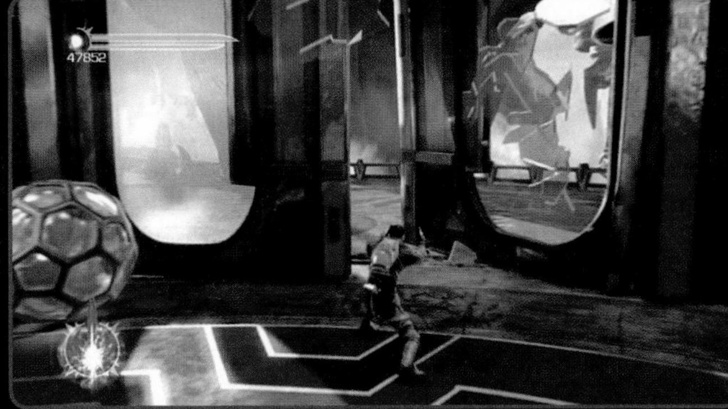

Crush the creeps crowding the hall, and make a left at the end. There you will find a large sealed doorway. Blow it open and exit the palace.

HOLOCRON

As soon as you exit the hall through the busted doors, make a sharp left. The next holocron is sitting just outside. Grab it to claim the Fury saber crystal.

Outside you're bombarded from above by several jumptroopers! Don't bother trying to grab them with the Force. Instead, zap them all with Force Lightning and short out their jet packs. When you do, they go haywire and crisscross each other, then explode.

After taking the jump out of the troopers, use Force Grip to disrupt the red force field in your way. Use the Force to destroy the next batch of enemies from afar, and sprint down the walkway to the next large circular area.

An AT-MP slowly lumbers out from around the corner. Stay back and wait for it to approach. Block its blaster fire and wait for it to fire missiles at you. When it does, bounce the missiles back at the machine until it's scrap metal.

Inch up to the platform's edge and use Force Grip to throw nearby objects at the enemies perched on the ledge above you. Use Saber Throw to bring the platform down, then double-jump onto the fallen platform to once again reach the higher walkway.

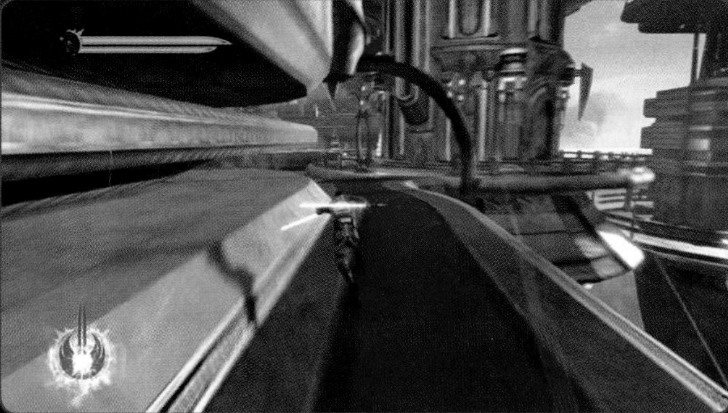

Dash down the long, curved walkway and avoid getting sniped by the scout troopers. Mind Trick them into becoming allies, then destroy the other enemies on the walkway. Stay near the center of the walkway and let the enemies come to you.

Don't speed to the left or right. If you do, the AT-MPs will pick you up from afar. Instead, use Force powers to throw enemies over the side, turn them on each other, or fry them. After you've destroyed all of the Imperial troopers, turn left and follow the path to the next walkway.

Bounce the missiles back at the clanker and blow it up! Disable the walking pile of scrap metal before the trio of riot troopers rushes out and attacks. Either slice them all to pieces or use Mind Trick to turn them on each other.

Make a right into the next large chamber, and use another globe statue to destroy the enemies inside.

HOLOCRON

When you remove the large red globe from its base, you'll reveal the next holocron. Hop onto the statue's base to grab the holocron and unlock the green Healing saber crystal.

The scout troopers at the hall's end on the right are crack shots with their sniper rifles. Quickly dash down and deny the scouts enough time to hone in you. When you reach them, use Mind Trick to turn them into allies.

Set the scouts loose on the other enemies, and wait for the Imperial riot troopers to rush in. Turn them into allies as well, then rush out of the walkway on the left behind your temporary group of protectors.

Rush into battle behind your makeshift allies, and use your Force powers to weaken the incoming waves of foes. Quickly traverse the short walkway to avoid being hit by the two AT-MPs ahead and get out of their firing range. Fry the walker on the right first, while the other mob distracts the clanker on the left.

JEDI WISDOM

You don't have to use an AT-MP's missiles against the walker; you can also toss the missiles at other enemies or even other walkers!

When you destroy the two clankers, an elevator at the platform's center delivers several Imperials. Rather than use your sabers, use Mind Trick on the first few riot troopers and let them take up the fight against the Sith acolytes.

JEDI WISDOM

The Sith acolytes resist all Force powers, including Mind Trick. Save your mind manipulation abilities for weaker foes like riot troopers, scout troopers, and stormtroopers.

After you destroy all the Imperials, the elevator at the area's center opens up, inviting you to trek higher into the baron's palace. Hop on and ride the elevator all the way up.

Exit the elevator and dash onto the long, cluttered bridge ahead of you. No sooner do you set foot on the bridge than a large gunship rises up from the side and attacks. Leap into a sprint and dash all the way down the walkway, staying ahead of the gunship's blaster fire as you go.

JEDI WISDOM

Don't bother with the stormtroopers on the bridge. Stop only to remove them if they're directly in your way and threaten to slow you down. If you can dash past them, do so. Don't engage in any unnecessary battles.

HOLOCRON

About halfway across the long walkway is another holocron. Jump into the air as you approach it, and dash toward it in midair to grab it. The holocron grants you a blue Energy Bacta Tank increase!

When you reach the end of the bridge, you manage to leap off the side and dive down to the area below for safety. Though the drop was steep, you safely land inside the baron's casino.

CHALLENGE UNLOCKED

After traversing the bridge safely, you unlock a new challenge! For tips and tricks on how to beat it, skip to the "Challenges" chapter.

JACKPOT!

The casino entrance is sealed. Unfortunately for a few troopers, they're sealed in the room with you. Dispatch them swiftly, then use a Force Push blast to blow open the doors to the casino.

The casino is split into two levels, with catwalks running above the edges of the casino floor. Scout troopers perch on the catwalks, so watch out for them while you battle enemies on the lower level. Use the globe statue at the room's center as a projectile, and knock the scout troopers off their perch.

ACHIEVEMENT/TROPHY UNLOCKED

If you weren't able to unlock the Strike! Achievement or Trophy earlier, this is a perfect place to do so. Hurl the center sphere at the trio of enemies on the left to bowl them over.

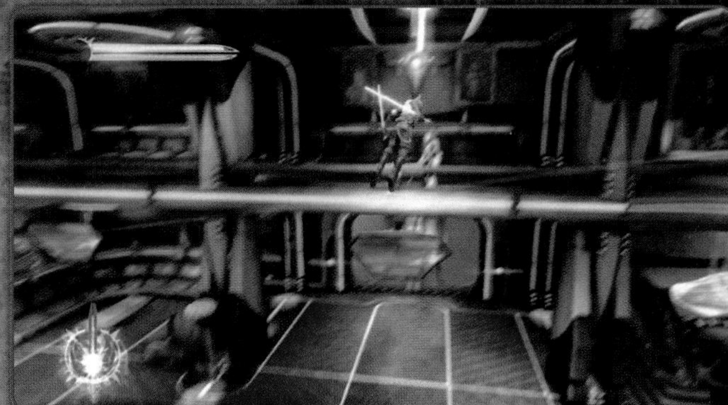

While the scouts are on the ground, rush around the lower level and eradicate the enemies around you. Use chained saber combos to take them out, then double-jump off the statue's base to reach the catwalks overhead.

Quickly cut through the scout troopers—or turn them into allies—then turn on the riot troopers patrolling nearby. Slice them up and clear the first area of the casino.

JEDI WISDOM

You can also use Force Grip to throw enemies into the red force field ahead of you. This is instant death for foes.

I
II
III
IV
V
VI
VII
VIII

HOLOCRON

There is a green holocron on the walkway above you, just in front of the red force field. Grab it after you've taken out the scout troopers; it will grant you a Health Bacta Tank increase!

With the room clear, go back down to the lower level and blow open the sealed door on the room's left side. Creep out and immediately scorch the jumptroopers flying overhead.

12

Make a right out of the door, following the walkway as it winds left, and eliminate the Imperials in your way. At the end of the path is a door along the right wall. Break it down with a Force Push blast and speed into the next part of the casino.

Step into the casino and hop onto the large pedestal near the center. Wait for the riot troopers to approach, and use Saber Throw to cause some damage. Use Mind Trick to turn the weakened troopers against each other, then press on, deeper into the casino.

A trio of Sith acolytes charges in for the attack. Take them out one by one. The three acolytes are strong, so split them up, using the parts of the casino as obstacles and eliminate each one.

Double-jump onto the upper level and approach the elevator on the room's left side. The top of the elevator car is attached by a short pipe. Use Saber Throw to slice through the pipe and send the car falling down. Jump down into the elevator shaft and reach the casino's lower level.

Make a right out of the elevator shaft, and slowly sneak out into the rows of casino machines. An AT-MP is hiding in the shadows and wastes no time in unleashing missiles on you. Dodge the first one, then Force Grip the others and throw them back at the machine.

Double-jump onto the top level, and Mind Trick all the scout and riot troopers into fighting each other. Sweep the area while they quibble, and take out all of the other low-level foes.

HOLOCRON

There's holocron floating over one of the bridges on the upper level. Grab it after you've taken out the Imperials in the room.

ACHIEVEMENT/TROPHY UNLOCKED

If you haven't already unlocked the Break the Bank Achievement or Trophy over the course of the battle, take a minute to destroy a few more game machines in this part of the casino. You'll unlock the achievement after destroying 10 game machines.

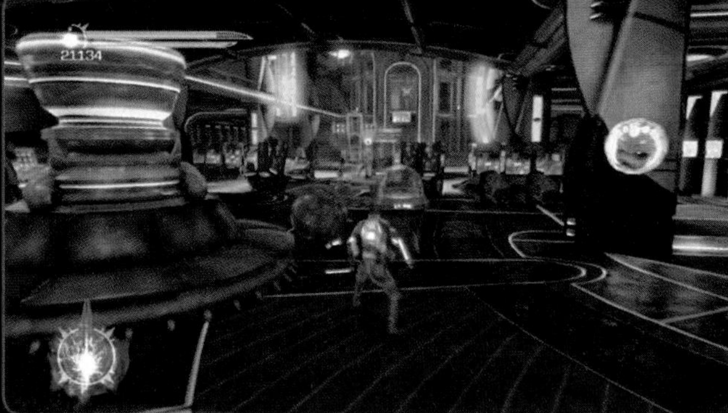

After destroying the Imperials, the red force field deactivates. Explore the casino further to find an AT-MP and several more Sith acolytes waiting for you. Use the game machines as weapons against the acolytes, but focus on the walker first.

You can also use the missile projectiles from the AT-MP against the Sith acolytes. If you take out the walker first, turn on the acolytes quickly and take them out. The longer you let them linger, the worse off you'll be.

Clear the area, then double-jump onto the top level. Follow the walkway to the room's far end, and drop the elevator at the end by severing the support cable with Saber Throw.

Drop down the shaft into a smoke-filled room, and slowly step into the haze. A carbonite droid is hiding in the smoke and slowly emerges as you step forward. Waste no time in engaging it in battle!

Force Grip the droid's massive shield, rip it away, and hit it with its own shield. Follow up your attack with Force Lightning and strafe around the clanker as you zap it. Stay on the move, whittling down the enemy with Force Lightning until you destroy it.

Deeper down the casino floor, another carbonite droid stomps into the room, followed by several Sith acolytes and Imperial stormtroopers. After entering, the droid turns around and seals the door behind it with carbonite.

Hide in the smoky upper level, and Mind Trick the enemies below to attack each other. While the stormtroopers distract the droid, jump down and take the battle to the acolytes. Eliminate them first, then bring down the droid.

Destroy the overgrown protocol droid, and use a Force Push blast to blow a hole open in the carbonite-sealed doorway.

HOLOCRON

At the end of the next hall is a large holographic projection of Jaba the Hutt and three casino machines. Destroy the three machines and a holocron appears above where they used to be. Jump up to grab it!

Dash down the hall and turn left at the end, just before you run into the Jabba holo-statue. Blow open the door and exit the casino.

ON THE TRAM

As soon as you exit, the large gunship strafes the bridge you're on and opens fire. Dash ahead of the fire and make it across the bridge before it collapses.

When you reach the end of the fallen bridge, you narrowly escape the gunship's fire! You mount a speeding rail transport, just like the one the baron used to escape, and speed down the rail to the city's other side.

Of course, the baron's men aren't going to give up that easily. As you speed along the transport, several waves of TIE fighters zoom in and attack. Use the Force to grip them in the air and destroy them before they cause too much damage to the tram.

JEDI WISDOM

You don't have to crush them to keep them from destroying the tram. Instead, try Force Gripping them and just letting them fall. This way, you can take out several in a short period of time. However, if you need to replenish your health, crush them to squeeze out every bit of health.

Fend off the TIE fighter swarms until the gunship resumes its attack. Turn around and face the gunship that zooms in behind you. Wait for it to open fire, and bounce its missiles back at it.

If it opens fire on you with blasters, move out of the way by backing up. Dodge the small batches of mines it drops, and focus on deflecting the missiles back at the gunship by blocking them away. After taking several hits with its own missiles, the gunship backs away.

CHALLENGE UNLOCKED

By defeating the gunship, you unlock a new challenge!

Despite your most heroic efforts, the tram takes too much damage and begins to go down in flames. It speeds along the laser rail but is clearly about to fall short of the docking pad. You jump out toward the docking pad, hundreds of feet away, and barely manage to land. It was a close call, but you've reached the opposite side of Tarko-se.

Cato Neimoidia

Having fought past the baron's guards, the Starkiller clone narrowly escapes a horrible death high above the Neimoidian planet. The speeding tram goes down in flames and almost takes the clone with it.

Were it not for his heightened abilities and Jedi-like reflexes, the troubled clone would have fallen thousands of feet to his death. But he is Starkiller's clone, and Starkiller knew the ways of the Force. That's how the clone was able to make the heroic leap off the tram and onto the Western Arch of Tarko-se City.

The Western Arch

LEGEND

- Waypoints (see corresponding images)
- Saber Crystal Holocron
- Green Bacta Holocron
- Experience Points Holocron
- Force Energy Holocron

MISSION DETAILS

OBJECTIVE

Cross the city of Tarko-se and reach the baron's arena to free General Rahm Kota.

ENEMIES ENCOUNTERED	HOLOCRONS FOUND
Imperial stormtrooper	1 holocron
Imperial riot trooper	1 Health Bacta holocron
Jumptrooper	1 Energy Bacta holocron
AT-MP	Chaos power crystal
TIE fighter	
Imperial gunship	

ON THE HUNT FOR THE BARON

As soon as you pull yourself up onto the docking platform, a transport of Imperial stormtroopers flies by and lands behind you.

HOLOCRON

There is a holocron sitting just on the other side of the small docking clamps. Grab it before you tear through the city.

Run up the incline leading back to the city proper. As you do so, a small group of Imperial riot troopers rushes down. Use Mind Trick on the first few and watch them turn around and head back.

Follow your "friends" up the walkway, and watch them slaughter each other with their electrostaff weapons. If any survive, use Force Grip to toss them or use Force Push to knock them over the walkway's side.

Sprint up the walkway and use Force Lightning on the jumptroopers hovering overhead. There are several scout troopers perched on the ledge above and to your right: Stay on the move to keep them from blasting you to bits.

Bully your way up the first walkway, and hold position at the center of the first circular platform. Use the Force to destroy the enemies as they pour down the opposite walkway, then rush up the path on the right.

About halfway up the walkway, a red force field activates and impedes your progress! Just then, several jumptroopers rise up from the sides of the walkway. Scorch them, then use Force Grip to bring down the field.

Sprint across the next circular platform, ignoring the TIE fighters that zoom by overhead, and reach the next area. A carbonite droid waits to attack. Turn the tables on it, and rip off its massive shield before you attack it with Force Lightning, saber combos, and projectiles.

Destroy the droid and wait for another transport to arrive with Imperial troopers. Mind Trick the riot troopers as they disembark their transport, then leap into the air to zap the jumptroopers in midair. With the jumptroopers taken care of, return to any riot troopers that haven't thrown themselves over the ledge and take them down with saber combos.

Clear the area, then use Force Grip to bring down the red force field.

Slowly cross the next short walkway. Watch the skies as you go—another transport will kindly drop more Imperials in your path. Once again, take out the jumptroopers first by zapping them out of the air; then run your lightsabers through the rest of the soldiers on foot.

Edge to the far right end of the next platform. It's a dead end, but enemies on the far left won't be able to target you in this location. Use Mind Trick to turn the remaining foes into allies, then rush out of the platform's right side to meet the enemies on the far left head-on.

First focus on the AT-MP. Deflect the walker's missiles back at it. Keep a safe distance from the metal menace, and use its missiles against it and the riot troopers that rush across the next bridge. Destroy every enemy on the bridge until you reach a red force field near the end.

CLONER'S CAUTION

There is a group of scout troopers on a bridge on the far right of your location. If you stand still too long, they'll pick you off!

Stand just left of the pylon along the bridge's right to block the scout troopers' view of your position. Once you're in the scouts' blind spot, use Force Grip to take down the red field.

Dash around the corner to the right, and head to the walkway where the scout troopers are perched. Use Force Grip to throw a nearby crate at the scouts, then throw the rest over the ledge.

HOLOCRON

After clearing this walkway, use Force Grip to move the large box back across the walkway and place it next to the three stacked boxes behind you. Jump onto the box stack, then turn right. Double-jump dash onto the ledge behind you and approach the far edge. Jump over the side to grab the holocron!

When you reach the next area, you find two carbonite droids and several Imperial troopers. Remove the droids' shields immediately, then use Mind Trick to turn the rest of the Imperials on the overgrown clunkers.

ACHIEVEMENT/TROPHY UNLOCKED

This is a great place to begin working on the Shattered! Achievement or Trophy. Coax the carbonite droids into spraying you with carbonite, then dash around the area so that it sprays the stormtroopers nearby. Once they are frozen, shatter them with a blow of your sabers.

The droids will eliminate the lower-level enemies, leaving you to face the two monsters on your own. Strafe around both droids and whittle them down with Force Lightning. Finally, rush in and take them down with saber combos.

No sooner do both droids go down than several more Imperials touch down on the platform. Use a combination of saber combos and Mind Trick to get rid of them. Use Force Grip to bring down the next red force field, and speed up the next walkway, back into the city interior.

HOLOCRON

You see the next holocron, a blue Energy Bacta Tank increase, as soon as you enter the room. Grab it before the gunship zooms by and blows the windows open.

The gunship blows open the windows, allowing nearby jumptroopers to shoot at you from outside the building. Edge up to the windows and fire a few blasts of Force Lightning outside to fry the jumptroopers' jet packs.

With the jumptroopers no longer a threat, turn around and face the oncoming wave of riot troopers. Turn your foes into friends and let them battle it out with each other. Wait to see who ends up the last trooper standing and congratulate him...with your lightsaber.

BRIDGE OF DESPAIR

Follow the hallways through the city to a long bridge heavily occupied by enemy forces. The bridge is stocked with barricades and Imperial troopers. Mind Trick the first few to get them out of your way, and quickly head toward the large barrier protected by the blue force field.

Use the smaller barricades as protection from the scout troopers near the large barricade. Tuck yourself behind the small barricades, turn toward the edges of the bridge, and electrocute the nearby jumptroopers.

When you destroy all of the enemies on this section of the bridge, the blue field is deactivated. Use a Force Push blast to blow down the large barricade, then speed into the next section of the occupied bridge.

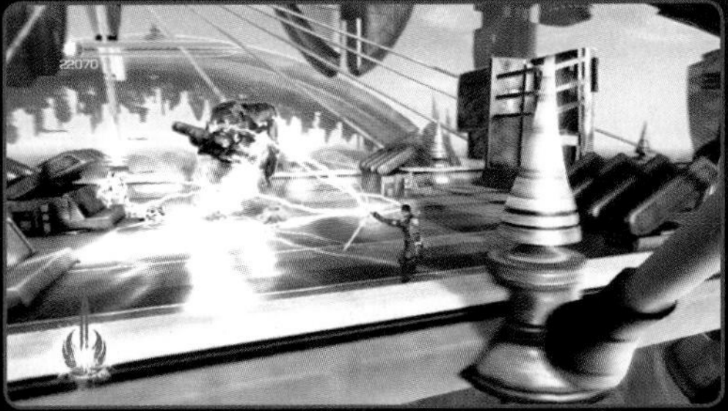

The next section is guarded by several more Imperials and a carbonite droid. Before you rush into the next area, stay near the partially demolished barrier and rip off the droid's shield.

Use Mind Trick on the weak-minded Imperial soldiers nearby; they will turn on the mechanical menace, distracting it. Take your saber and Force Powers to the droid while it attacks its allies.

Destroy the droid, then venture farther down the bridge. When the squad of jumptroopers leaps into the air ahead of you, bring them back down with a Force Lightning blast.

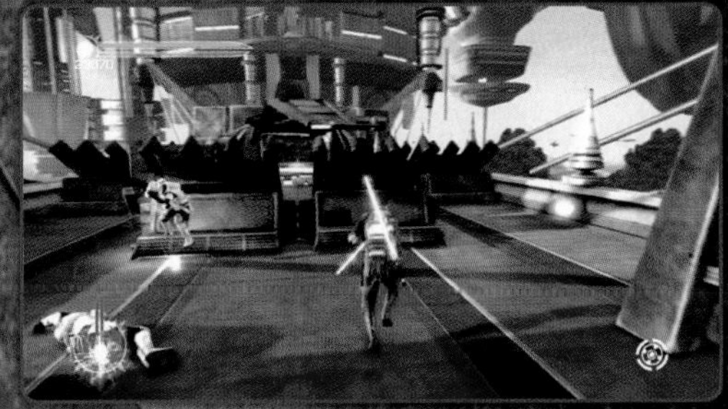

Blow through the next large barricade, and jump over the small barriers in your way. This time you're greeted by two large carbonite droids and a squad of Imperial soldiers. Do as you have done before: Mind Trick the Imperial soldiers and turn them on the droids or each other while you rip off the droids' shields and get to work them.

If the scout troopers near the next large barrier open fire on you, rush them and cut them down, then return to the larger droids.

JEDI WISDOM

If you're having too much difficulty taking down the droids and Imperial soldiers in this section, use Force Fury to augment your Force powers and fry everyone nearby with Force Lightning.

HOLOCRON

A green Health Bacta holocron is sitting near the center of this bridge. Grab it after the battle with the two carbonite droids.

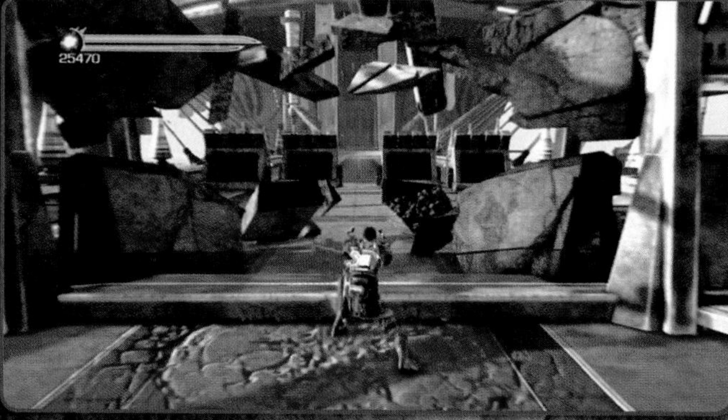

Once again, blast down the large barricade and eliminate the Imperial troopers behind it. Dash to the bridge's end, where several small barricades are lined up in a row.

GUNSHIP BATTLE

When you reach the end, an explosion rocks the bridge. It crumbles beneath you, and the gunship slowly rises out of the dust. This time you can't dash away; you're trapped!

Sprint back to the four small barriers and hide behind one. When the gunship opens fire with its blasters, the barrier will protect you. Stay hidden behind it until the gunship stops firing.

When it does, rush out of your protective cover and use Saber Throw to slice a part of the gunship's turret. Your attack won't completely disable it, but it will damage it. After taking a bit of damage to its turret, the gunship switches to missiles.

Use Force Grip to grab the missiles in midair and throw them back at the gunship. If it fires more than one at a time, use your blocking to bounce one back and double-jump into the air to avoid the rest.

JEDI WISDOM

Do not hide behind the four barriers to avoid getting hit by the missiles. Not only do you need to be out in the open to deflect the missiles back at the gunship, but also the missiles will instantly destroy the barriers; you need them for protection against the gunship's less powerful blaster fire.

8

After suffering several of its own missiles, the gunship becomes susceptible to a Force Grip attack. Follow the onscreen commands to grab the gunship and slam it left against the nearby tower.

With one booster down, the gunship resumes its blaster-turret attack. Duck behind another barrier again and repeat the same series of attacks on the gunship as before. When you slam the gunship into another tower and destroy the second booster, it finally goes down.

Cato Neimoidia

Once again, the Starkiller clone finds himself in a perilous situation. Having just defeated the Imperial gunship, he scrambles across the faltering transport and leaps across its top.

As the ship continues to fall, he flies across the sky and lands inside a tall, shaftlike tower. The tower leads down to the main arena. He's arrived at the Tarko-se arena.

The Tarko-se Arena

LEGEND

- (#) Waypoints (see corresponding images)
- Saber Crystal Holocron
- Experience Points Holocron

Both the Saber Crystal and Experience Points holocrons can be found in the drum-lke area before entering the arena.

MISSION DETAILS

OBJECTIVE

Fight your way through the arena and reach the baron. Free General Rahm Kota.

ENEMIES ENCOUNTERED

Imperial stormtrooper

Imperial riot trooper

Jumptrooper

Gorog

HOLOCRONS FOUND

1 holocron

Corrosion saber crystal (light red)

MEET THE GOROG

The vent deposits you at a gated drumlike area deep beneath the Tarko-se arena. When the gate drops, you see a hanging skeleton of a massive creature. Drop down and locate the elevator platform nearby.

HOLOCRON

There are two holocrons in this drum area. The first is on the second floor of the drum across from where you enter. To reach it, ride the elevator platform up, then double-jump dash over to a small ledge on the drum's right side. From there, double-jump dash again onto the walkway where the holocron sits. Grab it to unlock the Corrosion saber crystal.

The next holocron is on the level above the first. To reach it, hop back on the elevator platform and ride it even higher than before—but not all the way up! This time, double-jump dash directly onto the floor with the holocron. Grab it to gain more experience points.

JEDI WISDOM

If you ride the elevator lift up to the arena without getting the holocrons first, you'll have to replay the level in order to acquire them.

Step onto the platform and ride it up to the arena. The massive arena is full of spectators, but only one matters. The baron, safe atop his viewing deck, has had enough of your meddling.

With no one left to oppose you, the baron orders his Neimoidian attendee to send out the Gorog. The Neimoidian is shocked at the request. He insists that the arena's restraints are not ready for the Gorog to be unleashed.

Still, the baron insists. His fury may be the only thing that matches the Gorog's. Meanwhile, down on the arena floor, you join General Rahm Kota, who is very pleased to "see" you.

Just then, the sliding door across the arena opens, releasing a large, hungry...rancor? You relax your defensive stance somewhat, relieved that the beast that ambled out was a measly rancor. But before you can leap to the attack, a large three-fingered hand rises over the rancor and smashes it completely.

The rancor disappears into a pit. That is when the rest of the beast hoists itself out of the hole. The Gorog is a massive monster, as big as the arena itself! When it sees you, it lowers its rancor-sized head and roars. You're in for a fight!

The Gorog is a titanic brute. Despite having a huge cranium, it doesn't seem to have much to fill it. Luckily, that means it doesn't exactly have a sophisticated repertoire of attacks.

The Gorog begins its attacks by sweeping its hand across the arena to swipe you away. It immediately follows up its attack by slamming down the other hand—the one he didn't use to swipe. Double-jump dash over his swiping hand, then dash away from the slamming attack.

Wait for the monster to raise its hand to attack again, and hit it with Force Lightning and Saber Throw attacks. While its hand is in the air, look for the red shadow it casts on the ground. If you're in the shadow, you'll get smashed, so dash out of the way!

Continue dodging the Gorog's attacks until it gets so angry that it roars at you. If the beast's roar hits you, it'll knock you down but won't dish out much damage. To stay on your feet, block the roar with your lightsabers and counterattack with Saber Throw and Force Lightning.

Continue dodging and counterattacking until the Gorog slams its hand down again. When it does, bombard the Gorog's fist with Force Lightning attacks!

Eventually, the shackles around the Gorog's fist absorb enough electricity that they become magnetic. Seize the opportunity and use Force Push to slam the hand back until it is locked in place against the magnetic lock high above the arena.

Repeat this process with the second hand, using mostly Force Lightning or lightning-infused attacks until you charge the second manacle. Once it's fully charged, Force Push the hand in place until it is locked.

With both of the Gorog's hands locked against the arena supports, its head is defenseless. Zap it with Force Lightning or slice it with Saber Throw, then use Force Grip to grab its head and slam it into the ground! Not only does it anger the Gorog greatly, but it also inflicts major damage.

After slamming its head into the ground, the Gorog becomes so angry it rips its hands off the supports and begins attacking again! Repeat the process a second time; power its manacles, attach them to the supports, and slam its head.

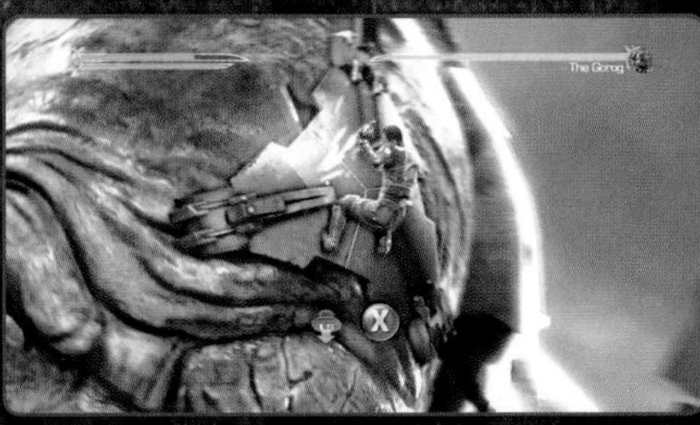

Your second round of attacks weakens the Gorog even more. So much, in fact, that you can leap onto its head and run your sabers directly into its brain. Perhaps a lobotomy will calm this titan.

Leap onto the Gorog's head and carefully follow the onscreen commands until you rip off the metal plate on the creature's head. When you stab the monster's massive head, it rears back in anger, plucks you off its arm as you try to escape, and flings you across the arena.

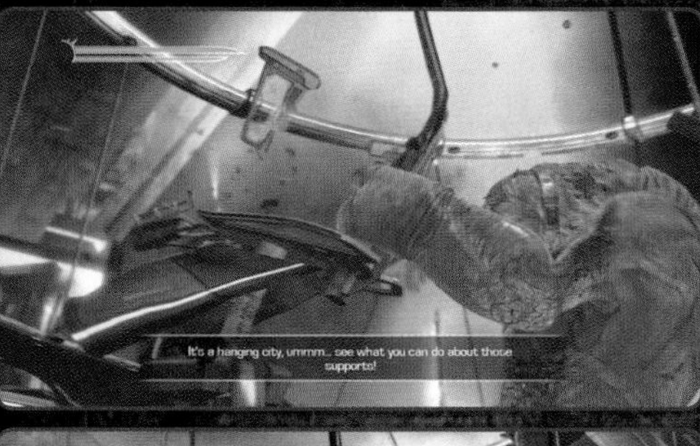

Rather than lobotomize the beast, you just made it even more angry! It begins to tear through the arena as you dust yourself off, having been thrown onto the upper levels of the structure.

In order to bring the monster down, you'll have to bring the city down on top of it. Rush to the right and do away with the nearby stormtroopers—simply Force Push them off the walkway.

Once again, double-jump dash the monster's swiping attack. Fry the Gorog with Force Lightning and weaken it again. You won't cause much damage, but you will make it angrier. Anger it enough to make it tear down the structure on the right.

When it does, rush around to the rear of the structure, fighting past stormtroopers as you go, and climb to the top. As you reach the top, the Gorog grabs ahold of the support. Strike down its hand and make the Gorog tear the structure loose.

CLONER'S CAUTION

Beware of the jumptroopers hovering around the top of the platform. Zap them with Force Lightning to get them out of the way before you attack the Gorog's hand.

The Gorog tears off the structure's support, forcing you to hop down onto the next section of the arena. Dash toward the stormtrooper squad, and take them all down quickly before returning your attention to the Gorog.

Resume your attack on the Gorog, and lure it toward the next tower. Rush up the tower and strike it down. This time, the beast tears off the support and everything begins to crumble. Storm across the falling platforms until you reach the baron's viewing room.

When you land, you find the baron and his protection detail in a battle with Master Kota! The battle is short, as you deflect the troopers' blaster fire back at them. The Gorog smashes through the room, and the baron plunges directly into the monster's massive mouth!

The arena supports finally give away, and everything begins to fall to the planet's surface! The monster grabs Master Kota and takes him down the miles-long plunge to Cato Neimoidia below.

THE PLUNGE

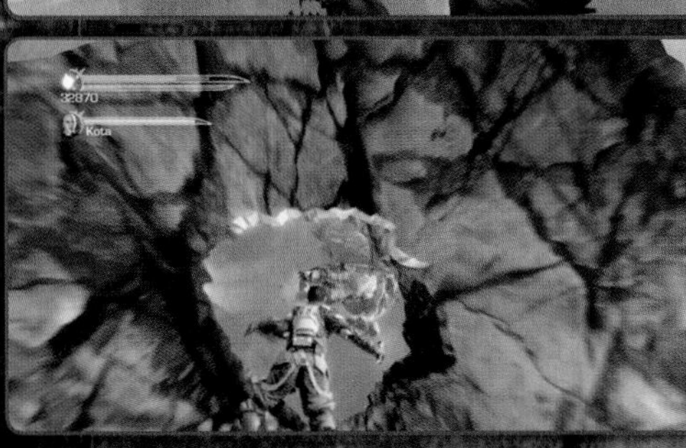

Without hesitation, you leap down, chasing after the plummeting beast. The debris from the falling city flies up at you at dangerous speed. Use Force Push blasts to destroy the debris as it flies at you and get it out of the way and use dash to speed up your descent

However, don't use Force Push repeatedly; you'll use up all your Force Energy. Instead, carefully choose the pieces of debris to destroy. Demolish the large pieces and dodge the smaller ones. Some pieces are so big that you may have to blast them twice to destroy them. Others may be easier; blast them once to punch a hole, then fly through the hole to avoid taking damage.

ACHIEVEMENT/TROPHY UNLOCKED

If you reach the Gorog without taking any damage from the debris, you'll unlock the Stay on Target Achievement or Trophy!

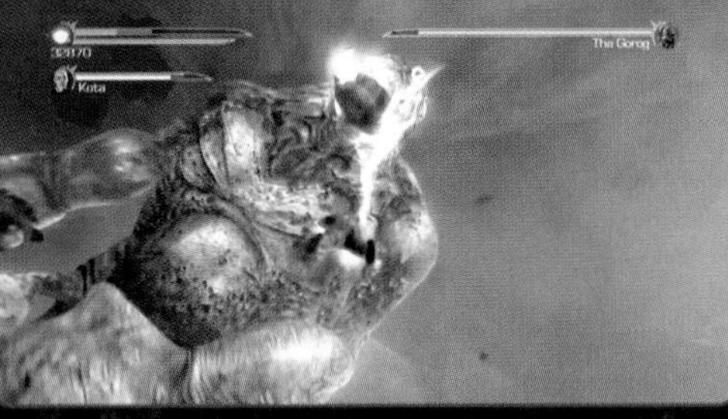

Dodge and destroy the debris as you descend, and reach the Gorog. Waste no time in launching your attack; the Gorog grasps Kota and squeezes the life out of him in the process!

Glide up and down, avoiding the Gorog's sweeping attacks as you fall, and bombard the beast with blasts of Force Lightning. Saber Throws are also very effective against the mindless brute. Attack and evade as you fall.

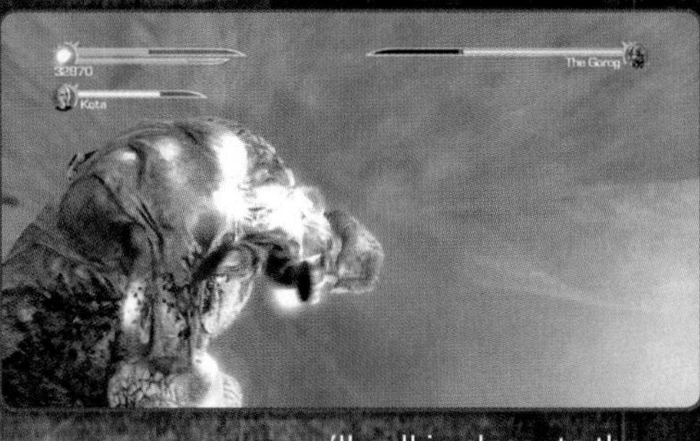

If the Gorog swats you away, you'll fall back a little bit and lose precious time; remember, Master Kota's life hangs in the balance, so be quick! When you regain your composure, you'll pull in closer to the Gorog's ugly face. Use Force Lightning up close to burn massive amounts of health from the monster's Health bar.

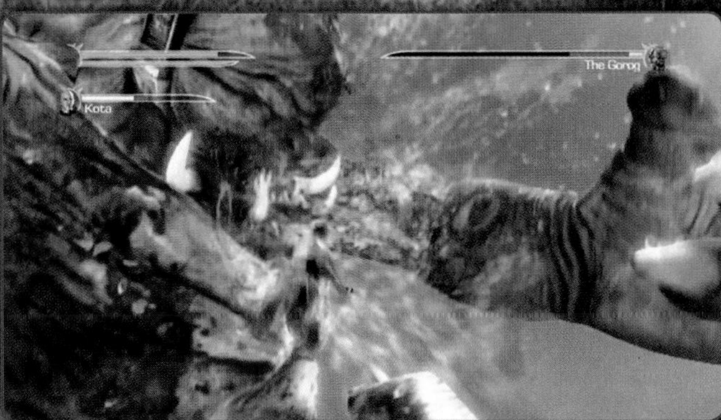

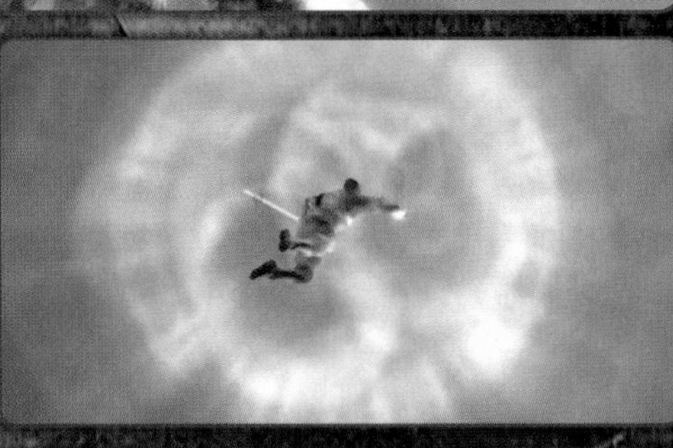

Eventually, the monster manages to pull away, and you're forced again to battle through the debris. Obliterate the chunks of rock and city until you reach the monster a second time. Resume your attack and electrocute the Gorog's head until it can take no more.

Finally, follow the onscreen command to create a Force funnel around yourself and speed toward your falling foe at superspeed. You fly down so quickly that you burst through the Gorog, finally killing it and forcing it to release the Jedi.

As you and Master Kota free-fall to the planet's surface below, you realize that you've no way to survive this. Luckily, the *Rogue Shadow* (Starkiller's ship) is nearby and zooms in just in time to pluck you from your free fall. You speed away to safety with Master Kota.

Dagobah

Safe in the *Rogue Shadow*, the clone quickly begins to look for Juno. Of all of Starkiller's memories, it is those of Juno that drive him. Unfortunately, Master Kota has long since lost communication with her. With the Rebel fleet scattered across the Outer Rim, he was unable to keep track of her, especially after his capture. Regardless of Juno's location, Master Kota wants the clone to lead the rebellion.

Starkiller's clone refuses. He may have Starkiller's memories and feelings, but he is not the same person. When he tells Kota that he's nothing more than a clone, the Jedi Master refuses to believe it.

Kota insists that the clone join them and lead the fight, but the Starkiller clone insists that he needs guidance. Leading the fight was Starkiller's destiny, and if he is nothing more than a clone of the original Starkiller, he must find his own way.

He begins his search in Dagobah.

MEANWHILE...

Back on Kamino, Darth Vader meets with the bounty hunter Boba Fett. The two plot to hunt down the rogue clone, but he's had a few days lead in his escape. The Dark Lord quickly formulates a plan to draw the escapee to him, rather than chase him.

The Vision

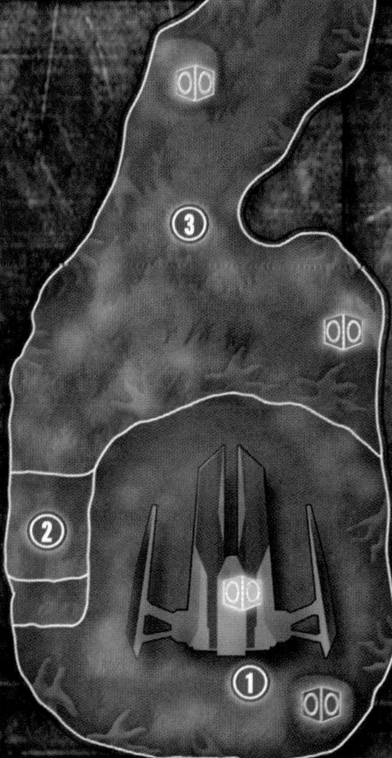

FINDING YOUR PATH

When you arrive in Dagobah, you find a dark and dank planet. The marshy landscape is perfect for hiding, and yet, for some reason, it seems like the perfect place to find oneself.

HOLOCRON

As soon as you disembark the *Rogue Shadow* in Dagobah, circle around to the back of the ship. Jump onto the large boulder, then bound up to the top of the ship. There, floating high above the *Rogue Shadow,* is the first holocron—a holocron.

The second holocron is hidden underneath the large boulder you used to jump onto the ship. Use Force Grip to lift the boulder and move it out of the way. Underneath you'll find a blue Energy Bacta Tank holocron.

Double-jump onto the ridge to the ship's left and trek deeper into the Dagobah jungle. Just above the ridge is a small hut tucked away in the corner.

HOLOCRON

The next holocron, a green Life Drain saber crystal, is sitting just to the right of the hut's entrance. Grab it before you continue into the jungle.

MISSION DETAILS

OBJECTIVE

Meditate in the Dagobah jungle and find your way.

ENEMIES ENCOUNTERED

None

HOLOCRONS FOUND

2 holocrons

1 Health Bacta holocron

1 Energy Bacta holocron

Life Drain saber crystal (green)

Focus saber crystal (light blue)

3

Follow the path left of the hut deeper into Dagobah.

HOLOCRON

After making a left at the hut, use Force Grip to lift the large boulder on the left. Underneath is a green Health Bacta Tank holocron. Continue following the path until you come across another holocron. Grab it. This one is a light blue Focus saber crystal.

Finally, grab the next holocron farther along the path, just before you enter the cave.

4

Approach the entrance to the cave and meet Master Yoda. As you are about to enter, he greets you with a sly smile. He knows something that you don't; you're about to find a part of yourself that has been lost.

Enter the cave. As you traverse the darkness of the cave, hands reaching out from the jungle vines begin clawing at you. You whip your lightsaber around, lighting the dark and revealing several other Starkiller clones begging for help!

You ignore the trapped clones and proceed farther into the deep black of the cave. In the end, you find a pitch-black area dimly lit by a mysterious, glowing fog at your feet.

In the distance, you see the silhouette of a feminine figure. As the scene comes into focus, you can finally see that it is Juno. Suddenly, as if a holographic display was suddenly switched on, the area around Juno materializes.

She's in a ship, giving out commands to the rest of the crew. They're under attack! A nearby explosion rocks the control room where she's stationed, and she's shot. As she stumbles away from her assailant, the ship begins to fade...until eventually, she fades too. The vision is over and your purpose is now clear. You must save Juno Eclipse.

When you emerge from the darkness, Master Yoda is waiting outside. He insists that you follow this vision. And you agree.

The Rebel Ship *Salvation*

Having found his purpose, the clone reunites with General Kota and heads to the Rebel ship *Salvation*. There, Captain Juno Eclipse commands a portion of the ragtag Rebels.

If the clone's vision was true, then the ship would be under attack. Since there was no sign of attack, then the vision must not have come to pass yet.

The duo docks inside the *Salvation* and quickly begins their trek to the control room aboard a moving platform. As they make their way, General Kota explains that the Rebels are slowly losing heart. Less and less fighters are willing to do what needs to be done.

But with a Jedi on their side, surely the rest of the Rebel fighters will jump at the chance to bring down the Galactic Empire. When the clone reminds Kota that he's just a clone, Kota refuses to put stock in that fact. With little else to convince Kota, the clone hands over a data cylinder with coordinates and schematics for the secret cloning facility on Kamino.

An explosion rocks the ship before the daring duo's platform reaches its destination. The assault from the clone's vision has begun!

Aboard the *Salvation*

See map on next page

MISSION DETAILS

OBJECTIVE

Fight your way to the ship's control room where Juno Eclipse is stationed.

ENEMIES ENCOUNTERED
- Terror spider droid
- Terror trooper
- Terror giant
- Terror walker

HOLOCRONS FOUND
- 2 holocrons
- 1 Health Bacta holocron
- 1 Energy Bacta holocron
- Regeneration saber crystal (light green)
- Wisdom saber crystal (white)

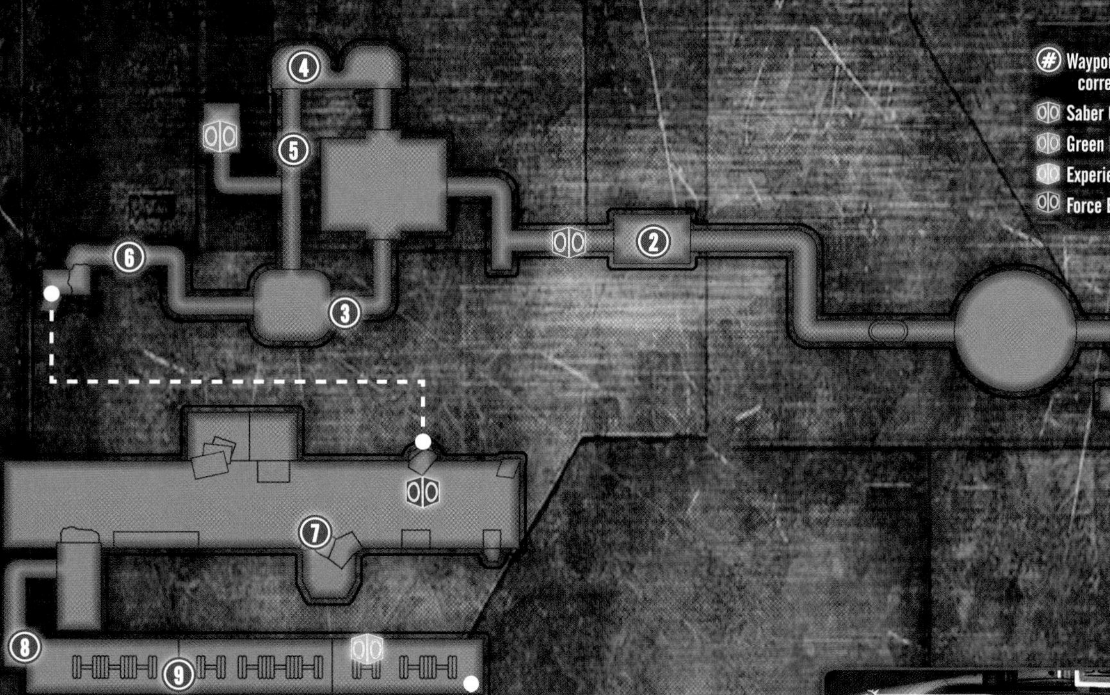

Grab the sealed door with the Force and lift it. Beyond the sealed door is a large room. Go inside.

VISIONS FULFILLED

Hop off the platform and sprint up the entry to the hall on the left. There are no enemies nearby, so follow Master Kota down the corridors as they wend to a dead end.

Upon entering the room, you find a squad of Rebel fighters tossed about. You slowly patrol the room, careful not to get ambushed by any rogue Imperials. Suddenly, out of the smoke, a hand claws at your feet.

You drop the saber to strike, only to find that it's your combat training droid! When you ask it about Juno, it informs you that a bounty hunter has taken her to the hangar bay on Deck 7!

TO THE RESCUE

Begin your trip to the hangar bay by using a Force Lightning shock to power the fuse just left of the door. Once the fuse is charged, pass through the sliding door, deeper into the ship.

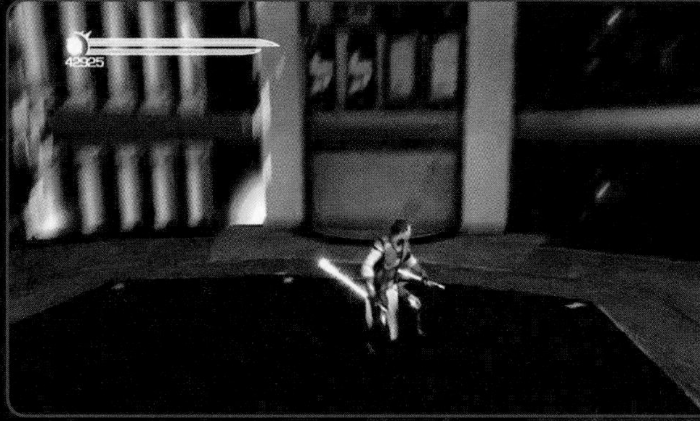

Round the corner and use Force Grip to pick up the fuse sitting on the ground. Move it over to the fuse slot left of the next door and slip it into place. Once in place, shock it with Force Lightning to power up the door.

Run down the hall and step onto the elevator platform at the end. It lowers you a few levels and quickly loses power, sending you plummeting down several levels.

JEDI WISDOM

Every chance you get, destroy the walls of the ship to acquire valuable Force Points.

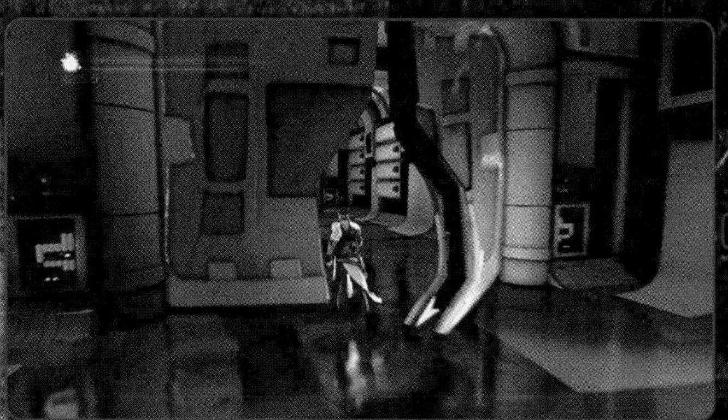

When the platform reaches the bottom, double-jump up to the next corridor. Follow the corridor to a long, curved hallway with windows lining the right side. Use Force Grip to peel open the door at the end and enter the hall.

Rush to the hall's end and peel another door open with the Force.

Rush inside and immediately use your Force Lightning, saber combos, and Force Push to destroy the small army of terror spider droids waiting for you. Once you've taken out the first batch of foes, a whole new batch drops in from above.

The spiders slowly begin to circle around you, when suddenly you have a flashback. You remember your Force Repulse ability just in the nick of time! Use it to obliterate the entire group of terror spider droids. Continue using Force Repulse until you've destroyed all of the terror spider droids in this room.

JEDI WISDOM

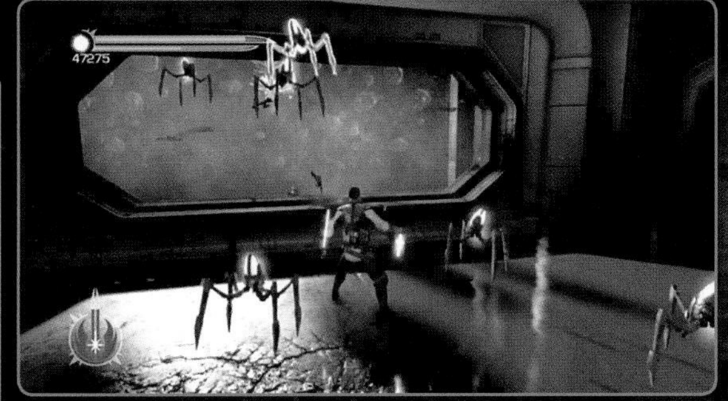

You can also break open the window in this room to blow the terror spider droids into space. However, you can do this only once; the broken window is instantly replaced by a force field.

CHALLENGE UNLOCKED

By defeating all of the terror spider droids in this room, you unlock a new challenge!

Once again, grab the nearby fuse and slip it into the slot just left of the next door. Power the fuse with a lightning shock and open the next door.

HOLOCRON

The first holocron is in the room immediately following this door. Grab it as you pass through this short hall to unlock the Regeneration saber crystal.

Drop onto the elevator platform at the end of the next hall, and ride it down, deeper into the heart of the ship. As you descend, several more terror spider droids drop in on you from above. Use the large elevator platform to your advantage, and wait for the spiders near the center of the lift. As they circle around you, destroy them with Force Repulse.

Dash down the corridor ahead of you, frying the little pests as you go. If you're surrounded by them, you know what to do. Speed right around the next corner and follow the corridors to a large, wide-open room with several tanks in it.

ACHIEVEMENT/TROPHY UNLOCKED

To unlock the Master of Disaster Achievement or Trophy, destroy all of the coolant tanks on the ship, beginning in this room.

Make a left in this large room and pass through the flaming door. When you reach the end, you find a blue force field blocking your path. On the other side is Juno, unconscious! There's no way to reach her from this area, so turn around and backtrack to the previous room.

A shadowy figure appears at the far end of the large room. However, before you can see it clearly, the mystery fighter disappears! He quickly begins to stalk you in the smoky room. Raise your sabers to block before it attacks. When the terror trooper reappears, either shock it with Force Lightning or use Mind Trick to distract it. Follow up your Force attack with saber combos and take it down.

After destroying the terror trooper, several more terror spider droids appear. Dispatch them quickly, then speed over to the fuse wedged into the right of the broken, flaming door. Grab it with the Force, slip it in the slot to the left of the door across the room, then charge it with Force Lightning.

Several more terror troopers appear behind you while you attempt to power the next door. Turn around and use Mind Trick on them when they appear. The terror troopers won't immediately turn into allies or attempt to destroy themselves, but they will experience pain before your suggestion sets in. Rush them and cut them up as they struggle with Mind Trick.

JEDI WISDOM

Terror troopers can't disappear if they're stunned by Mind Trick.

Pass through the newly unlocked door into the next section of the ship. Several more terror troopers appear. Some of these throw fireballs and electricity. Wait for them to appear out of thin air and use Force Lightning and Mind Trick to stun them. Finish them off with saber combos, then make a left down the long hall.

Turn left at the end of this hall, and follow it to a room where several more terror spider droids attack. Clear the room quickly and find another discarded fuse and a sealed door.

HOLOCRON

Instead of using the fuse on the nearby door, Force Grip the fuse and maneuver it into a small room om the right. Pop the fuse into the slot in this room, charge it, and open the next door. Inside are three tanks. Use Force Repulse to destroy them, and grab the green Health Bacta holocron sitting in the center tank. Remember to remove the fuse before you leave this room; you'll need it for the next door.

ACHIEVEMENT/TROPHY UNLOCKED

If you've been destroying all coolant tanks as you go, these should be the last three coolant tanks to get the Master of Disaster Achievement or Trophy.

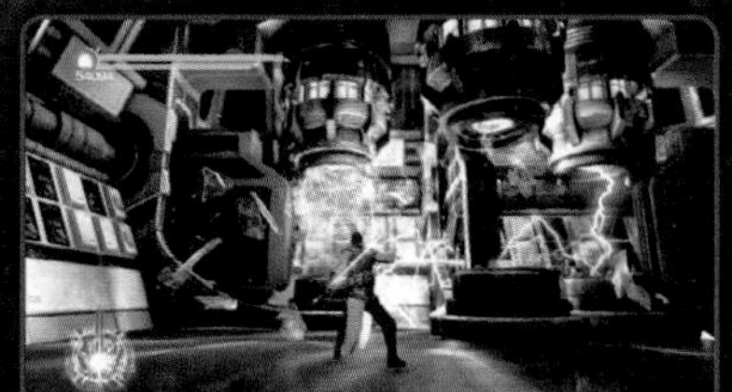

Place the fuse into the slot and power it up. Enter the now-unlocked door to find a small area blocked off by transparent view screens. On the other side, you see Boba Fett escorting Juno.

Use a powerful Force Push blast or saber strike to break through the screens and give chase. Take out the terror troopers in the room, then turn and use the Force to lift the door on the right.

Follow the halls to a long room. After you enter, an explosion at the room's far end hints at a massive menace waiting for you in the distance. The room's far end is demolished instantly, and a large sweeping beam fills the hall.

Rush to the hall's end and destroy the terror spider droids in your way. Make a left into the passage created by the melted hall. Make an immediate right, through another large, melting hole in the wall. Follow the path of destruction out to a long canyonlike section of the ship that is marked by several similar burned holes in the wall.

ACHIEVEMENT/TROPHY UNLOCKED

Destroy all of the terror spider droids in this hall. If you don't unlock the Arachnophobia Achievement or Trophy by now, you should be close. Crush as many spider pests as you can until you get all 200 you need for the unlockable.

Edge out onto the first platform and double-jump dash across the chasm onto the next ledge. Turn around and locate the next ledge farther along the chasm. Once again, double-jump dash across to reach another small ledge.

HOLOCRON

There is a blue Energy Force Bacta Tank holocron just beneath the first ledge leading out into the chasm. Double-jump dash across the chasm, then turn around to see it. Jump onto the rickety platform, grab the holocron, then quickly jump back onto the ledge above you.

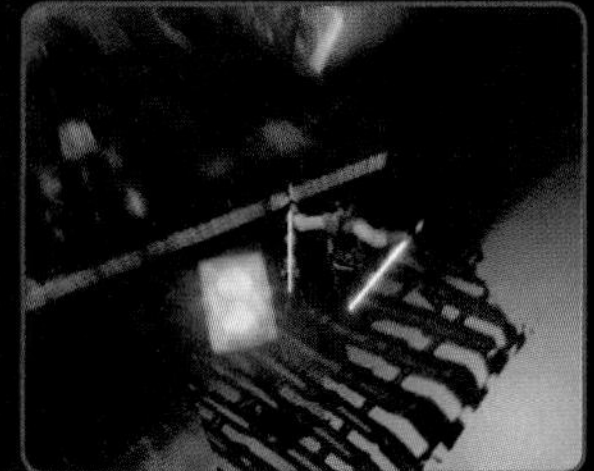

Continue zigzagging across the chasm, hopping from platform to platform, until you reach a room with a small pile of fuses in it. Grip one and float it across the chasm into the next room. Drop it, then double-jump dash into the next room and pop it into place.

Charge the fuse, open the door, and go through. Jump up the stepped ledges on the left and carefully creep out to the edge. Locate the rickety platforms across the gap and double-jump dash onto them. Quickly traverse the platforms before they give way, and reach the end of the canyon. Make a left back and reenter the main section of the ship.

Turn right in the ship and follow the long curved hall to its end. Drop down the shaft there and reach the gearworks area of the ship.

GEARWORKS

The gearworks is a very dangerous area of the ship. Several red force fields surround electrical blasts, and huge spinning cogs churn nearby. Wait for the electrical blasts to stop, then dash past the blast tubes.

On the other side, the path splits in two. On the right is a spinning cog firing electric bursts inside of it. On the left is another red electrical tube. Wait for the red electric field on the left to stop, then dash past to the room's center. Turn right and hop over the small spinning rotor.

At the room's far end is a rotor spinning at great speed. Use Force Grip to bring the rotor to a screeching halt, then jump through the small gap it creates to the other side of the gearworks. This time, the red tubes are firing too quickly to dash past them. Instead, go to the left and wait for the spinning cog to stop and the lasers to deactivate.

HOLOCRON

There is a holocron sitting between the spinning cogs on the room's left side. Wait for the cogs to stop spinning, then quickly dash through to grab the holocron, earning you experience points.

Carefully dash through the cogs once they've stopped spinning, and reach the room's far end. Drop into the shaft to reach a small terror spider droid–infested room. Demolish the little pests with Force Repulse, then continue traversing the gearworks.

Fight through the spiders to the rear of this room, past several more spinning cogs. Use the Force to stop the rapidly spinning rotor along the back wall and hop through into the next room. Wait for the rows of red tubes to stop firing, then dash past them.

The room's far end is crawling with more terror spider droids. Use Force Repulse to dispatch the terror spider droids and drop down the next hole.

ENGINE ROOM

After the drop, you find yourself in a short, white hall. Run to the end and pass through the sliding door to reach the engine room. The engine blasts on the room's right side, while several enemies wait for you below.

HOLOCRON

Before dropping down from your platform, turn right and locate the platform next to you. Jump across, then turn left and locate the holocron floating above the engine nestled in the right wall. Creep out to the platform's edge, then double-jump dash toward the holocron and grab it for experience points.

If you miss the holocron on your first attempt, you can try again once the room is clear. You can also try to leap out from the opposite platform if that helps.

JEDI WISDOM

If you land on the holocron in this room, you can then double-jump dash across the room to the next platform and bypass all of the enemies in this room!

There are three different types of enemies in the engine room: terror spider droids, terror troopers, and a terror giant. First take out the spider droids; if they grab ahold of you, they'll distract you long enough for the other foes to really cause some damage. Repulse them, then dash away from the terror giant to avoid getting hit.

With the spiders squished, lock on to the terror giant and fry it with Force Lightning while you strafe around it. Don't stand in place, lest you make yourself a target for the other foes in the room. Whittle the monster down and stop to use Mind Trick on the terror troopers only after you've gained some distance from the terror giant.

The terror giant is very fast, so stay fleet-footed and use leaping Lightning blasts to stay above the dangerous droid and avoid its stabbing attacks. Eventually, the terror giant takes enough damage for you to finish it off.

JEDI WISDOM

The terror giant is so strong that it will get stuck in the ground if it misses you with its stabbing attack. Take advantage of this and rush in with Lightning-infused saber combos while it is stuck.

With the terror giant out of the way, turn on the terror troopers and cut through them. You can also use the flame jets in the room as booby traps for your enemies by luring them over the flames as you fight.

With the room clear, use Force Grip to lift the platform on the left. Jump onto it, then jump right, onto the platform above you. Make a left into the next room to find a large circular elevator room.

Ride the elevator to its end, then reach the docking bay. Just as you arrive, Boba Fett makes off with Juno in the *Slave I*. Though your rescue attempt was a failure, you still have a chance to save Juno. You order Kota to begin the assault on Kamino; you will join it soon.

While you discuss the details with Master Kota, a huge spiderlike droid, the terror walker, sneaks away behind you. You give chase and follow it to a nearby section of the hangar bay.

BOSS BATTLE: TERROR WALKER

When you reach the sneaky spider clunker, you find that it's not like the other terror spider droids. It's much, much bigger. The ship-sized walker doesn't waste any time in attacking. You dodge the mechanical monster's laser beams and retaliate with Force Push blasts, but they do no damage.

Suddenly, the machine rises several feet in the air, activates its shields, and begins stomping toward you, while several of its little terror spider droid minions scurry in for the attack.

JEDI WISDOM

If you haven't already upgraded your Force Lightning or Saber Throw, now is a good time to do it. Both attacks are vital in this battle.

The terror walker's shields are too strong for you to penetrate with your attacks. To disable the menace's shields, dash around the center of the room—destroying terror spider droids as you go—and use Force Grip to lift the large power nodes out of the ground around the center generator. Once all four nodes are lifted, the generator overloads and disables the terror walker's protective shield!

JEDI WISDOM

Lure the terror walker to the opposite side of where you want it positioned. It will slowly stomp behind you. Once it is where you want it, dash away to the opposite side of the generator and safely lift the power nodes out of the ground.

When all four nodes are yanked out, the center generator emits a powerful electromagnetic pulse that disables the walker's shields. Dash toward the terror walker and attack one of the monster's legs. If it lifts its leg, rush to one on the opposite side and resume your attack.

Drop the terror walker so its head section is on the ground, then rush in with Lightning-infused saber combos, Force Lightning blasts, and Saber Throw attacks. Throw everything you've got at the mechanical menace.

Eventually, the terror walker gets back on its legs and begins stomping around. To make matters worse, several more enemies join the fight. Dash away from the mob and reach the outer wall.

Use Force Lightning attacks to stun the terror troopers and slash through them, and use saber combos on the spider droids. Since the terror walker is up and about, don't waste time using attacks that hurt only one kind of enemy. Force Repulse is not as effective against terror troopers, and Mind Trick has no effect on spider droids, so stick with Force Lightning and get both at the same time.

Distance yourself from the walker and hit it with Force Lightning every chance you get. Dash away from the walker's laser attacks. If it lifts its legs, move away and leap over the shock-wave attack it fires when it slams its legs down.

JEDI WISDOM

If you have a full Force Fury meter, this is a great time to use it. You'll be invulnerable to your enemies' attacks and have increased Force Lightning to zap all enemies at once!

Dash around to the rear of the monster and resume your attack on its hind legs. Switch from leg to leg until you bring it down a second time. Take the attack to the walker's head and resume chipping away at the machine's health.

This time, the walker gets up as several fuses pop out of their slots along the outer wall. The walker's shields power up, and it begins its rampage again. Rush back out to the outer wall and replace the fuses in their slots, then use Force Lightning to charge them.

JEDI WISDOM

There are three ways to approach this task. Dash around the room and replace the fuses one by one, without charging them. Then dash around a second time and charge each one. This way, you won't be standing in one spot for too long, allowing enemies to surround you. Another way is to replace the fuse and charge it immediately before moving on to the next one. This method is slightly more dangerous but will allow you to resume your attack on the walker more quickly. The fastest way to do this, however, is to pick up each fuse with Force Grip and zap it with Force Lightning as you slip it into the slot. This will charge the fuse before it's even in the wall!

CLONER'S CAUTION

Be careful of the terror troopers and terror spider droids. They're not going to let up on you while you replace the power fuses. Take them out with saber combos, or they'll take you out first!

After you replace all the fuses in their respective slots in the wall, the terror walker's shield deactivates again. Lure the vulnerable monster over to the explosive crates along the outer wall and use them to damage the droid monster's legs some more.

If the center generator, which is still malfunctioning, sends out a radial pulse, leap over it and attack the terror walker again.

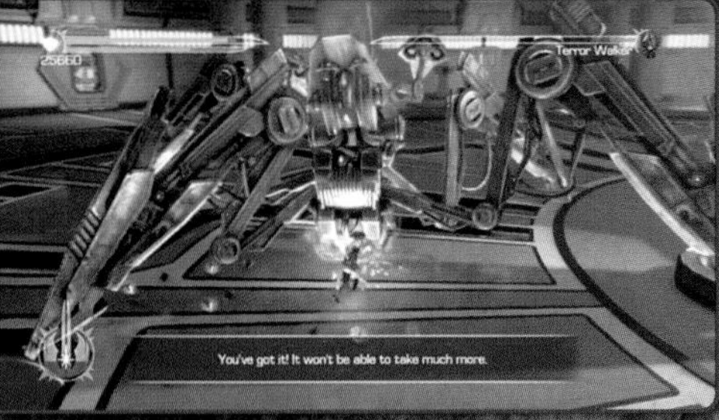

Resume your attack on the walker, targeting its body with Force Lightning and its head with Saber Throw. Pummel it until it drops, then target the head section again. After a flurry of Force-infused attacks, the walker is yours for the taking.

With the walker out of energy, follow the onscreen prompt to take control of the massive mechanical monster and guide it around the room. Use the walker's lasers to destroy the terror giants that suddenly appear in your way.

With no more terror giants, turn around and target the center generator. Move the walker over the generator and attack. The attack finally destroys the terror walker, sending it, and you, flying across the room. Approach the fallen walker and use Force Grip to lower its body section. Double-jump onto the body, then into the hole in the wall. Follow the path out of the walker's room and into the next section of the *Salvation*.

ACHIEVEMENT/TROPHY UNLOCKED

To unlock the Droid Rage Achievement or Trophy, destroy all of the terror giants in the room while on the terror walker.

HOLOCRON

After exiting the room with the terror walker, grab the Wisdom saber crystal holocron in the dark room of smoldering rubble.

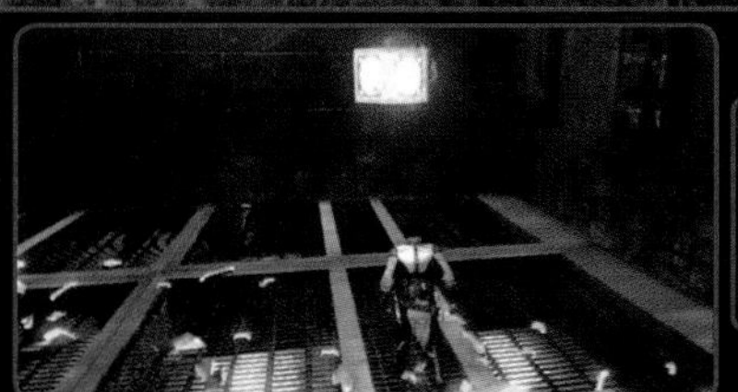

The Rebel Ship *Salvation*

The *Salvation* jumps to light speed as the Rebels initiate their attack on the Kaminoan cloning facility. When they reach Kamino, the rest of the Rebel fleet is engaged in heavy battle with Imperial forces!

Massive Star Destroyers float high above the battle while TIE fighters and Y-wings trade blaster shots. Inside the *Salvation*, the clone prepares to make his way back onto the planet's surface to find Juno.

Battle for the *Salvation*

LEGEND

- Waypoints (see corresponding images)
- Saber Crystal Holocron
- Green Bacta Holocron
- Experience Points Holocron
- Force Energy Holocron

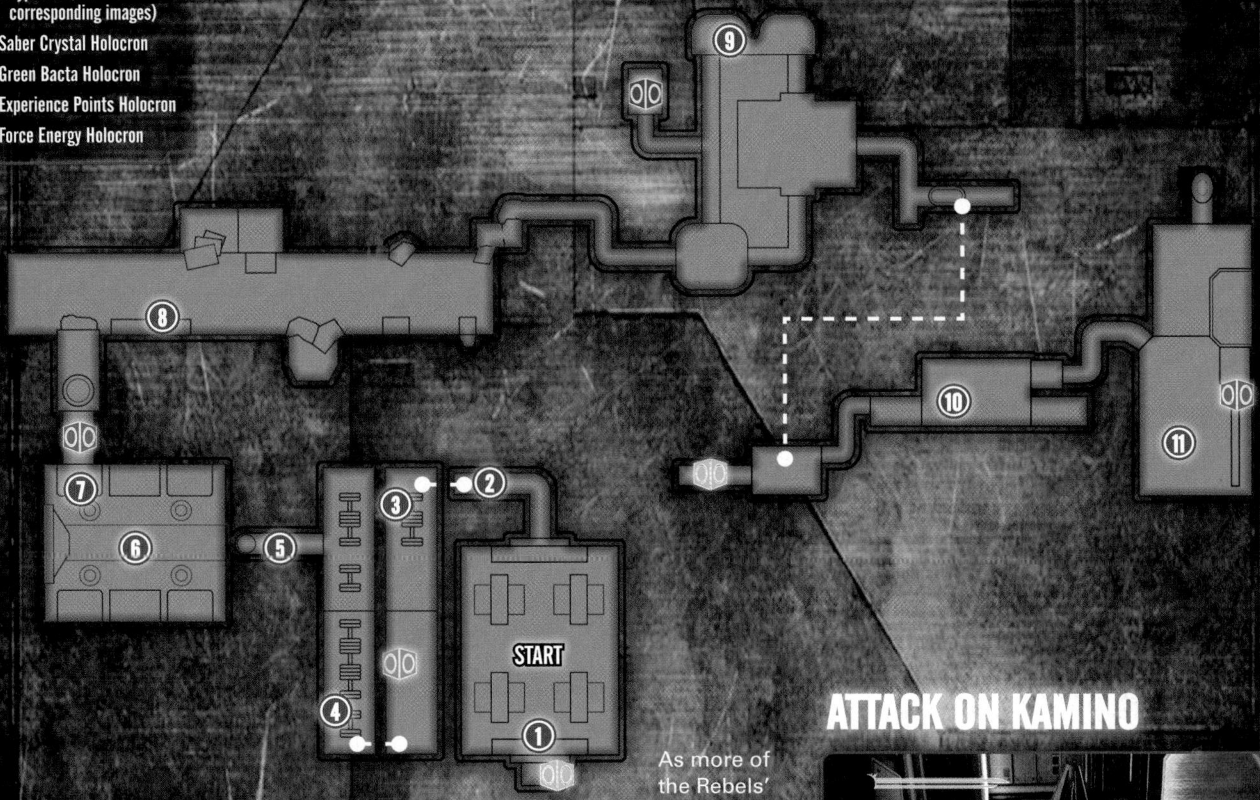

START

ATTACK ON KAMINO

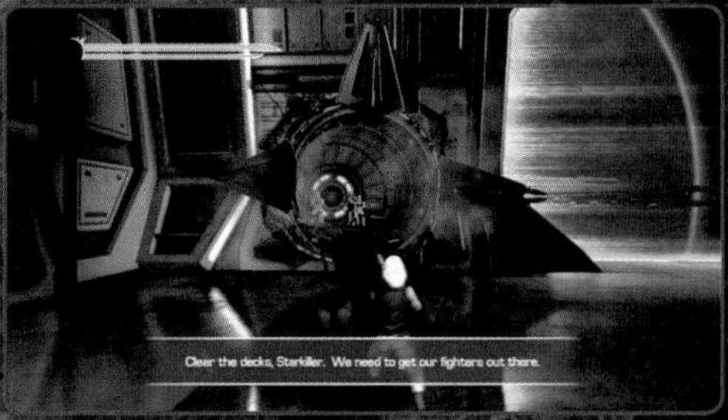

As more of the Rebels' Y-wings attempt to launch from the *Salvation*, they're met with blaster fire and are immediately destroyed. Suddenly, an Imperial transport pod crashes into the *Salvation*'s deck, delivering Imperials onto the ship!

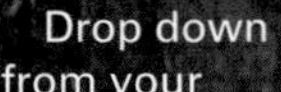

Drop down from your position and speed across the bay toward the pod that just landed. Hit the stormtroopers with a Force Push blast and take them out.

With the Imperials out of the way, turn your attention to the saber guard. Either engage him in saber combat or use Mind Trick to turn him into an ally.

MISSION DETAILS

OBJECTIVE

Fight your way to the *Salvation's* bridge where Juno Eclipse is stationed.

ENEMIES ENCOUNTERED

- Imperial stormtroopers
- Jumptroopers
- Imperial riot troopers
- Terror troopers
- Terror spider droids
- Scout troopers
- Saber guards
- AT-ST
- AT-MP
- Incinerator wardroid

HOLOCRONS FOUND

- 2 holocrons
- 1 Health Bacta holocron
- 1 Energy Bacta holocron
- Meditation saber crystal (blue)
- Healing saber crystal (dark green)
- Incineration saber crystal (unstable red)

Just then, a second pod delivers even more Imperials onto the deck. If you used Mind Trick on the saber guard, follow him to the second pod and use Mind Trick on the new saber guard. Allow them to destroy the rest of the Imperial forces, then take out any remaining enemies.

Use saber combos, Force Repulse and Force Lightning to sweep the deck clean of all Imperials before more arrive.

JEDI WISDOM

There are a few Rebel fighters on the deck too. If you help keep them alive, they'll aid you in the battle by firing on the Imperials!

With the first few batches of bad guys out of the way, a new, larger transport crashes into the side of the ship and clamps down on the top of the hangar bay. The pod's door swings open and delivers a squad of Imperials, an AT-ST, and an AT-MP!

Use Mind Trick on the Imperials and turn them into distractions for the walkers. You'll need to take out the AT-MP first; it's quicker and can easily pepper you with missiles.

Turn on the AT-ST and use the Force Lightning to fry it. Rather than stand in the open and take incoming fire, position yourself between the walker and an object for protection or stand high atop one of the platforms in the hangar bay.

JEDI WISDOM

If you have a secure position, you can also take advantage of the AT-MP's attacks and use the missiles against the AT-ST and other nearby enemies.

Work quickly and take out the AT-ST, then turn on the AT-MP. Bounce its incoming missiles back at it and blow it up!

When the second large pod crashes into the ship, it delivers even more enemies. This one carries two AT-MPs, an AT-ST walker, and several Imperials. Approach this battle just as you did the other one. Mind Trick the Imperial soldiers, then turn on the AT-MPs. Before you do, though, take out the scout troopers on the upper level.

Jump atop the large platforms in the bay—the AT-MPs won't be able to reach you as easily there—then double-jump dash from the platform onto the upper level where the scout troopers are perched. Take them out any way you like.

HOLOCRON

In the small pod on the upper right corner of the bay is a holocron that will earn you experience points. After taking down the scout troopers, examine the ledge's left side to find the pod attached. Step inside and grab it!

JEDI WISDOM

You can also use the R-22 Spearheads hanging overhead in the bay as huge explosives against the walkers below. Jump onto the platform, Force Grip it to yank it off the support, then hurl it at the enemies below.

From the safety of the top platform, use the Force to destroy the remaining walkers below, finally clearing the deck. Before leaving the deck, use Saber Throw to slice off the docking clamps from the pods.

Hop onto the platform on the left and follow the hallway to a large tunnel leading back toward the gearworks. Jump in and follow the tube all the way back.

GEARWORKS REVISITED

Upon landing, you find two saber guards. Mind Trick them both and watch them fight it out. When only one is left, scorch him with Force Lightning!

Approach the red firing tubes at the room's far end, and either Mind Trick the enemies on the other side, or grab them with the Force and yank them into the tubes. With the enemies gone, grab the large cog sitting on the ground and place it in the center of the spinning rotor nearby.

The rotor's electrical conduits overload with the cog in place and allow you to pass through the rotor to the other side of the red tubes.

Force Grip the large spinning rotor in the next room and force it to stop. Jump into the room's other side and use Force Repulse to quickly disable the enemies nearby.

Walk to the room's left side and peer through the large spinning rotor again. Locate the cog on the other side, then move it into the center of the rotor, just as before. Overload the conduits, then jump onto the other side.

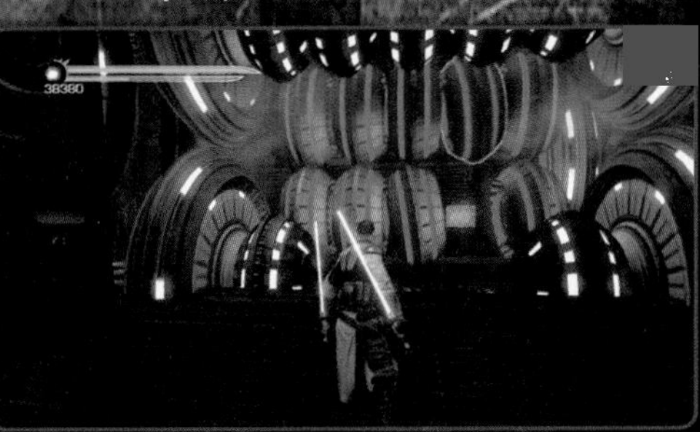

Head over to the unstable engine parts ahead (they're glowing red) and zap them with Force Lightning. The charge blows them up and clears a path farther into the gearworks.

HOLOCRON

After destroying the rows of unstable engine parts, pick up the green Health holocron in the corner.

Drop into the shaft at the room's end and make your way across the next section of gearworks by placing the cog into the rotor on the right.

Face the AT-MP in the next area, and fire its missiles back at it. Force Grip the next rotor and stop it, then rush into the next section of the gearworks.

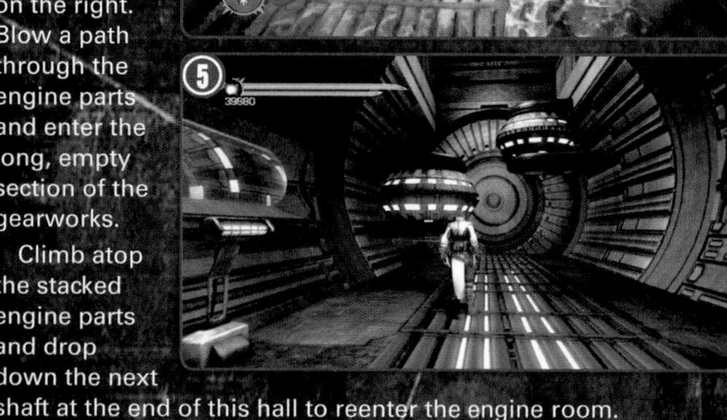

Use Force Repulse to destroy the Imperials in the next room, and use Force Lightning to destabilize the engine parts on the right. Blow a path through the engine parts and enter the long, empty section of the gearworks.

Climb atop the stacked engine parts and drop down the next shaft at the end of this hall to reenter the engine room.

ENGINE ROOM

When you arrive in the engine room, Master Kota locks it down until you clear it out. Use Mind Trick on the enemies below and wait for them to do most of the work for you.

Drop onto one of the platforms below and bounce the AT-MP's missiles back at it. Stay above the ground level and use Force powers like Lightning and Mind Trick to eliminate the enemies from a perched position. When the area is clear, you can drop down to the area the enemies were.

If you can't manipulate or fry everyone from your elevated position—some enemies may be hard to see—then drop down only after you destroy the AT-MP. The saber guards won't hesitate to gang up on you. Take your sabers to the remaining enemies and put them away.

After you've cleared the engine room of enemies, Kota unlocks the room and removes the blue force field from the upper platform. Double-jump onto the top platform and follow the hall out to an elevator platform.

HOLOCRON

There's a Meditation saber crystal holocron in the hall. You can't miss it, so grab it on the way out!

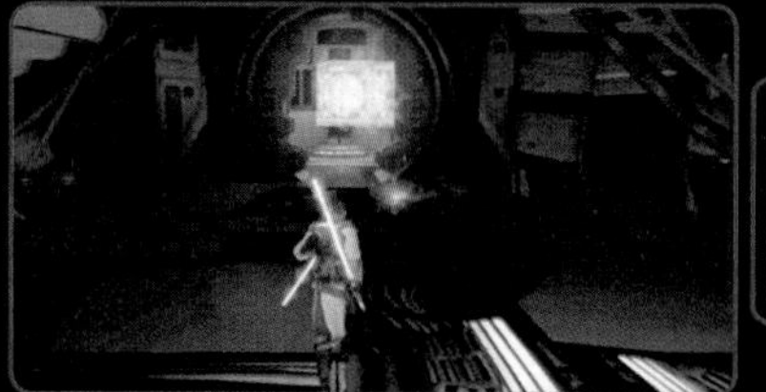

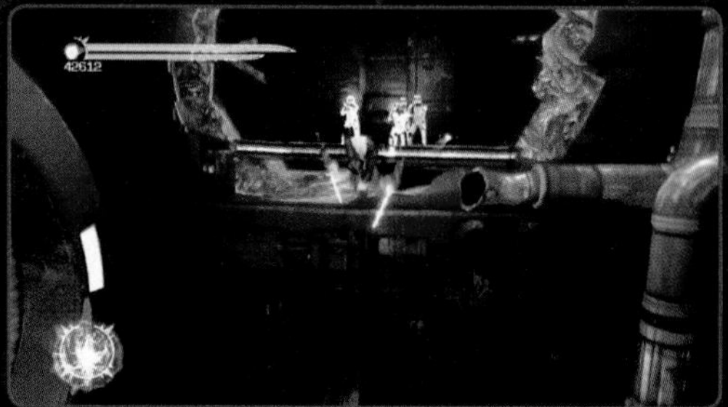

Ride the platform up to a small room with a huge gaping hole in it. Double-jump toward the hole and use Force Repulse to knock the nearby Imperials away. Step on the ledge where the Imperials were perched.

You're back in the long, canyonlike chasm inside the ship. Turn right and locate the large catwalk overhead. Use Force Grip to lower it, then double-jump dash onto it and take out the two scout troopers. Electrocute the jumptroopers in the air as you go; otherwise, they'll blast you to pieces.

8

Lower the next catwalk and dash across it. Make a left into the next section of the ship and hop down. Take out the lone scout trooper near the next large hole in the wall, and creep to the wall's edge.

Double-jump across the chasm into a small room crowded with Imperials. Take them out any way you'd like, then exit the room and zigzag across the chasm, zapping jumptroopers as you go.

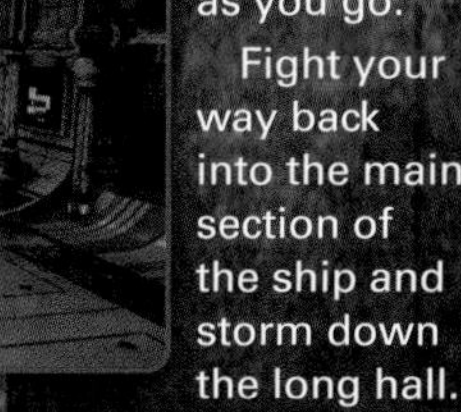

Fight your way back into the main section of the ship and storm down the long hall. A pod crashes into the side of the ship again, this time delivering a large incinerator wardroid.

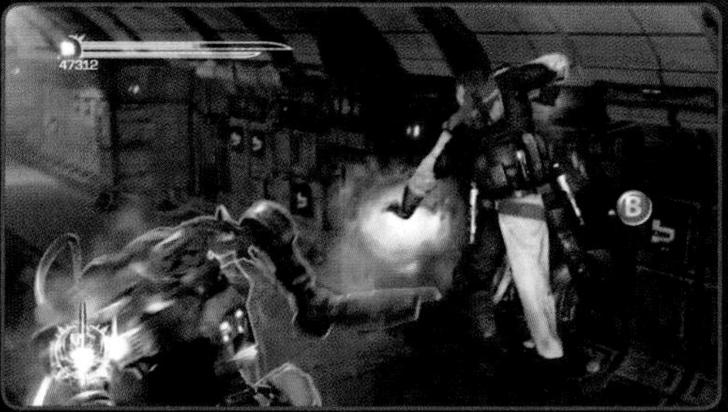

Battle tactics against the incinerator wardroid are the same as against its carbonite cousin: rip away its shield, fire its projectiles back at it, and take it down with Force Lightning or lightning-infused saber combos. Once its ready to drop, follow the onscreen prompts.

HOLOCRON

After you destroy the wardroid, be sure to sneak into its pod and grab the Incineration saber crystal holocron.

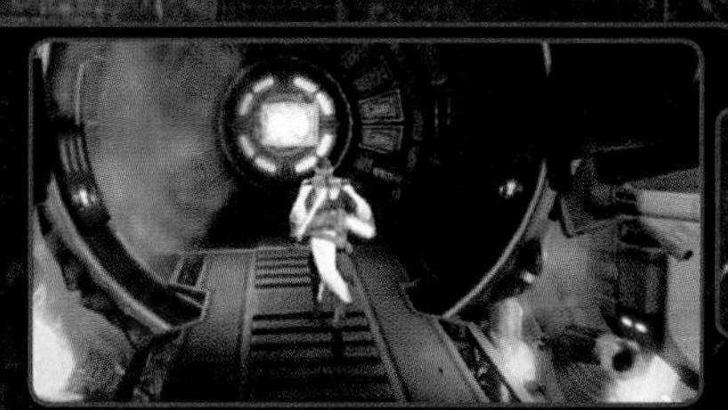

Follow the hall out to a large room with another incinerator wardroid and several saber guards. Target the wardroid first. Use its fireball projectiles against the nearby enemies, then against the wardroid itself.

Mind Trick the saber guards and allow them to distract the wardroid. While it is firing on the saber guards, zap it with Force Lightning and weaken it.

Rush in as soon as the onscreen command pops up, and finish off the wardroid. Pick up the nearby fuse and slip it into the slot to the left of the door.

Battle your way down the hall, through several more Imperials and a few terror troopers. Turn the terror troopers into allies and watch them tear apart the lesser Imperials.

HOLOCRON

Return to the small room off to the side where you previously picked up the Health holocron. The room is already open, and the center tube, still demolished from your last visit, now has a blue Bacta Tank holocron!

Keep battling down the hall until you reach a room full of Imperials, mostly scout troopers. Take out the scout troopers first, then turn on the stormtroopers and crush them.

JEDI WISDOM

Try throwing enemies into the electrical currents in the nearby tubes for some creative battle techniques.

Eventually you reach a room with an incinerator wardroid and several Imperial squads. Mind Trick the lesser Imperials, including the saber guards, and let them fight it out amongst themselves.

Watch as your enemies tear each other apart, then take on the wardroid. Rip off its shield and fry its circuits with Force Lightning. Bring it down, then continue your trek across the *Salvation*.

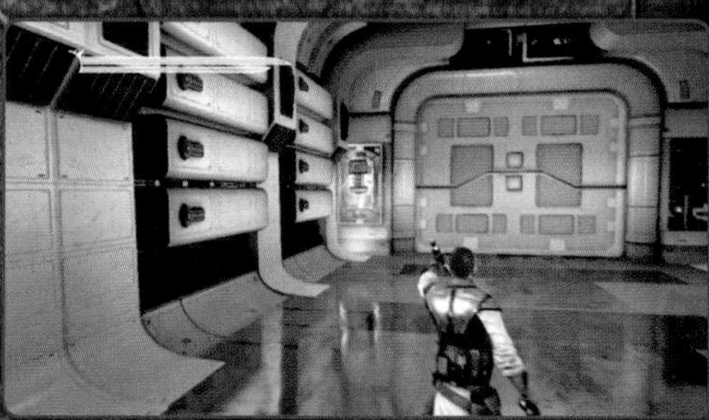

Grab the fuse in the room and float it over to the next sealed door. Pop the fuse in place, charge it with lightning, and get moving!

Follow the hall as it winds around to a broken elevator platform. Lift it out of the way and drop into the elevator shaft.

HOLOCRON

After dropping into the elevator shaft, turn around and locate a niche above you. Jump in and follow it to its end to find a holocron!

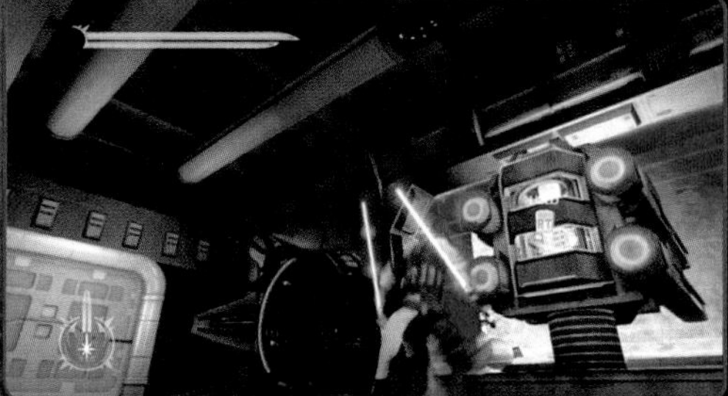

Double-jump dash onto the next hallway entrance and dash down the long ruined hall. Sprint to its end until you find a room with a turbo laser. Demolish the enemies in the room, then turn to the turbo laser, remove the protective cover of the power fuse, and hit it with Force Lightning. The lightning activates the laser, and it fires on the neighboring Star Destroyer!

After firing at the Star Destroyer, use Force Grip to yank out the fuse from the turbo laser mechanism. Move the fuse into place on the door nearby and power it up. Enter the next room to find even more Imperials!

The room is occupied by an incinerator wardroid, saber guards, and several Imperial troopers. Take out the smaller enemies first, leaving the droid for last so you can face it one-on-one.

There are several more turbo lasers in this room. The first two blow up before you can use them. Approach the third one and use Force Lightning to activate it and fire on the Star Destroyer some more.

When you're done, remove the power fuse and place it in the fallen turbo blaster. Activate it with lightning, and it will blast a hole open in the far door. Walk into the demolished hallway and follow it toward another hangar bay.

Before dropping into the bay, locate the two AT-MPs below. Destroy them with their own missiles, then drop down and wipe the area clean of all Imperials.

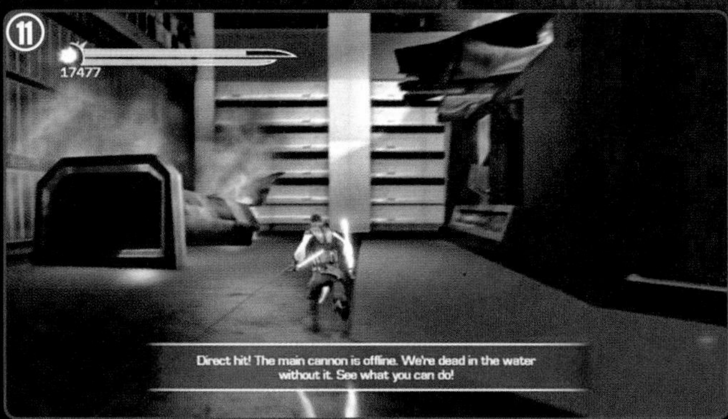

Make a left and approach the rear of the bay. When you do, the Star Destroyer blasts the *Salvation*'s firing solution and deactivates it. Make a right at the rear and double-jump onto the top of the firing solution.

HOLOCRON

Before powering the massive cannon, sneak around to its left side. Use Force Grip to stack the two large boxes, then climb onto the gun. Double-jump out onto the stack of boxes, then double-jump dash out to the holocron floating overhead.

Stand between the two large coils and follow the onscreen commands to power them up and fire on the Star Destroyer.

ACHIEVEMENT/TROPHY UNLOCKED

When you bring down the Star Destroyer, you unlock the Crack the Sky Achievement or Trophy!

When you're done, go into the elevator at the room's rear and ride it all the way up. Follow the hall to the next platform transport and ride it as it speeds across the *Salvation*.

Use Force Repulse to destroy the terror spider droids that attack and shift from side to side as you dodge the explosions in the transport tube. If the view shifts right, then you move left. Reach the end of the transport and join Master Kota and the combat training droid in the control room.

Kamino

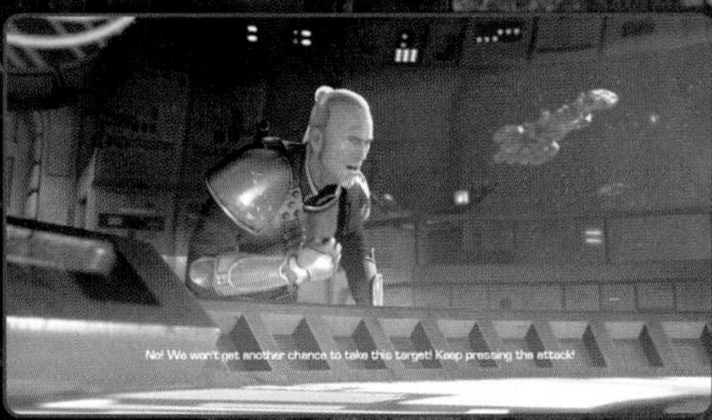

As the *Salvation* nears the planet of Kamino, it begins to take too much damage. The Rebel Alliance, on the verge of retreat, would give in now if not for the determination of General Kota. He orders that they press the attack.

Not only is the *Salvation* losing its shields, but also the planetary shield is preventing them from making an assault. The Starkiller clone insists that Kota get to the *Rogue Shadow*. While Kota and the rest of the crew abandon ship, Starkiller's clone will stay behind and manually drive the *Salvation* into the Kaminoan cloning facility!

The Return

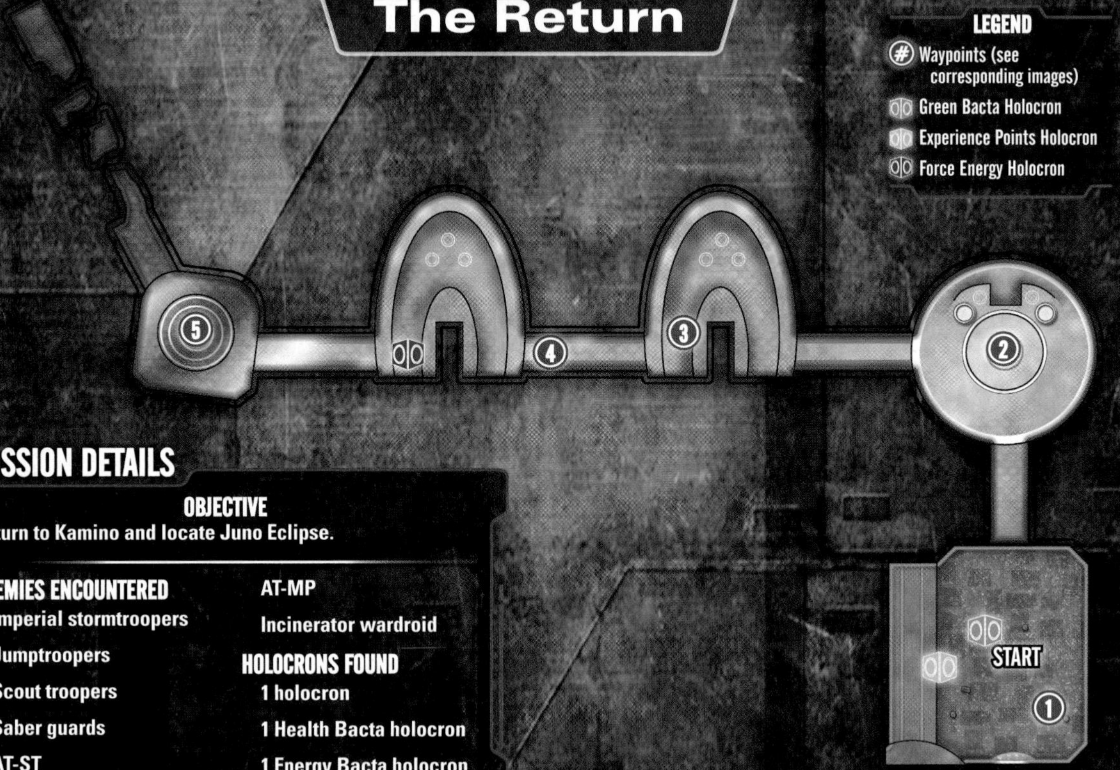

LEGEND

- # Waypoints (see corresponding images)
- Green Bacta Holocron
- Experience Points Holocron
- Force Energy Holocron

1 2 3 4 5 START

MISSION DETAILS

OBJECTIVE

Return to Kamino and locate Juno Eclipse.

ENEMIES ENCOUNTERED

- Imperial stormtroopers
- Jumptroopers
- Scout troopers
- Saber guards
- AT-ST
- AT-MP
- Incinerator wardroid

HOLOCRONS FOUND

- 1 holocron
- 1 Health Bacta holocron
- 1 Energy Bacta holocron

ROUGH LANDING

The *Salvation* is going down hard, so you take position near the view screen. Follow the onscreen commands to move the debris out of the ship's way and clear a path to the Kaminoan surface.

Continue following the onscreen commands when the ship breaks the planet's surface, and exit the ship! Glide alongside the *Salvation* and dodge the falling debris.

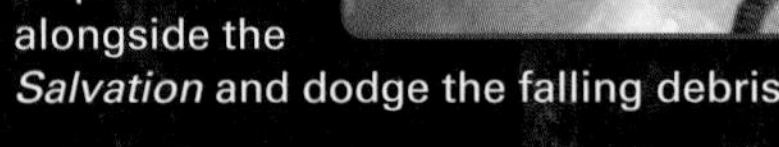

JEDI WISDOM

You can also use Force Push blasts to destroy small chunks of debris on your descent.

Eventually the *Salvation* crashes into the facility, causing a massive explosion. The crash alerts the Imperial forces on the ground, and several swarms of TIE fighters attack. Use the Force to destroy them as they approach and clear a path down.

You land in the same square where you first encountered the carbonite droid. Only now it is covered in debris and more is still crashing around you. Ignore the debris shower and head toward the AT-ST.

Bounce its Thermo Detonators back at it and knock it with scraps of metal lying around. Whittle down its defenses, then follow the onscreen commands to take it down.

HOLOCRON

There's a green health Bacta holocron sitting high atop a tower of debris. Either climb up the trash around the tower or use the neighboring trash tower to hop atop an AT-ST. Next, double-jump dash off the AT-ST, toward the green holocron.

There's another holocron floating high above the room's left side. To reach it, climb atop the trash heap to the holocron's right, then double-jump dash to reach it and receive experience points.

Take out the other AT-ST in the room while deftly avoiding the blaster fire from the nearby gun turrets. Stay out of the red targeting reticules while you zap the walker. Take it down quickly. When you do, you're attacked by AT-MPs. Take them out by zapping them with Force Lightning. If you try to Grip their missiles and hurl them back, you may take fire from the gun turrets.

After eliminating all of you enemies, use the debris to reach the walkway to the left of the area. Fight past the scout troopers and other enemies as you approach the blue force field.

Turn to the force field and use Force Grip to destroy the gun turret. Drop back down to the ruined area below, and sprint across to the other side and take out the second turret the same way.

With the coast clear, use Force Grip to remove the large chunk of debris from the exit and leave this room. Dash down the hall and hop onto the elevator at the end.

The elevator takes you up to the security towers. Master Kota battles the Imperials in the opposite tower.

Run around the room and Mind Trick as many enemies as you can. Let your new small army do most of the work while you sweep up the rest of the fiends. Concentrate on the saber guards first, then the scout troopers, leaving the lesser stormtroopers for last.

CHALLENGE UNLOCKED

When you clear this room of enemies, you unlock a new challenge!

3

With the room clear, the nearby door slides open. Several stormtroopers dash in. Rush the soldiers and cut them down on your way to the room's exit.

Dash across the hallway, frying jumptroopers and saber guards as you go, then enter the next tower.

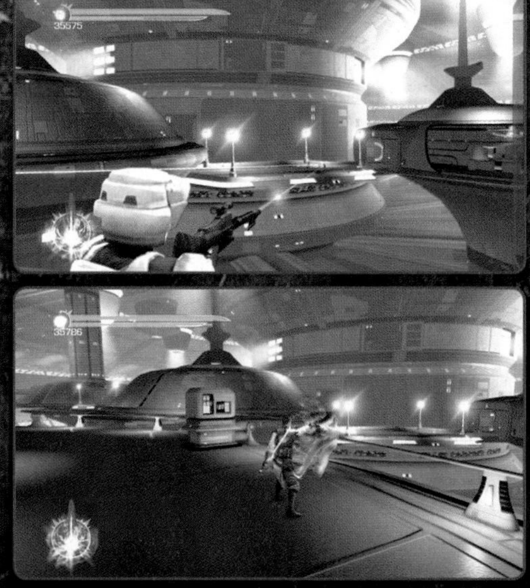

While you're battling through the hall, Master Kota and his troopers are pinned down by nearby scout troopers. Speed into the next tower and pass up the incinerator wardroid. Make a beeline toward the scouts in the tower, and destroy them to clear Kota's path.

Finally, turn on the wardroid and take it down. Use strong saber combos, Force Lightning, and Saber Throws to thoroughly crush it.

Enter the next hall and meet the incinerator wardroid head-on. Rip off its shield and get to work just as you have done before. The hall is also inhabited by saber guards, stormtroopers, and nearby jumptroopers. If you have a full Force Fury meter, feel free to use it now and shred everyone all at once.

4

If you don't have Force Fury available, dash past the first batch of enemies and take out the scout troopers first. With them gone, zap the jumptroopers next, then Mind Trick the saber guards. Finally, take out the wardroid.

As the wardroid comes tumbling down, a bombing run swoops by and demolishes the next bridge. You have to find another way around!

Enter the next tower while Master Kota finds another route for you. Keep yourself busy with the squad of Imperials. Cook the creeps with Force Lightning and clear the tower.

HOLOCRON

There is a blue Energy Bacta holocron on the far right side of this tower's upper level. Jump onto one of the display consoles, then double-jump onto the small ledge jutting out to the room's center. Follow the ledge to the far right and find the holocron.

While you're busy cleaning out the towers, Kota and his men storm across a distant platform. Before they can reach their destination, however, they're ambushed by two transports carrying several Imperials.

Edge out to the broken window and wait for a TIE fighter to zoom by. Grab it in midair with Force Grip, then hurl it at one of the attacking dropships. Take out both dropships with TIE fighters to free Kota and his men.

Enter the next hallway and cut through the saber guards. Run them down with your sabers, then take out the scout troopers and jumptroopers nearby.

In the next room, which is a large circular chamber, two incinerator wardroids await. Rip off both of their shields right away, then use Force Lightning to fry both of their circuits simultaneously.

Strafe around the monsters with your lightning crackling, and stop only to bounce their flaming projectiles back at them. When the jumptroopers join the fight, switch back to Force Lightning and burn them down.

When the room is clear, the door opens, allowing you to see the demolished bridge. Master Kota runs out and uses the Force to create a makeshift bridge from the debris.

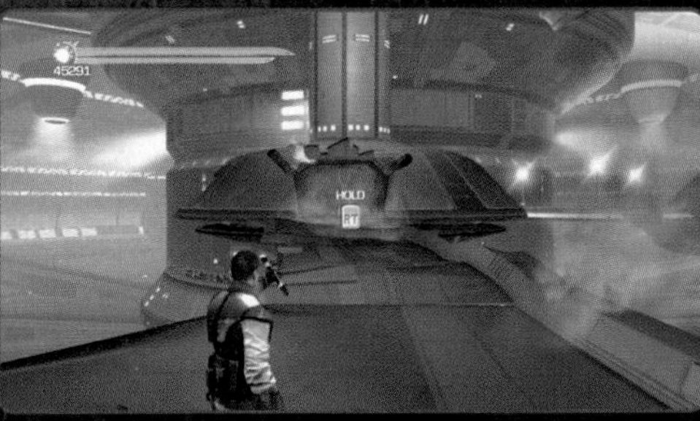

Use the Force to lower the large bent platform, then dash across the floating debris to the other side.

ACHIEVEMENT/TROPHY UNLOCKED

When you reach the other side of the bridge, you unlock the Meeting of the Jedi Achievement or Trophy!

Kamino

As Master Kota and Starkiller's clone approach the city's main access ways, they find that the path ahead is locked down. The clone leaves the Jedi Master behind and sets off to find Vader.

If anyone is going to find a way up to the top of the city and rescue Juno Eclipse, it's him. He steps onto the nearby elevator platform and rides it up.

The Confrontation

See map on next page

DESTINY FULFILLED

Leave the room via the hall ahead of you and follow it out. As you dash down the hall, Master Kota contacts you on the radio and tries to convince you to join the attack. Your mind is set, however. You're not here to put an end to the Empire; you're only here to rescue Juno from Vader.

The hall leads back out to the rainy Kaminoan landscape. Turn right as you exit and locate the walkway beneath you. Drop down and get to work on the Imperials in your way.

The first batch of Imperials is accompanied by a terror giant. Use Mind Trick on the stormtroopers and allow them to distract the giant temporarily while you use the Force to destroy the terror giant.

Farther down the walkway are several scout troopers. If you approach them straight on, they'll blast you to bits. Instead, zigzag-dash up the walkway until you reach them; then utterly demolish them.

Double-jump onto the raised area ahead, and edge close to the other side. Below, you'll see two AT-MPs stomping out of a door on the right. Stay atop your platform and wait for the walkers to bombard you with missiles. Reflect the missiles either with the Force or by blocking them back, and destroy the walkers.

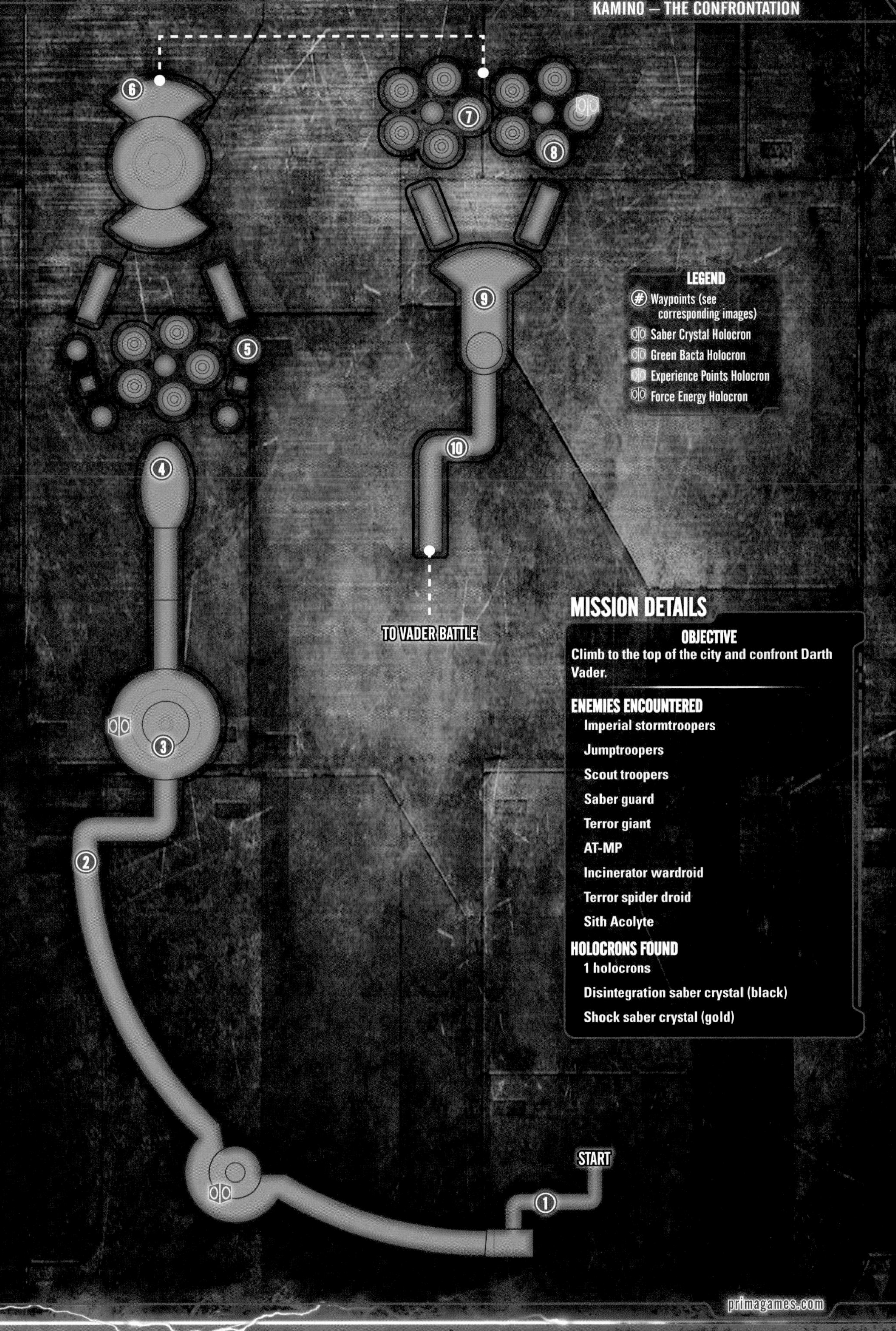

MISSION DETAILS

OBJECTIVE

Climb to the top of the city and confront Darth Vader.

ENEMIES ENCOUNTERED

- Imperial stormtroopers
- Jumptroopers
- Scout troopers
- Saber guard
- Terror giant
- AT-MP
- Incinerator wardroid
- Terror spider droid
- Sith Acolyte

HOLOCRONS FOUND

- 1 holocrons
- Disintegration saber crystal (black)
- Shock saber crystal (gold)

Drop back down to the walkway, and follow it up to where it bends left. Greet the attacking Imperials with Force Lightning blasts and burn them up!

HOLOCRON

There's a nearby holocron just before the path turns left. Use Force Grip to move a large crate to the base of the upper round platform. Double-jump from the crate onto the round platform and grab the Disintegration saber crystal holocron.

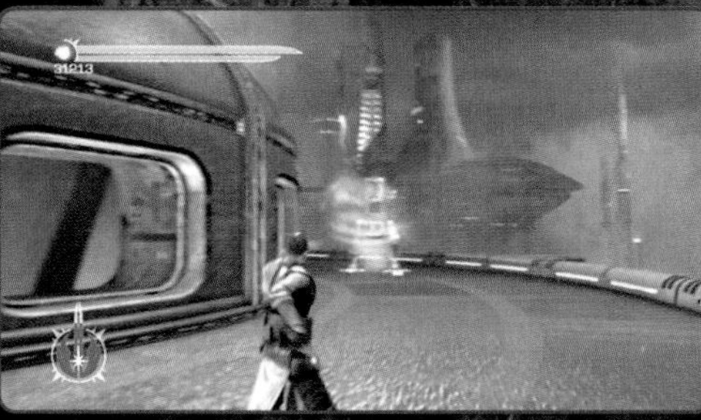

Resume your attack on the Imperials. Drop back down and take out another terror giant. With the terror giant out of the way, turn your attention to the next two AT-MPs. Blow them up, then continue up the walkway.

ACHIEVEMENT/TROPHY UNLOCKED

There are several large electrical coils lining the walkway. Use Force Grip to throw 10 enemies into the coils and unlock the Amplified Achievement or Trophy.

Just before you reach the next passageway along the walkway, you encounter another vicious terror giant. Bring the giant down, then sprint into the next large corridor.

There are several Imperial stormtroopers in the hall. Make short work of them as you traverse the bending hall, and follow it to the large open elevator room.

The elevator lowers you into a room with a hulking incinerator wardroid! Tear away its shield and weaken it with Force Lightning blasts. Back off before it retaliates, then use Force Repulse to destroy the terror spider droids as they approach.

Several short walls line the sides of the large, circular room. Use them to protect yourself from the wardroid's attacks while you take out all of the terror spider droids. Once the room is clear of spiders, finish off the wardroid.

I II III IV V VI VII VIII

JEDI WISDOM

You're temporarily trapped in this room until you destroy all enemies. Therefore, now is a good time to unleash Force Fury if you have it.

If you don't have Force Fury, use the wardroid's fireballs as projectiles against it and other enemies.

HOLOCRON

After defeating the enemies in this room, scour the room's edge. You'll find a red holocron that unlocks the Shock saber crystal.

THE CLONING SPIRE

Exit the room and speed down the hall. As you do, General Kota contacts you, begging you to join the fight. You tell him that you can't, that you must save Juno. You then press on, deeper into the facility.

The halls lead to a tall room with several spinning platforms leading up to a sealed door. Use Force Lightning to fry the jumptroopers' jet packs and send them flying uncontrollably around the room.

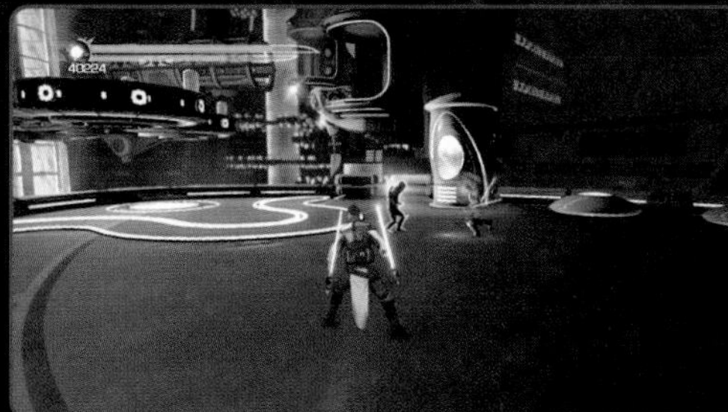

After you dispatch the jumptroopers, several pods rise from the ground along the edge of the platform and deliver Sith Acolytes and saber guards. Use Mind Trick on the saber guards and let them either attack the acolytes or throw themselves over the edge.

With the saber guards occupied or eliminated, turn on the acolytes. Use strong saber combos to take them down quickly.

As you eliminate enemies, more emerge out of the pods to take their place. Hold position near the platform's edge and use your Force powers to destroy the foes as they pop up.

With the first few waves of enemies out of the way, several terror troopers join the fight. Handle them quickly any way you choose. After cleaning out the majority of the enemies on the platform, a stepped platform rises out of the far end.

JEDI WISDOM

Since you're fighting atop a platform, your best bet to quickly dispatch enemies is to toss them over the edge.

Hop up the stepped area and approach the large spinning platforms ahead of you. Jump onto a platform as it passes you by and ride it right. When it gets near an open pod on the right, double-jump dash into the pod and turn left.

5

Run across the floating droid's flaps and jump into the next pod. Turn left again and locate the long, hanging tunn[illegible]mp into it and run across to the other side. Double-jump onto the curved walkway on the tunnel's other side, then follow it left.

Turn left at the walkway's end and speed down the next hanging tunnel. Double-jump dash out of the tunnel into the next open pod and locate the next floating droid on the left.

ACHIEVEMENT/TROPHY UNLOCKED

Be very careful as you navigate the tunnels, pods, and floating droids. If you make it to the top of the spire without falling, you unlock the Top of the World Achievement or Trophy!

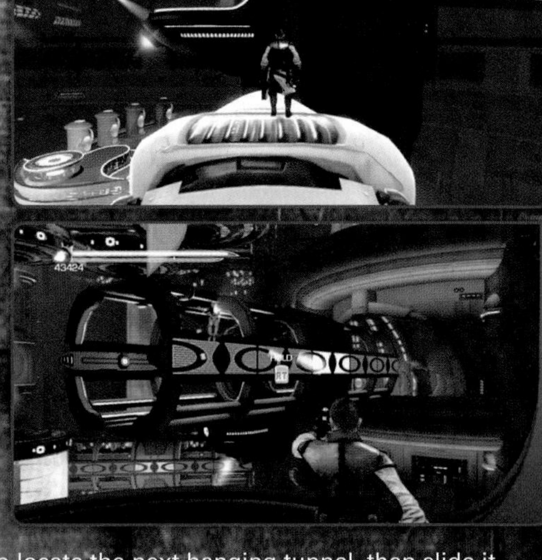

Once again, locate the droid and run across it to the next open pod. This time, the hanging tunnel is floating over your head.

Use Force Grip to lower the tunnel into position, then jump in and run across. Find the next droid, run across it again, and jump into another open pod. Look left from this pod to locate the next hanging tunnel, then slide it right into place so you can dash across.

There are several jumptroopers patrolling the spire. Use your Force Lightning to bring them down as you go up.

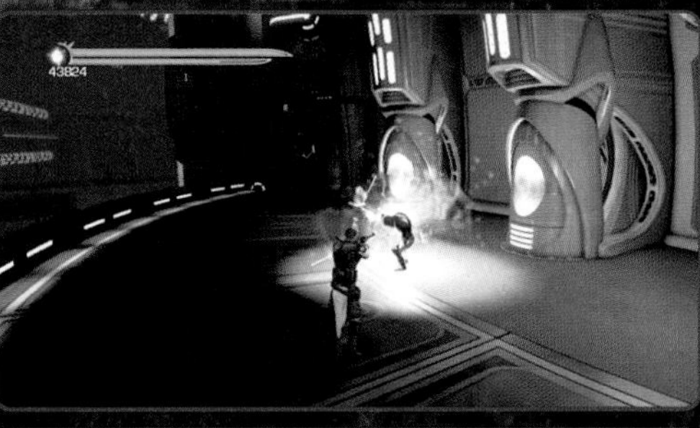

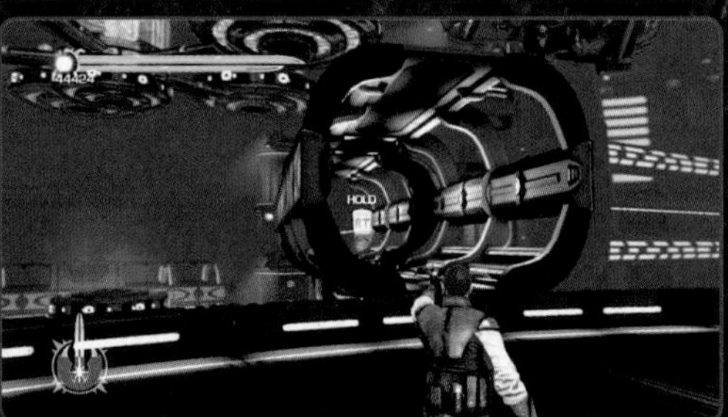

Reach the next curved walkway and engage the three enemies waiting for you. Use Mind Trick on the two saber guards and let them work on the acolyte. Finish him off, then slide the tunnel you just crossed right so it lines up with the next open pod.

Follow the tunnel to the pod, then run across the next droid to find another open pod. Use the Force to lift the tunnel below you into place, then dash across.

Hop across the last few floating droids until you reach another set of spinning platforms. Ride the platforms around until you come across one more droid. Run across the droid's flaps into another pod, then turn right and dash across the final tunnel.

A pair of Sith acolytes ambushes you on the next walkway. Use saber combos to cut them down, then use Force Grip to pry open the sealed door.

Enter the next room, a large chamber with an electrical current at its center. Get to work on the warriors inside. Use Force Lightning, saber combos, and Force Grip to throw enemies into the current. You can also use Mind Trick on them and let them tear each other apart. When the room is clear, use the Force to open the door and exit into another tall room with spinning platforms.

JEDI WISDOM

The pods lining the room will deliver swarms of Sith acolytes and saber guards, so stand your ground and dispatch your enemies quickly before they fill the room and overpower you.

6

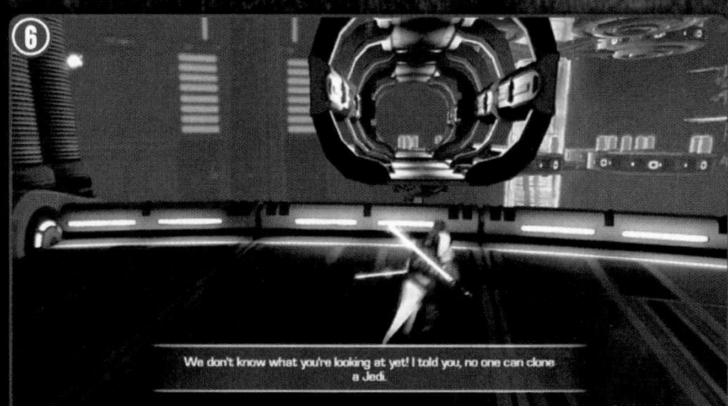

Back inside the spire room, walk over to the new tunnel on the left and go through it. Follow it to the other side, where you'll find the first of many spinning platforms. Jump onto it and stay still as it spins clockwise.

Wait until you reach the next floating droid. Jump onto it, then use it to reach the next series of platforms.

7

When you land on the platforms, several terror troopers will attack. Hold your own on the platform's center, and shove the terror troopers off to dispatch them quickly.

Continue using the floating droids to reach the platforms, and climb higher and higher in the spire. Be sure to stand near the center of the platforms as you go so that you don't fall over the side when battling the terror troopers.

HOLOCRON

Just before you reach the top of the spire, you'll come upon another stationary set of platforms. Battle the terror troopers on the platforms, then locate the yellow holocron inside one of the cloning tanks.

8

When you reach the large tunnel overhead, double-jump dash into it, then follow it out to the next walkway with a door at the far end.

CHALLENGE UNLOCKED

Upon reaching this walkway, you unlock a new challenge!

Finally, open the door with the Force and go inside, where there's another elevator platform.

WALKING IN THE DARKNESS

The elevator lifts you up to a new section of the facility. Walk forward and enter the smoke-filled room.

Slowly traverse the smoky room. Follow the path past several cloning pods and through the winding halls. Each step you take brings another painful memory from Starkiller's past. Approach the exit on the room's far left.

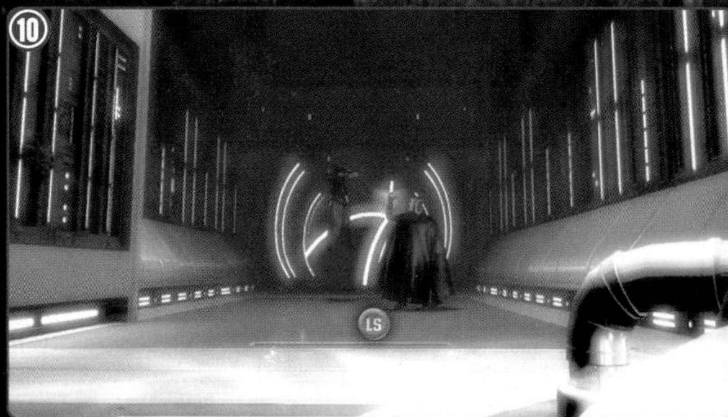

As you stalk the room, Vader emerges from the shadows and attacks you! Follow the onscreen commands to shake loose, then exit the passageway to find the next tall chamber of the spire.

The towers inside the spire are full of tubes with Starkiller clones in them. High atop the towers, standing defiantly on one of the rotating platforms, is Darth Vader. You jump onto the platform to attack.

Lunge at Vader and lash out with your lightsabers. Execute combos to inflict damage, but block when he counterattacks. If you engage in a saber lock, follow the onscreen commands to break free and kick him.

When Vader realizes that you're tougher than he expected, he summons the help of the clones in the nearby vats. Mind Trick them as they bust out of their tanks and let them loose on Vader.

Rush Vader while he's destroying the clones and strike at him while he's occupied. When he takes too much damage, he retreats to a distant platform. Walk up to the edge of your platform, and use the Force to bring down Vader's.

However, before you can reach him, he flees again to another distant platform. He Force Grips the platforms above you and brings them crashing down near you.

Jump up the fallen platforms and approach Vader. He begins to throw tanks at you to keep you at a distance. Use his projectiles against him by grabbing them with the Force and throwing them back.

Your attack forces the Dark Lord to back up a little bit. Once again, climb atop the fallen platforms and lunge at Vader. Lash out at him with your sabers until he summons more clones.

The blue clones are lightning charged and quickly begin to fire Force Lightning spheres at you. Dodge their attacks and either use Mind Trick or Force Push blasts to get rid of them. Engage Vader in lightsaber combat again until he retreats to another distant platform.

Use the Force to bring down Vader's platform and double-jump dash onto it. As you do, you're flooded with Starkiller's memories. When you come back to, you find that Vader has once again fled and is throwing more platforms at you.

Rush up the fallen platforms, tossing the cloning tubes back at Vader as you go, until you reach the top. Just before you reach Vader, he ambushes you with several more clones.

This batch of clones is a mix of saber combatants and Force Lightning wielders. Use your skills to destroy the clones or let them destroy themselves.

With the clones out of your way, resume your attack on Vader. Follow him as he attempts to flee to nearby platforms and cut him down. When he attempts to let another batch of clones loose on you, dispatch them just as you did the others.

Continue to strike down Vader. If he uses Force Grip to choke you, follow the commands onscreen to shake loose, then resume the attack.

JEDI WISDOM

You can use Force Fury during the battle against Vader, but he'll only flee while your Force Fury runs out. Instead, save it to use against the clones.

If you engage Vader in a saber lock, follow the commands until you overpower him again until he flees. Use Mind Trick to turn the next batch of clones on Vader while you attack him from behind.

Finally, whittle Vader's health down until he runs away again. Give chase! When you catch up to him on the nearby platform, you have another vision. You see Juno in your arms, her life slipping away. The moment of hesitation is just what Vader needs to take the advantage.

He strikes you down and retreats on a floating droid. When you come back to, you see Vader escaping, so you hop on a droid and fly after him!

CLONER'S CAUTION

Warning! The following section contains spoilers. If you want to proceed with the walkthrough without spoilers, then skip to the "Vader Battle" section for tips on defeating the Dark Lord. If you don't mind spoilers, read on.

THE CHOICE

When you finally catch up to Vader, he offers you a choice. Either bow before him or let Juno die. He lifts her in the air to display her to you while you make your choice.

You drop your lightsabers and fall to your knees, vowing to do his bidding. Vader lets go of Juno, but she picks up one of your lightsabers!

Before you can stop her, Vader lashes out, sending her flying across the facility. When she lands, her body is thrown across a distant platform surrounded by electrical currents. She lies there, limp and lifeless.

You grab your sabers and attack, but Vader is too powerful. He tosses you away like a rag doll. You land on Juno's platform, with Vader not too far behind.

VADER BATTLE

Vader is highly skilled in manipulating the Force. His knowledge of the dark side is enough to render most of your Force attacks useless. Instead, focus on lightsaber combat. Use lightsaber combos to drive Vader back toward the outer rim of the platform.

Strike him down until you engage him in a saber lock. Follow the onscreen commands to overpower the Dark Lord and knock him into one of the electrical towers.

When he does hit an electrical tower, engage him in lightsaber battle again. Get into a saber lock and overpower him a second time.

CLONER'S CAUTION

Stay away from Vader as he prepares to use Force Repulse on you. He'll knock you off your feet! And don't use Force Lightning. He'll only turn it against you.

Repeat the process of striking Vader down with your lightsaber, then overpowering him in a saber lock. Knock him against the electrical towers until he takes too much damage.

Eventually, he'll throw you over the side of the platform, but you'll grab hold of the beams. Follow the commands as they appear onscreen to dodge his attacks and get the upper hand.

Once you've got the upper hand, repeatedly blast Vader with Force Lightning by following the onscreen prompts, ending the Dark Lord's reign.

With Vader at your feet, you're faced with making a choice. Strike him down and avenge Juno's death or allow him to live so that the Rebel Alliance can interrogate him? The choice is yours....

NEIMOIDIAN NOTES

Since there is no gameplay after you make this choice, we will not continue and reveal either ending. Instead, we leave it up to you to find out.

ACHIEVEMENT/TROPHY UNLOCKED

By making the red selection, you unlock the Betrayed by Rage Achievement or Trophy. If you choose the blue selection, you'll unlock the Measure of Mercy Achievement or Trophy. To unlock both, simply reload the game at this point and make a different selection than you did the first time!

WELCOME TO THE WII

Welcome to the Wii section of the walkthrough. Before you get started, take some time to learn the subtle differences between this and other versions of the game. Even though the story remains the same, the levels, items, controls, and even some of the Force powers are different in the Wii version.

Items

Scattered throughout your adventure are several collectible items. Keep your eyes open to find the following:

Health Bacta Tanks: These red tanks increase your maximum health.

Force Energy Tanks: These blue tanks increase your maximum Force Energy.

Holocrons: All holocrons grant you 500 experience points. Some have the added bonus of also unlocking art gallery images.

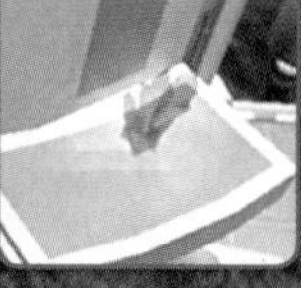

Power saber crystals: All power saber crystals appear as black crystals when you encounter them. Each power crystal has a different effect when applied to your lightsaber.

Color saber crystals: Color saber crystals appear as the same color as the color you unlock. For example, if you find a red color crystal, it unlocks the red color for your lightsaber. These crystals merely change the color of your lightsaber, and that's all.

POWER CRYSTALS

There are 12 power crystals available in the Wii version of the game, each with its own special effect. Since you can equip one power crystal in each lightsaber, you can have up to 144 different combinations of effects! Play around with different power crystal setups to find a combo that suits your combat style.

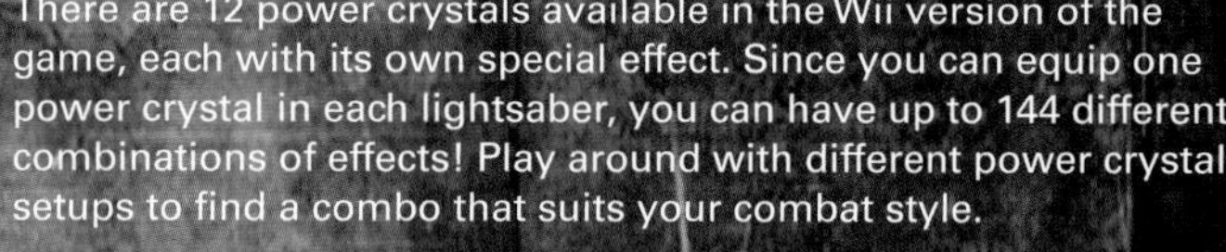

JEDI WISDOM

To learn more about the power crystals, check the "Becoming Starkiller" chapter.

Heads-up Display (HUD)

1. **Health bar:** This displays your current health. Don't allow this to deplete completely or you'll rejoin the Force....
2. **Force Energy meter:** This displays how much Force Energy you currently have. You use Force Energy to execute Force attacks. Once depleted, the Force Energy replenishes on its own.
3. **Force Points:** This shows you how many Force points you gain by defeating enemies. The more creatively you dispatch your foes, the more you build up your Force points multiplier.
4. **Force Rage meter:** This meter fills up over time as you combat enemies. Once it's full, you can unleash your Force Fury.
5. **Combo meter:** The Combo meter is broken up into different ranks. Each rank will allow you to execute a Lightsaber Special attack, each more powerful than the rank before it!

Controls

Since many of you are returning to the world of *Star Wars: The Force Unleashed,* we're going to keep the basics brief. For advanced combat tactics, skip to the "Becoming Starkiller" chapter. If you're new to the *Star Wars: The Force Unleashed,* make the most of the following pages.

Basic Movement

WALKING AND RUNNING

Action	Command
Walk	Press ◎ lightly
Run	Press ◎ firmly

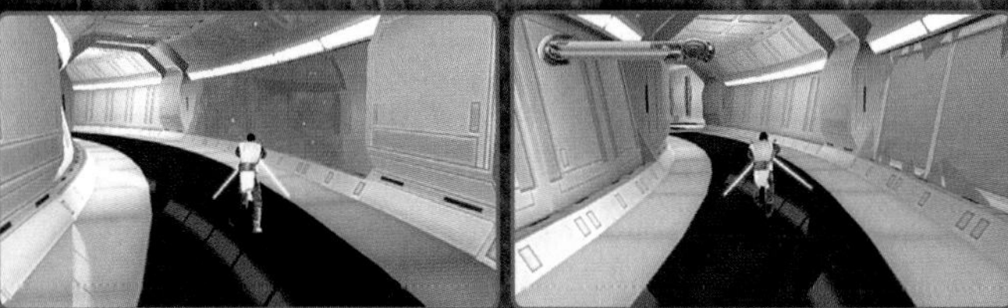

Movement is simple. Simply press the movement Control Stick in the direction you want to go. To walk, press it lightly. To run, press it firmly. The main difference between walking and running (aside from getting to your destination more quickly when running) is that walking allows you to deflect blaster fire more efficiently while blocking.

JUMP AND DOUBLE-JUMP

Action	Command
Jump	Ⓑ
Double-jump	Ⓑ, Ⓑ

Jumping and double-jumping is a basic skill that often plays a very necessary role throughout your adventure. While navigating platforms, be careful not to double-jump past your target. Usually you can time the second jump in your double-jump so that you can reach landing targets near or far. Practice this ability frequently so you don't die needlessly down the line.

In battle, use your jumping ability to get a better vantage point on your enemies. Leap over their heads and come down on them with devastating attacks.

JEDI WISDOM

Pair your double-jump with Force Dash to execute double-jump dash. This maneuver can help you reach distant areas and enemies!

LIGHTSABER BLOCK

Action	Command
Lightsaber Block	Tilt the Wii Remote sideways

Just because you're now an ultrapowerful clone strong in the ways of the Force doesn't mean you can rampage through everything. You must still block enemy attacks! By blocking, you can deflect enemy blaster fire as well as handheld weapon attacks. Keep your Wii Remote tilted sideways as you run and you'll constantly have a defensive posture when entering new areas.

CAMERA CONTROL

Action	Command
Look left and right	⊕ and ⊖, respectively
Center camera	Tap Ⓒ

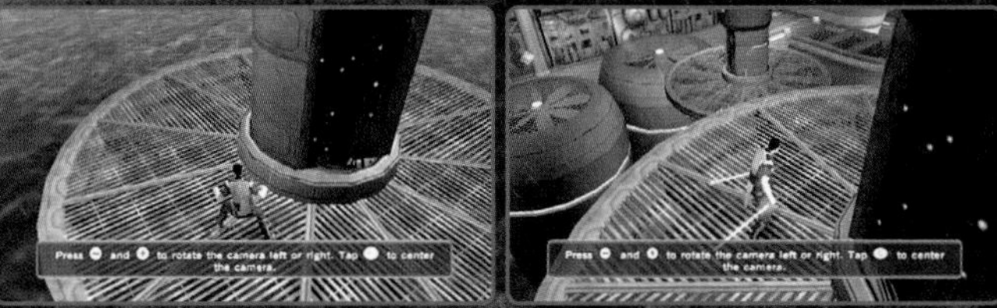

Camera control is essential for navigating the complicated locales you'll traverse. Move the camera around to get a better view of the area around you. You can use this to spot hidden holocrons and items and to look around corners. When paired with Force Vision, you can see things you normally wouldn't with the naked eye!

FOCUS THE FORCE

Whenever you want to focus your Force powers more accurately, bring up the aiming reticle by pointing the Wii Remote at the screen. This will make a blue circle reticle appear on the screen. Aim the reticle at the desired target and execute your Force power, be it Force Push, Force Lightning, or Force Grip.

This aiming reticle is extremely useful in blasting through doors, hitting specific enemies in a group, grabbing platforms, and lighting up switches.

Force Powers

You have the same Force powers as the original Starkiller. In fact, you even have Force powers that he didn't! Read on to learn more about all of your Force powers and how to use them effectively.

FORCE DASH

Action	Command
Dash	✚

Force Dash isn't a typi[illegible]l attack. In fac[illegible]t doesn't have to be used as an attack; it's a very handy way of covering a lot of distance in a little bit of time. However, you can also use Force Dash to barrel through small groups of enemies!

FORCE LIGHTNING

Action	Command
Force Lightning	Hold Ⓩ and shake the Nunchuk

This is one of your most powerful Force powers. At lower levels, it can stun most enemies and electrocute weaker stormtroopers. When upgraded, it can bring down even large war droids with sustained Lightning blasts.

FORCE PUSH

Action	Command
Force Push	Shake the Nunchuk

Force Push is one of the most effective powers against all enemies. Use it to bully enemies around and shove them off ledges and high platforms. You can also add Force Push to the end of saber combos to blast enemies away. Force Push is necessary for bringing down large obstacles, blowing down doors, and moving objects out of the way quickly.

FORCE GRIP

Action	Command
Force Grip	Press and hold Ⓒ
Move gripped object	◎ or move the Wii Remote
Throw	Hold Ⓒ, move object toward target, then release

Very few enemies have a suitable defense against Force Grip. Once they're in your grip, they are helpless and at your mercy. Enemies and items can be moved around or even tossed aside. Force Grip is also useful in moving objects, opening doors, and tearing away war droids' shields. Force Grip enemies and hurl them over ledges or into lethal objects such as flame jets, fans, and explosive objects.

JEDI WISDOM

You can also electrocute enemies while they're in your Force Grip. To do so, execute Force Lightning while holding an enemy with Force Grip.

CLONER'S CAUTION

While Force Gripping something, your movement is restricted and you'll only be able to walk slowly, so be careful!

SABER THROW

Action	Command
Saber Throw	Hold Ⓩ, then thrust the Wii Remote

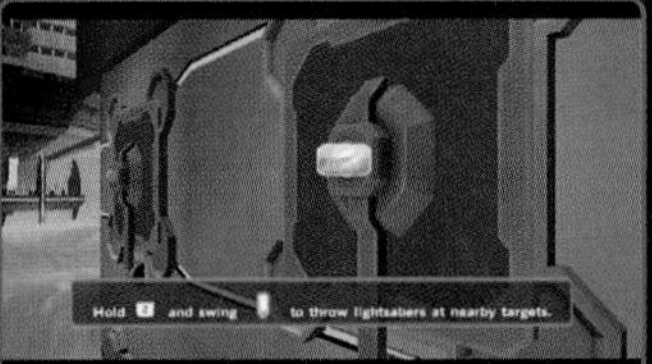

Saber Throw is a great power that can dish out decent damage from afar. Many enemies, like war droids, are far too dangerous to take on hand-to-hand. When in combat with these large clunkers, keep your distance and use Saber Throw to slice them from afar. Saber Throw is a great ranged attack, but keep in mind that while your lightsabers are in the air, you'll be defenseless to blaster fire and other enemy attacks. You can also use Saber Throw to solve environmental puzzles and chop down structures.

FORCE REPULSE

Action	Command
Repulse	Hold Z and A, then shake both

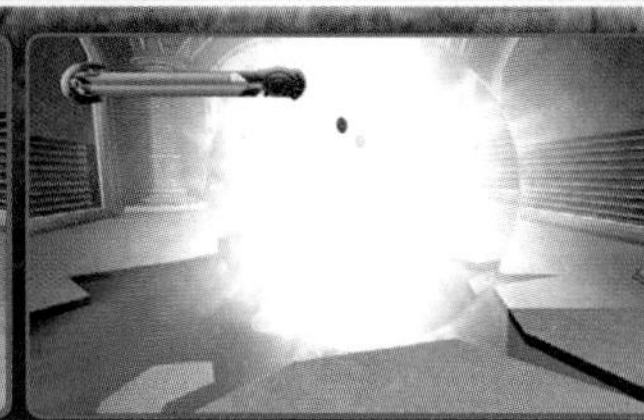

Force Repulse isn't just another Force attack; you can also use it as a defensive maneuver against enemies. Charge Force Repulse to gather your Force Energy around you like a bubble, then release it to cause a Force explosion that radiates 360 degrees around you. While it may not immediately destroy most enemies (though it is very effective against lower-level enemies like terror spider droids), it is very useful in repelling foes as they surround you.

MIND TRICK

Action	Command
Mind Trick	Aim the Wii Remote, then press ✚

Mind Trick is one of your sneakiest skills. With it you can eliminate enemies without ever swinging your lightsaber! Mind Trick allows you to fool your enemies into thinking what you what them to think. You can convince enemies to turn on their comrades, making them temporary allies! This skill is especially useful when facing several different types of enemies at once. Use it to turn a few strong enemies on weaker ones, or use it to turn many weak enemies on a few stronger ones.

FORCE VISION

Action	Command
Force Vision	Press ✚

A Jedi doesn't need eyes to see; Master Kota is living proof of that. He relies on the Force to guide him. Like Kota, you can activate your Force Vision to allow you to see things that otherwise would not be visible to you. Once this skill is active, enemies and grippable objects are highlighted in bright blue. However, your Force Energy slowly dwindles while your Force Vision is active, so keep an eye on it. If you use other Force powers while Force Vision is active, your energy will deplete even quicker.

WALKING IN STARKILLER'S SHADOW

A long time ago in a galaxy far, far away....

The galaxy is on the brink of civil war. Inspired by the sacrifice of DARTH VADER's secret apprentice, a ragtag Rebel Alliance plots to overthrow the evil GALACTIC EMPIRE. Imperial forces in relentless pursuit of the Rebels have captured the Jedi Knight RAHM KOTA. Its general lost, the Alliance fleet has vanished. While the Empire searches for the Rebels, Darth Vader has put a dark plan in motion that will bring an end to his apprentice's legacy....

Prologue

The ocean world of Kamino isn't known for its picturesque weather. As the TIE Advanced fighter makes its descent, it's greeted by a sheet of rain so thick the secret cloning facilities below nearly disappear. However, this is no typical TIE Advanced fighter; it belongs to someone very special.

As the TIE Advanced fighter touches down on the landing pad the stormtroopers that guard the secret cloning facility scurry into place.

Imperial stormtroopers line the halls of the facility as Darth Vader coolly trundles past them toward a distant corner of the labs that only he and a few others have access to.

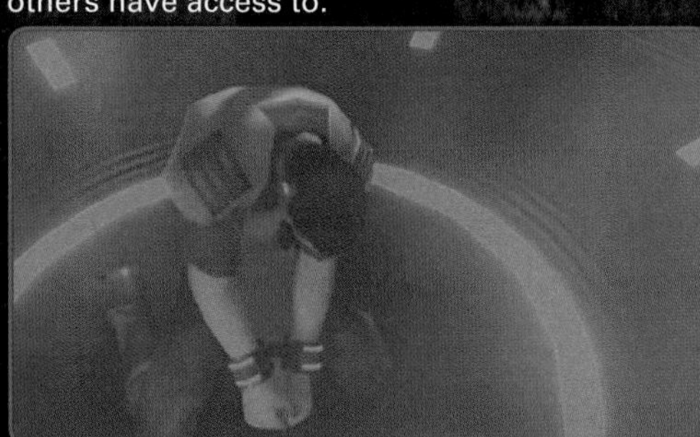

When he reaches his destination—a holding pit—a familiar face stares up at him from the depths. It's Starkiller's face, but not quite the same person. The clone of the once-secret apprentice is shackled and weak. Despite his connection to the Force, Starkiller's clone is unable to free himself from Vader.

The Sith Master has a mission for his new minion. Starkiller's old Jedi mentor, General Rahm Kota, has been captured. He's being held captive on Cato Neimoidia. The clone's mission, once his training is complete, is to travel to Cato Neimoidia and execute Kota.

As the Starkiller clone shakes the memories from his head, Vader tries to convince him that they're not truly his memories to own. A side effect of the cloning process and a remnant of the training process, the memories should soon fade.

Vader hands the Starkiller clone a pair of lightsabers, prompting him to cut loose of the memories and truly shake free of his progenitor's "weakness"—that is, his feelings for Juno Eclipse. Just then, several Combat Training Droids approach and engage their holo-training systems.

JEDI WISDOM

The following teaches you lightsaber and Force power combat. Use this section to get comfortable wielding dual lightsabers and manipulating the Force.

Combat Training

Begin to develop your skills by letting your dual sabers loose on the Combat Training Droids within the holding cell. Concentrate on the Rebel fighters and strike them down with lightsaber attacks.

When the next batch of Rebels appears, turn to your Force powers. Follow the onscreen commands to fry them with Force Lightning. The Rebels, or rather the combat training droids, are weak, so a blast of Force Lightning or two will defeat them instantly.

JEDI WISDOM

To more precisely aim the Force, point the Wii Remote at the screen. This will bring up a blue circle reticle that you can use to target enemies and objects.

Dispatch the Rebel scum with Force Lightning until a new squad arrives. This time, practice blocking to deflect blaster fire back at your holographic foes. Finish tearing through the Rebel soldiers by stringing together saber attacks to build up your Combo meter.

Once you've built up the combo meter, follow the onscreen commands to execute a Lightsaber Special. These special attacks can strike down multiple enemies with over the top finishing moves. As you chain together more combinations of attacks on enemies your Combo Meter will increase. Each rank in your Combo Meter will execute a different finishing move. A higher Combo Meter gives an XP multiplier and allows you to pull off more powerful Lightsaber Specials.

JEDI WISDOM

The Combo meter won't stay full forever once you've filled it up. If you don't use it to execute Lightsaber Specials, then it will slowly drain, so be sure to use it whenever you can.

When you finish, the room is littered with the bodies of the demolished training droids. Darth Vader rejoins you and brings one last person for you to strike down. Just as your lightsabers are about to tear through her skin, she screams in terror and you stop. It's Juno!

Vader insists that you strike her down and do away with Starkiller's feelings that echo inside of you. When you resist, Darth Vader takes matters into his own hand.

Disturbed, Vader then decides that you, like the clones that came before you, are of no use to him. Angered at Vader's apathy towards Juno and knowing that you'll likely be killed as yet another failed experiment, you lash out with Force Lightning.

Before he has a chance to retaliate, you jump out the window and take your first step toward freedom.

Awakening

LEGEND

- Checkpoints (see corresponding images)
- Power Crystal
- Power Crystal (Unleashed Mode)
- Green Color Crystal
- Holocron
- Bacta Tank
- Blue Tank

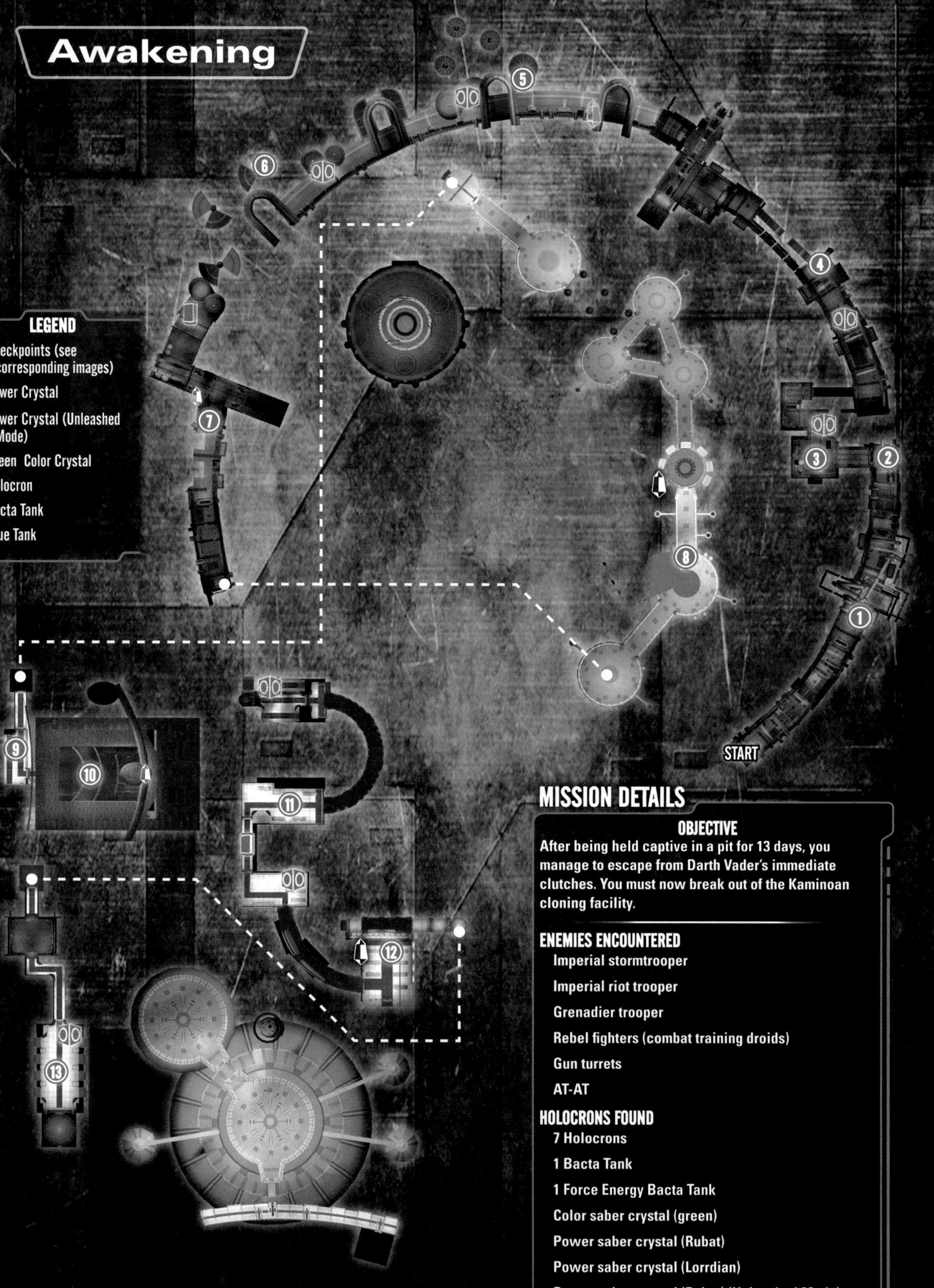

MISSION DETAILS

OBJECTIVE

After being held captive in a pit for 13 days, you manage to escape from Darth Vader's immediate clutches. You must now break out of the Kaminoan cloning facility.

ENEMIES ENCOUNTERED

- Imperial stormtrooper
- Imperial riot trooper
- Grenadier trooper
- Rebel fighters (combat training droids)
- Gun turrets
- AT-AT

HOLOCRONS FOUND

- 7 Holocrons
- 1 Bacta Tank
- 1 Force Energy Bacta Tank
- Color saber crystal (green)
- Power saber crystal (Rubat)
- Power saber crystal (Lorrdian)
- Power saber crystal (Rubat) (Unleashed Mode)
- Power saber crystal (Lorrdian) (Unleashed Mode)

Free...for Now

Though brave and bold, your escape is also hasty and extremely dangerous. You've managed to get away from Darth Vader, but now you're in a trench on the cloning facility's outer rim that is infested with Imperials!

Run straight ahead, toward the large raised platform, and double-jump onto it. Double-jump across the gap onto the next platform, then reach the sealed door at the far end. Stand in front of the door and follow the onscreen commands to Force Push it open.

JEDI WISDOM

If you're having a hard time hitting the door directly with Force Push, aim the Wii Remote's reticle at the door. When the blue circle is on the doorway, execute Force Push for a direct hit.

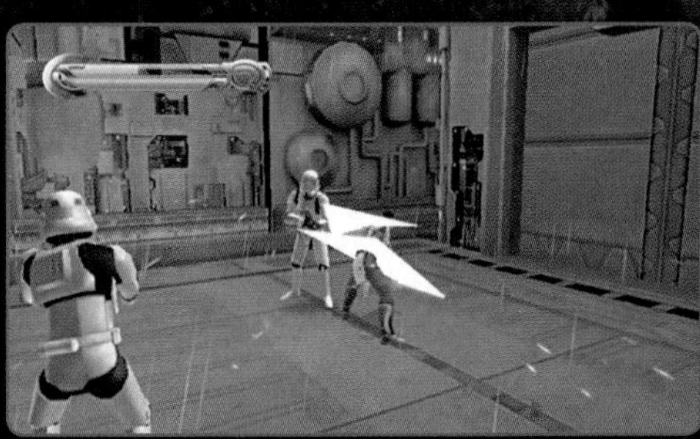

Rush into the next compartment of the facility and tear through the first batch of Imperial stormtroopers. Run your sabers through them to take them out. Try to destroy all three at one so they don't split up and pick you apart with their blasters.

JEDI WISDOM

You can also use Force Push to blast them into the gap just right of the next doorway. Be careful not to fall in, however. You'll die instantly.

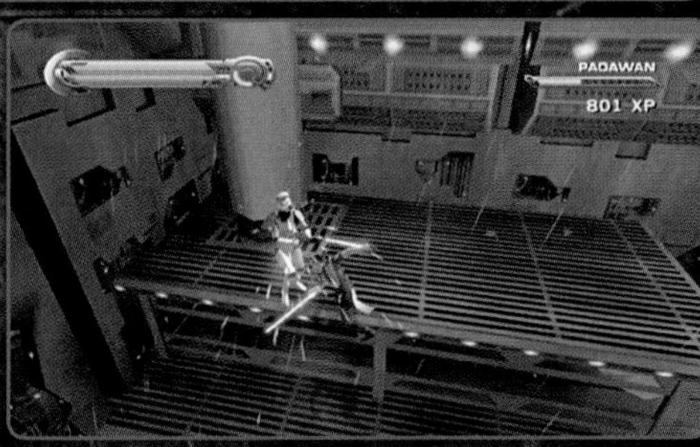

Blow open the next doorway and greet the stormtrooper battalion that rushes through the hatch on the right. Execute saber combos to put the enemies down quickly; then turn on the next few that rush out of another nearby hatch.

When you destroy the stormtroopers, the hatch at the room's far end slides open and several more stormtroopers rush out. Deal with them quickly, then hurry to the grenadier trooper perched atop the small platform ahead of you. Rush him and slice him up before he can cause any damage with his thermal detonators.

JEDI WISDOM

If he manages to knock you down with a grenade, rapidly shake the Wii Remote and Nunchuk to get up and hurl your lightsaber at him. You can execute this move any time you get knocked down.

Double-jump over the series of platforms until you're in a long section of the facility with several venting fans protruding from the walls on either side of you.

Upon landing on the other side, practice your Force Grip and hurl the nearby objects at the door on the left. Pick up objects with Force Grip, then quickly flick the Wii Remote in the direction you want to toss them. This will hurl the objects in that direction. Eventually, the door gives way, revealing a room swarming with Imperial stormtroopers. Rush in and get to business!

Make short work of the Imperial stormtroopers inside by using Force Push to blast debris at them. If that doesn't knock them out, then sprint toward them—with your sabers in blocking position—and execute a series of lightsaber combos to destroy them.

The room is large, so look out for stormtroopers near the edge. They can pick you off from afar while you attack their squadmates. If you find your health quickly depleting, use Force Push to knock the distant foes off their feet before you finish them off.

HOLOCRON

The door on the far right side of this room leads to a holocron. Destroy your enemies to open the door, then rush through to get 500 experience points!

Pass through the doorway on the right, then enter the narrow passageway protected by stormtroopers at the far end. Run down the hall with your sabers in blocking position, then slice up the Imperials as you emerge.

Upon exiting the hallway you enter an area with a Stormtrooper Commando at the far end. Use Force Grip to on a nearby piece of debris to throw at him.

As you let the grenadier feel your sabers' heat, several more stormtroopers rush out of a nearby hatch. Welcome them to the fight... with several lightsaber combos or a Lightsaber Special. Crush the Imperial scum, then double-jump over the next series of platforms to an area with a short bridge.

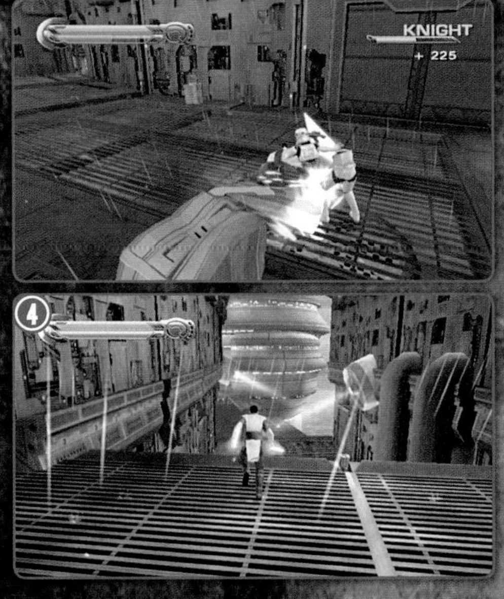

Several more stormtroopers wait to incinerate you, so use Force Push to blast them into the chasm below before heading across the bridge.

HOLOCRON

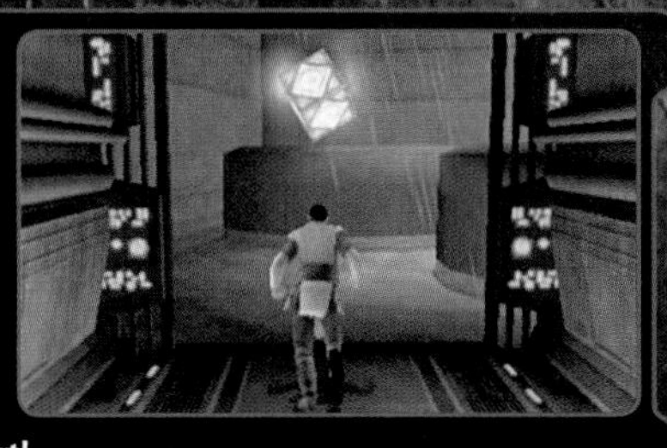

Just before the bridge, there is a small hole in the floor. Drop down the hole, then turn back around to find a tunnel behind you. Follow the tunnel to its end to locate the 2nd holocron. In addition to earning XP it also unlocks new concept art!

Double-jump across the small gap in the bridge and quickly slice up the stormtroopers on the other side.

Hop up the raised platforms until you reach a small room with a large fan in the far right corner. Dispatch all of the storm-troopers waiting to ambush you by either cutting them down with lightsaber combos or tossing them into the giant fan.

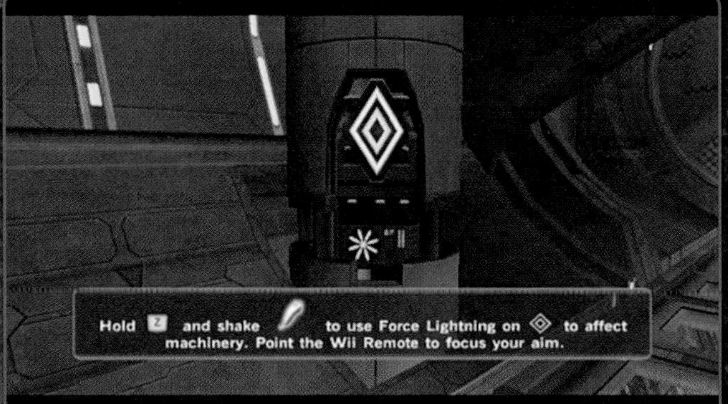

When you're done, target the diamond-shaped plaque to the fan's left and zap it with Force Lightning. The electrical current shorts out the fan, and it slowly comes to a halt, allowing you to pass its blades unharmed.

JEDI WISDOM

Take a minute to go into the Pause menu and select Customize. Select Force Upgrades and use your accrued XP to augment your Force power of choice! Upgrading your Force powers is the best way to make sure you always have the upper hand in combat.

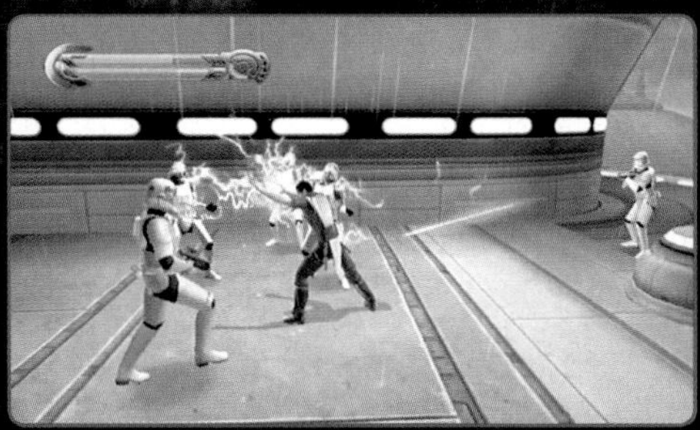

Run past the fan blades when it stops spinning and make a left. Climb up the stepped platform and sprint out onto the circular walkway. When you do, several more storm-troopers rush out. Zap them or slice them, then follow the walkway right.

ITEM FOUND

As the circular walkway turns left, back toward the main path, look to the right to find a green saber crystal. Grab it as you return to the main path.

Follow the path to the dead end, then look right. Just over the ledge is a large circular platform. Double-jump onto it and follow the series of circular platforms down and back around to the main path.

HOLOCRON

After following the circular platforms back to the main path, look left. Just left of the two large fan platforms is the next holocron. Jump off the left fan to reach it. This one is worth 500 experience points!

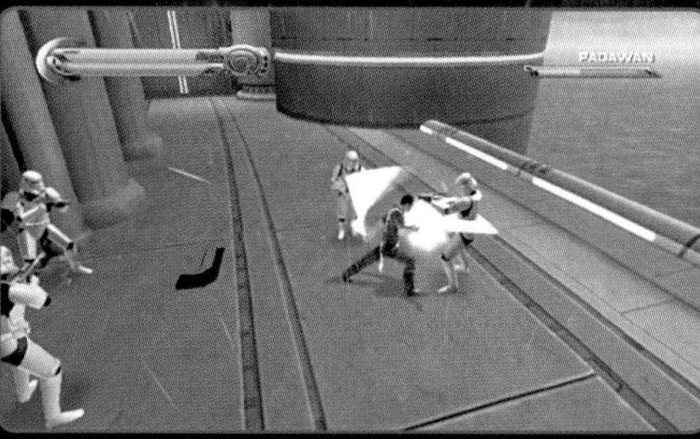

Once again, follow the main path until you reach a platform made of metal grating. Double-jump across the gap and turn left to find several Imperial stormtroopers and a Stormtrooper Commander in your way.

Slice through the Stormtrooper Commander first, then chop down the other weaklings. Resume your attack and Force Push through the door at the far end.

JEDI WISDOM

An alternate approach to this and some future encounters is to take out enemies of the same type—in this case, the regular stormtroopers—first, then target the tougher Stormtrooper Commander last. By doing so, you'll rank up your combo meter and earn more XP that you can use to purchase more Force Upgrades!

HOLOCRON

After blasting through the sealed hatch, make an immediate right. The next Experience Point holocron is just right of the busted hatch!

After crushing the hatch, follow the walkway to its end and look right. Locate the large quarter-circle platform, and use Force Grip and the Control Stick to move the platform from the right to the left creating a half-circle. Once you have locked it into place, double-jump to it then continue moving along the platforms, using Force Grip to slide them into place as you go.

ITEM FOUND

Once you've hopped across all of the half-circle platforms and reached the main path again, you'll find a glowing red Bacta Tank. Grab it to increase your overall health!

Double-jump down to the area below and quickly use Force Push to get the stormtroopers out of the way. Destroy them, then turn to the diamond-shaped plate along the far wall. Fry it with Force Lightning to stop the fan on the left; then pass by the fan blades to a small hallway.

Make a right out of the hall and exit to the Kaminoan rain. There's a group of foolish stormtroopers waiting to ambush you outside. Show them you can't be surprised; run out of the hall toward them and throw crates at them from afar to push them over the ledge's side.

7

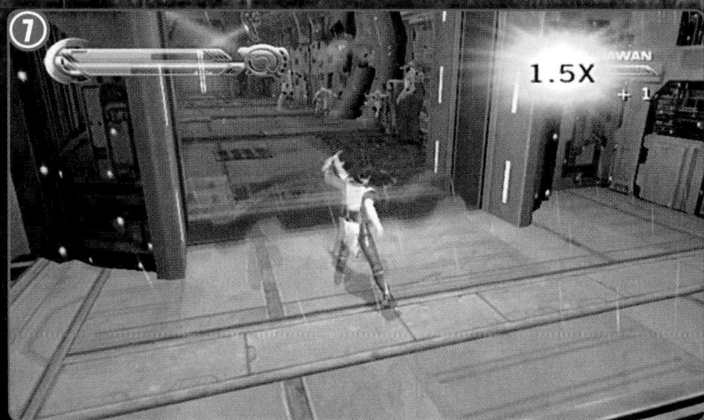

When you get rid of the first few fools, the hatch at the far end slides open, revealing several more troopers. Put them down quickly, then rush to the hall's end.

JEDI WISDOM

There are explosive barrels throughout Kamino that you can use as a weapon. Use Force Grip to pick them up then toss them at groups of enemies to dispatch them at the same time.

Just before you reach the next door, a shockwave from above drops rubble blocking your escape. Suddenly you hear a breathing apparatus and heavy footfalls behind you. It's Lord Vader!

You slowly rise into the air as Vader begins to choke the life out of you, but a well-timed Force Lightning attack sets you free. Follow the on screen commands to face off with Darth Vader. Just as you are about to get the drop on Vader a powerful force explosion sends you tumbling down a nearby shaft!

The drop deposits you on a lower level of the cloning facility exterior. Turn left and battle past the small squad of stormtroopers. Take out the grenadier trooper first!

Follow the walkway as it turns right, along a circular part of the building, and crush all Imperials in your way.

8

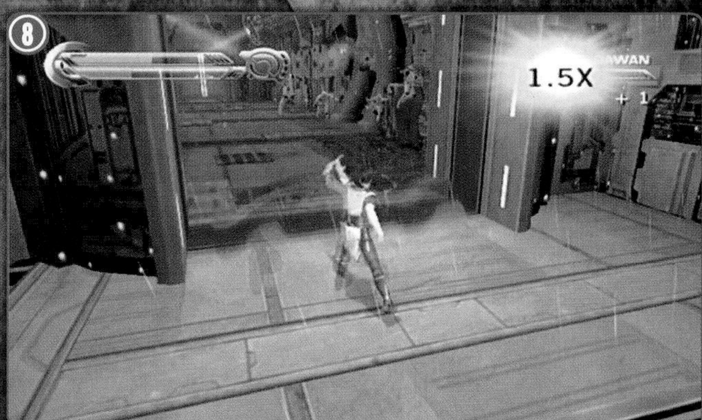

Use Force Push to knock the next batch of bothersome troopers off the long walkway, then make haste into the large elevator shaft at the walkway's end.

ITEM FOUND

Before entering the elevator, hop onto the ledge on the right of this tower. Follow the ledges up and around the tower to find the Rubat power crystal!

JEDI WISDOM

After acquiring the Rubat power crystal, go into the Customize menu and equip it! The crystal increases damage dealt with your lightsaber!

When you reach the top of the elevator, the door slides open to reveal another part of the facility exterior. It is here that you learn Force Dash, so use it down the long walkway toward the stormtroopers on the platform ahead.

The platform is attached to two walkways, both leading to the same junction. Pick either one and dash across to the troopers on the other side. Slice them up, and dash across the junction to the other side.

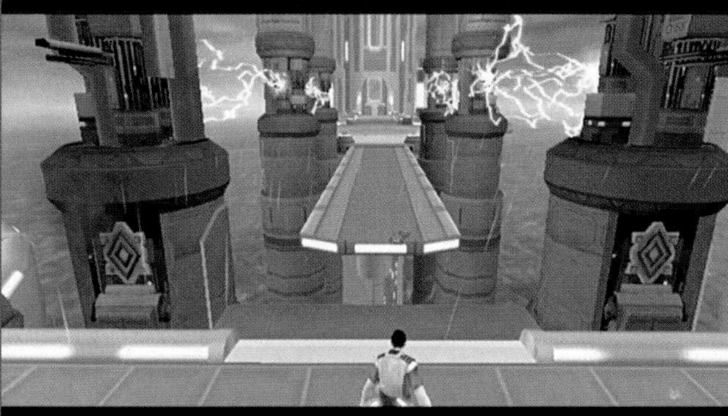

Once the coast is clear, use Force Lightning to activate the two diamond-shape plates nearby. The lightning powers the retractable bridge connecting your platform to the next one.

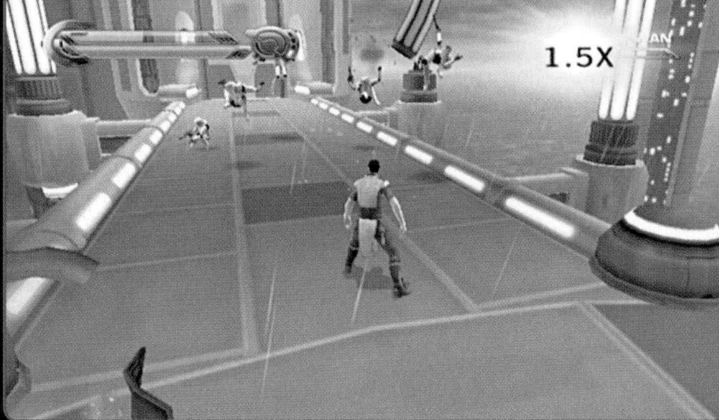

After crossing the bridge, a squad of Imperial stormtroopers rushes out of the nearby elevator. Force Push them off the walkway, then get into the elevator at the end, where several more troopers await. Crush them, and ride the elevator to the next section.

TRAINING GROUNDS

Force Push through the elevator doors and dispatch the stormtroopers in your way. When you do, the door on the left side of the room opens up to reveal a large courtyard used for Imperial training exercises.

The training yard incorporates two gun turrets located along the far wall and several retracting panels that rise up from the floor. To activate the panels, simply walk near them and they'll pop up!

Use this to your advantage by standing near the panels to protect you from the turret fire, then turn around and use the Force to grip the large lever on the wall and lower it. This deactivates the nearest floor panels and allows you to move one step closer to the turrets. Dash forward and approach the turrets. This time, another set of panels rises from the ground. Once again, stand near them and use Force Grip to lower the lever along the far right wall.

Dash forward and approach the turrets. This time, another set of panels rises from the ground. Once again, stand near the panels and use Force Grip to lower the third and final lever behind the turret on the right side.

JEDI WISDOM

Keep the battle with the droids near the panels so that you're not exposed to the turrets' blaster fire while you fight.

Destroy the turrets and any remaining training droids. Before you can escape this room, however, Darth Vader arrives and you face another battle. Follow the onscreen gesture commands to defeat Vader and quickly flee into the nearby elevator.

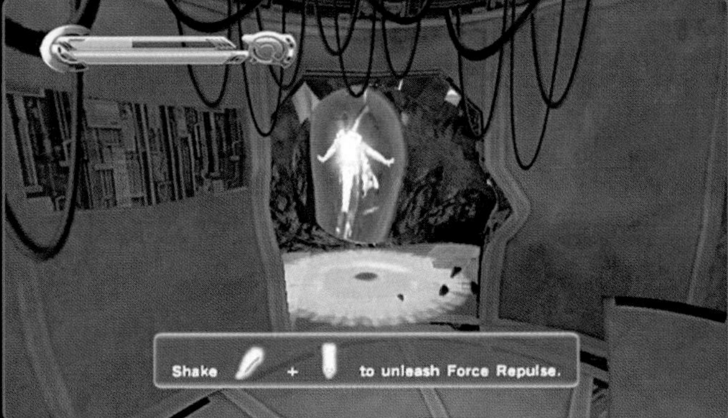

Luckily, the shaft crumbles around you, not on you. Force Repulse the debris away from you and create an exit from the busted elevator.

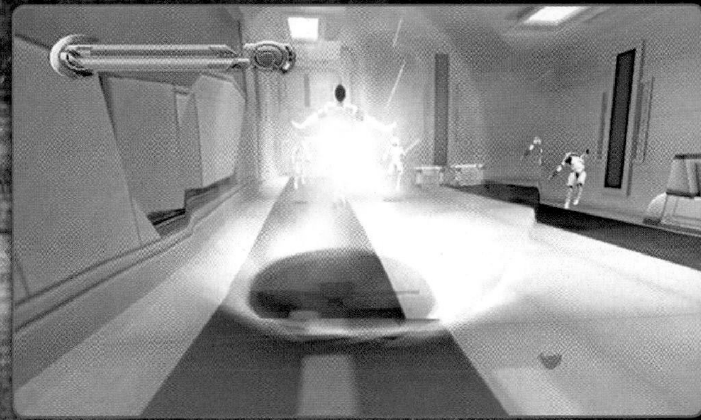

Exit the shaft and enter a small room with several troopers. Practice your new Force Repulse power on them and slam them against the walls of the room.

HOLOCRON

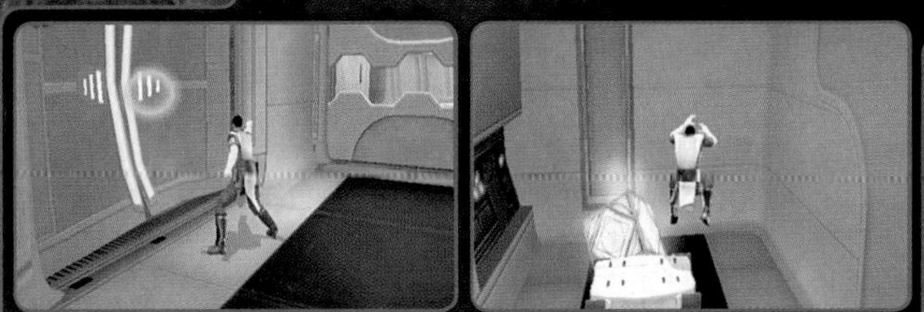

There is another holocron nearby. After destroying the enemies in the room, Force Push down the door on the left wall to find a smaller room. The holocron worth 500 experience points is hidden behind three small crates.

When the door along the far wall slides open, Force Push the troopers away. Dash toward them and cut them down, then continue dashing down the long, curved hall, dispatching foes as you go.

Upon reaching the hall's end, you're greeted by several Imperial riot troopers. These foes are armed with electrorods and are very skilled in weapon combat. Use Lightsaber Specials to whittle them down, then finish them off with strong saber combos.

JEDI WISDOM

Remember to use Recovery Attacks if they knock you down!

ITEM FOUND

The exit hall to this room has a blue Force Energy Bacta Tank. Grab it as you trek deeper into the facility.

Force Push through the next door and use Lightsaber Specials to chop down the enemies in the next room. They're all spread apart from each other, so link your attacks with saber combos to move around the room quickly.

HOLOCRON

The next holocron is located in the far left niche in this room. Remove the crates in the niche to find it. Not only do you get 500 experience points, but you also unlock new concept art!

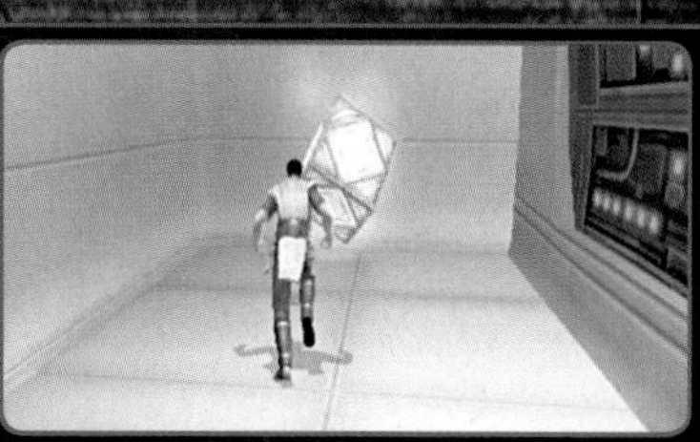

Make a right out of this room and dash down the long, curved corridor. The corridor leads to a two-level room where a squad of Imperial stormtroopers and riot troopers ambushes you. First take out the riot troopers on the lower level. Take the fight to the ledge beneath the stormtroopers so that you don't give the perched enemies a clean shot at you.

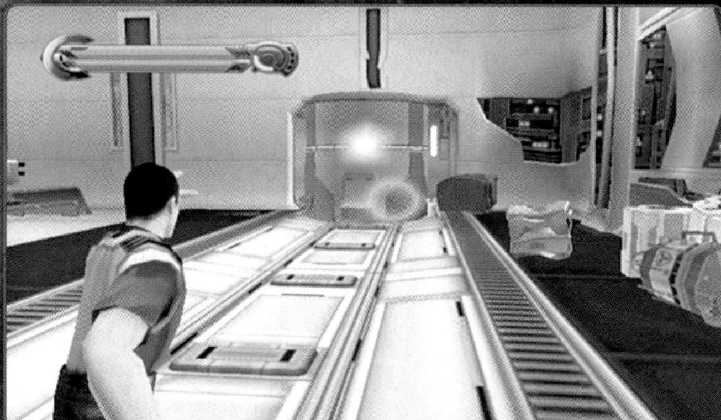

When the lower level is clear, turn left and use Force Grip to yank the large crate out of the wall. It's on a track, so pulling it out is easy.

ITEM FOUND

After you've pulled the crate from the left wall, explore the hole where the crate was. The Lorrdian power crystal is inside!

Use the large crate you just pulled out to double-jump onto the top level. Surprise the stormtrooper scum there with several saber strikes, then make a right down the hall into the next area.

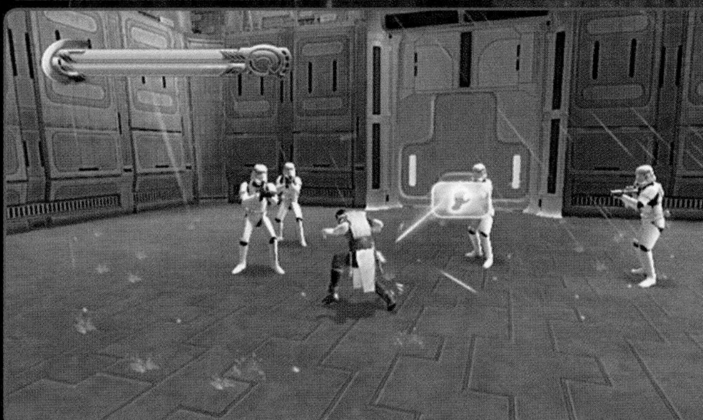

Approach the next elevator shaft. As you do, Vader once again sneaks up on you. Follow the onscreen commands to shove Vader away as you escape into the elevator. Ride the elevator all the way up and dash out.

Stand at the center of the stormtrooper squad and use Force Repulse to shove them all away. Rush the fallen foes as they stagger to get up and strike them down with your saber!

Use Force Grip to raise the hatch, then dash down the hall to a long room with gun turrets and several grenadiers and stormtroopers. Rush the turrets first and slice them up. With the turrets out of the way, turn on the grenadiers, then the weaker stormtroopers.

HOLOCRON

The next holocron is hidden behind three crates in the near, left corner of the room. Wait until you've cleared the room of all enemies before acquiring this Experience Points holocron.

Hop into the elevator at the room's far end and take it all the way up. It leads to a long, curved corridor full of stormtroopers. Either Force Dash past all of the enemies, or strike them down as you head to the far hatch.

When you exit the corridor, you find two large AT-ATs waiting to blast you down. Quickly follow the onscreen commands to crush them and bring the large nearby tower crashing down on them. The tower slows Vader's pursuit just long enough for you to steal his TIE Advanced fighter and escape Kamino!

Cato Neimoidia

High above the planet of Cato Neimoidia hangs the city of Tarko-se. There, in the Tarko-se arena, several of the most powerful warriors put their skills to the test (often unwillingly) against the galaxy's most fearsome creatures. Today, the crowd cheers for Tarko-se's greatest champion.

As the champion slowly steps forward, a pair of wild combatants leaps into a full charge. With one swift, fluid motion, the champion steps aside, swings his lightsaber, and strikes down the menaces.

The warrior, General Rahm Kota, [illegible] fazed [illegible] opponents size, speed, or strength. He's got the Force on his side.

Having struck down all of his opponents, Rahm Kota waves his fing[illegible]he spectator stands defiantly. He challenges the baron to t[illegible]him all he's got, so the baron unleashes the Corellian slice hounds.

As the baron contemplates his next move, a Neimoidian attendant delivers some troubling news. While the baron watched over his arena battle, a TIE Advanced fighter touched down in the plaza.

The baron hastily runs off to meet the TIE Advanced fighter's pilot but is surprised to find that it is not who he expected. Where the baron expected to see Darth Vader, he found instead a young but weathered boy resembling Starkiller, Vader's secret apprentice.

When the baron realizes he isn't going to face Lord Vader, he threatens Starkiller's clone to reveal the security codes to this sector. He knew that having captured Rahm Kota would draw Vader to him, but he'd never expected to see Starkiller...or his clone.

The devious despot eventually realizes he isn't going to get what he wants from the clone, so he orders his stormtrooper squad to open fire and retreats like the coward that he is. The baron makes a narrow escape just as his drawbridge retracts, leaving the Starkiller clone alone with the stormtroopers.

City of Bridges

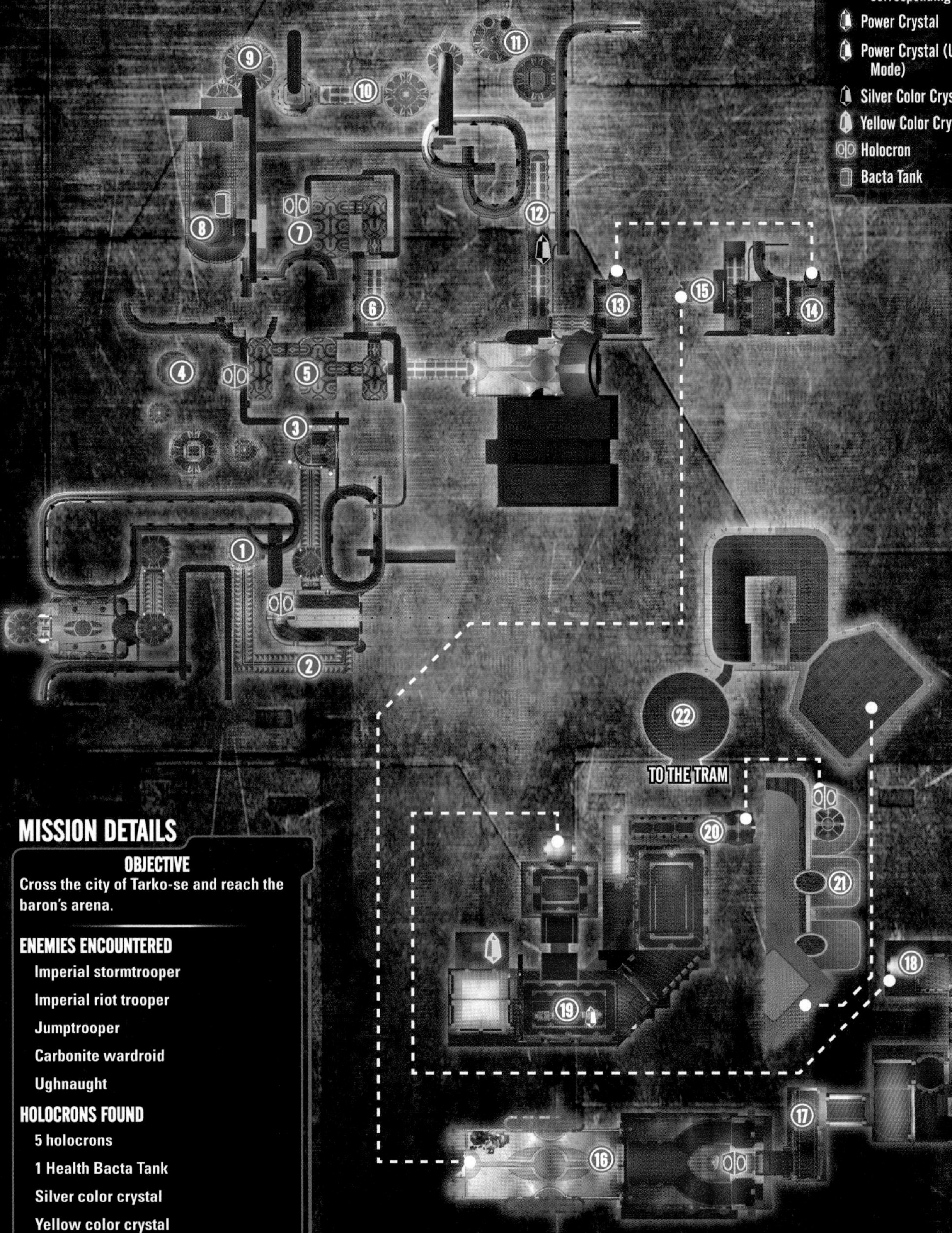

LEGEND

- Checkpoints (see corresponding images)
- Power Crystal
- Power Crystal (Unleashed Mode)
- Silver Color Crystal
- Yellow Color Crystal
- Holocron
- Bacta Tank

MISSION DETAILS

OBJECTIVE

Cross the city of Tarko-se and reach the baron's arena.

ENEMIES ENCOUNTERED

- Imperial stormtrooper
- Imperial riot trooper
- Jumptrooper
- Carbonite wardroid
- Ughnaught

HOLOCRONS FOUND

- 5 holocrons
- 1 Health Bacta Tank
- Silver color crystal
- Yellow color crystal
- Opila power crystal
- Opila power crystal (Unleashed Mode)

ARENA BOUND

The baron's first line of offense are Imperial stormtroopers and a stormtrooper commander. Lift your lightsabers to blocking position and reflect their blaster fire as you approach them. As soon as you reach them, let your lightsabers loose and strike them down.

While you fight the first few stormtroopers, a small complement of Imperial riot troopers arrives on the nearby elevator. Turn on them and use the Force to either electrocute them or toss them over the side of the platform.

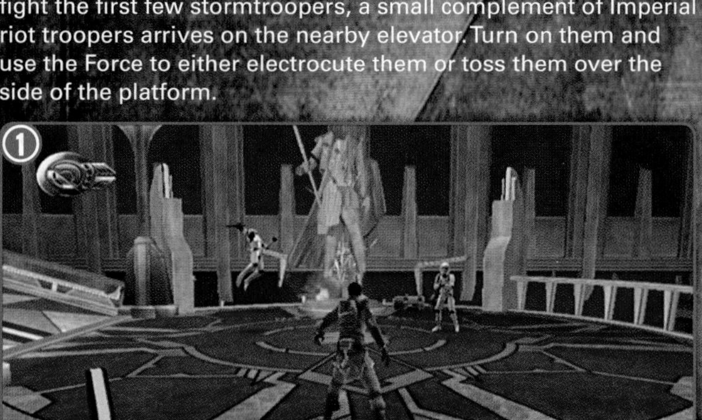

Step onto the elevator and ride it up to the next level. As you arrive at your destination, use a Force Push attack to send the two nearby stormtroopers flying.

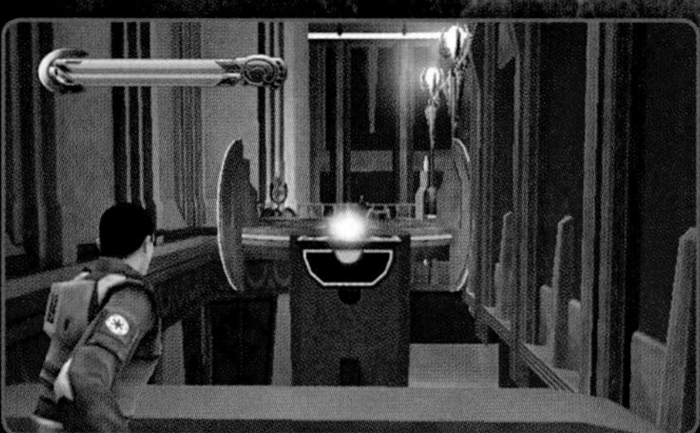

Make a left and sprint up the incline as you chase down the baron. You reach the top of the next platform to find the baron speeding across a retracting bridge. Use Force Grip to yank the retracting bridge and extend it across the gap.

Force Dash across the newly extended bridge, and run your sabers through the stormtroopers on the other side.

Make a right after the bridge and sprint across the next incline. Another group of riot troopers waits for you at the top of the incline. Force Push them off the bridge. If they don't all fall off, use Lightsaber Specials to attack them all at once and take them down.

Follow the bridge left and fight past several more stormtroopers. As you do, the baron calmly saunters onto his tram and speeds away. Meanwhile, the city's defensive turrets come back online and nearly blow you to little clone bits!

With the baron gone, you'll need a different way to reach him. The door ahead of you opens up, revealing a path into the Tarko-se facility, and several riot troopers come storming out. Welcome them with several saber strikes and slice them up.

HOLOCRON

The first holocron is hidden behind the tall statue on the left, just after the baron speeds away on his tram. Peek behind the statue before leaving this area.

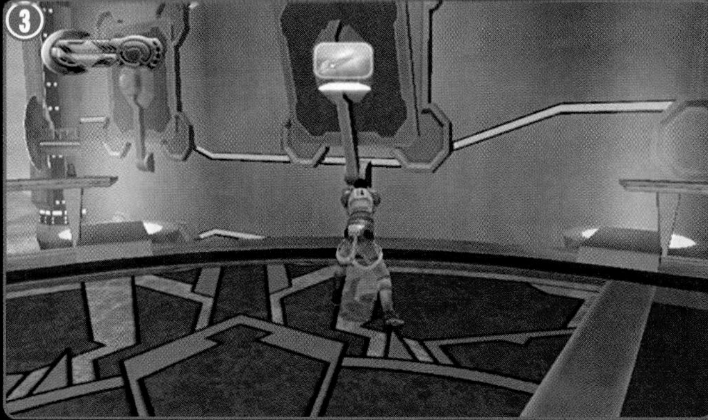

Speed into the next area, through the door where the riot troopers came out, and crush the remaining stormtroopers. There's an explosive tank on the right; use it to blow up the soldiers with one quick attack from afar.

At the top of the walkway, locate the locked panel along the far wall. Use Saber Throw to unlock the panel, and it will drop, turning it into a platform.

Jump onto the platform, then use Saber Throw to unlock the next wall panel on the left. Next, double-jump across to the nearby circular platform to the far left.

After you reach the circular platform, several jumptroopers immediately attack! Use Force Lightning to short out their jet packs and ground them. If any land on the platform with you, rush them and take them down with lightsaber combos.

Double-jump across the next few platforms, zapping jumptroopers as you go. Reach the final circular platform in this section, and turn right to find another retracted bridge in the opposite wall.

Use the Force to grip it and pull it out so it connects your platform to the far wall.

HOLOCRON

Before you cross the newly extended bridge, use Saber Throw to unlock the wall panel just right of the bridge. The panel reveals a holocron hidden inside a small wall niche. Double-jump dash onto the platform, then hop into the niche to grab it.

5

6

Cross the bridge and enter the city walls. Blow open the door on the left and pass through a small passageway into a room with more stormtroopers. Take them down easily with a few Force blasts.

Turn left and enter the next room. Attached to this small room are two bridges. The city's defense turrets blow up the one directly ahead of you! Turn left and dash across the next bridge while the turret destroys the bridge as you go.

Use Force Push to blow open the next door on the left and destroy the two stormtroopers in your way. Rush into the room and obliterate the squad of stormtroopers inside.

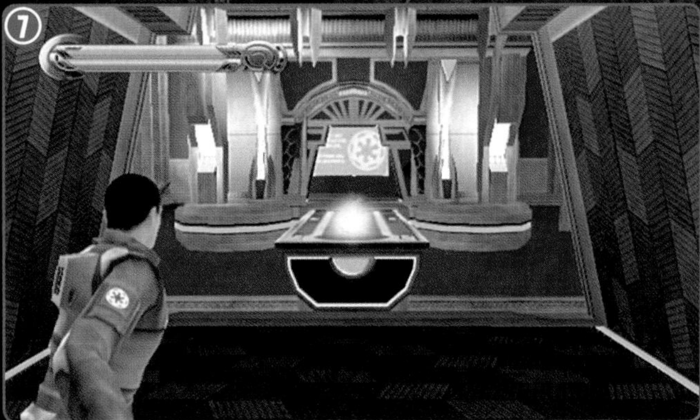

7

Walk up to the exit and locate the retractable bridge along the far wall. Force Grip it and pull it into place.

HOLOCRON

Before speeding across the bridge, walk onto it and turn right. Locate the next locked wall panel behind and to your right, then open it with a Saber Throw. Double-jump onto it, then hop up to grab the next holocron.

8

Run across the bridge and follow the small winding walkway down into a long room with three floating platforms in it.

ITEM FOUND

Don't rush across this room just yet. Instead, take a minute to grab the Health Bacta tank nearby. Pull the far left platform close and jump on it. Before it begins to slide back across the room, turn right and double-jump onto stationary middle platform. Finally, grab the platform on the far right and pull it into place next to the platform you're on. Double-jump onto it, then quickly jump onto the small ledge on the right wall to find the Bacta Tank.

Force Grip the far left platform and pull it toward you. Double-jump onto it, then onto the nearby middle platform. While on the middle platform, grip the far right platform and pull it toward you. Jump onto it and ride it across the room as it slowly floats back into its original spot.

Exit the room and jump down onto the platform below. An Imperial transport ship drops several stormtroopers onto it. Drop down on them with a savage downward blow of your lightsaber.

After landing, look up and locate the jumptroopers buzzing about. Zap them with Force Lightning, then turn back on the remaining Imperials and do away with them.

Follow the platforms around to another long bridge that is being guarded by the defense turrets. Take out the enemies on the bridge, then quickly dash across it while the turret attempts to obliterate you.

Use a Lightsaber Special to take out the next batch of stormtroopers before turning left and speeding across several more platforms. Reach a structure with three tall columns on it, each one taller than the next, and hop up the stepped columns, taking down stormtroopers as you go.

Hop across the columns onto another large circular support and wait for a transport ship to rise ahead of you. Force Grip the ship and bring it down!

With the transport out of the way, use the Force to pull the next bridge out and connect it with the platform you're standing on. Once again, dash across the bridge while the turret destroys it. Stay ahead of the turret blasts to keep from getting killed.

ITEM FOUND

There's a silver color crystal on the center of the bridge, near the left edge. Veer left as you dash across and grab it before the bridge is destroyed!

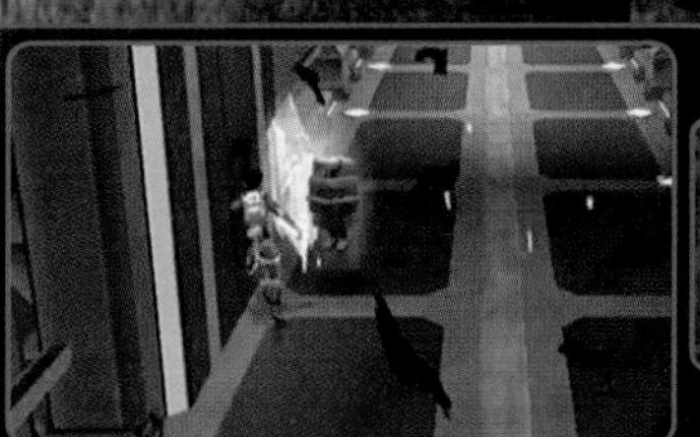

Make a left after crossing the bridge and blow through the sealed door with Force Push. Follow the passages to a small room with several stormtroopers and cut them down. Take out the turrets along the far wall while you fight the stormtroopers to keep from getting shredded by blaster fire.

When you take out the first batch of enemies, a small group of riot troopers arrives on the nearby elevator. Defeat them quickly, then hop on the elevator and take it up to the next level.

Exit the elevator and use Force Lightning to fry the bothersome Ughnaughts in the room. Rush the turrets and destroy them, then make a right into the next room. Crush the Imperials inside and exit the room to find a large gun turret.

Follow the onscreen prompts and destroy the turret. When you do, the explosion sends you falling down to the next section of the city.

TARKO-SE CASINO

Before you can proceed into the Tarko-se casino, a large carbonite wardroid comes ambling out of the door ahead of you. Quickly rip off its shield by Force Gripping it and flinging it away, then strafe around the massive menace while you zap it with Force Lightning. Bring it down and approach the door ahead of you.

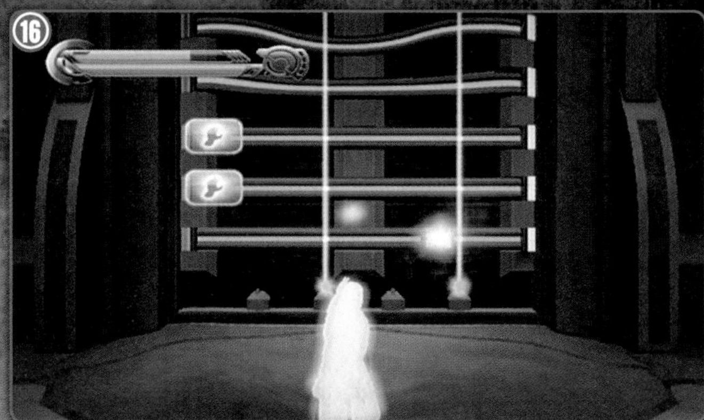

Do as Master Kota says and activate your newly acquired Force Vision. Use Force Grip while your Force Vision is active and slide the door's locks right, across the door, to unlock it. Only move the locks when the lasers aren't firing—avoid running it into a laser.

Rush through the door and take your lightsabers to the stormtroopers along the split staircase. Take them all down quickly with a few combos.

HOLOCRON

The next holocron is hidden behind the tall statue when you enter this room. Sneak behind the statue and grab it.

17

ITEM FOUND

The next power crystal is the Opila, located at the center of this room, underneath the force field. To grab it, approach the force field and use Force Grip to grab the sliding icons above the force field. Slide all of the V-shaped icons (the one with the two notches) into place until they "lock" and match all the way across. When you do, the force field deactivates. Just be ready for the Ughnaughts that come rushing out and attack. Use Force Repulse to destroy the bothersome little pests.

Follow the hall atop the stairs to another room, and use Lightsaber Specials to destroy the riot troopers. Continue exploring the casino, tearing through stormtroopers as you go. Tear through the casino until you reach a casino room with a force field at the center.

Hold position near this room's center as several waves of stormtroopers attack. The room is a large area with several doors along the wall; the enemies emerge from these doors. Wait for them to approach and build up your Combo meter. Fill it all the way to the Unleashed rank and use your strongest Lightsaber Special to dispatch enemies quickly.

18

After clearing the room of all enemies, go through the door on the left. Step on the elevator in the room and ride it up to the next section of the casino.

Rush down the steps after exiting the elevator and use Force Push to bully through the squad of enemies. When you reach the bottom of the stairs, tear them up with saber combos.

19

Shortly after clearing the room, a large carbonite wardroid comes ambling in. Rip off its shield and get to work on it immediately. Whittle down its health with Force Lightning, then finish it off with lightsaber attacks.

ITEM FOUND

Before continuing, stop and examine the room to the right at the bottom of the stairs. Use Force Vision to see through the door and unlock it. On the other side is a yellow color crystal!

Turn left at the bottom of the stairs, and follow the casino halls to a dead end. Use Force Repulse at the dead end to blow the roof off, then jump outside.

HOLOCRON

The next holocron is located above and to the left as you jump out of the casino. Hop up and out, then turn left to find it.

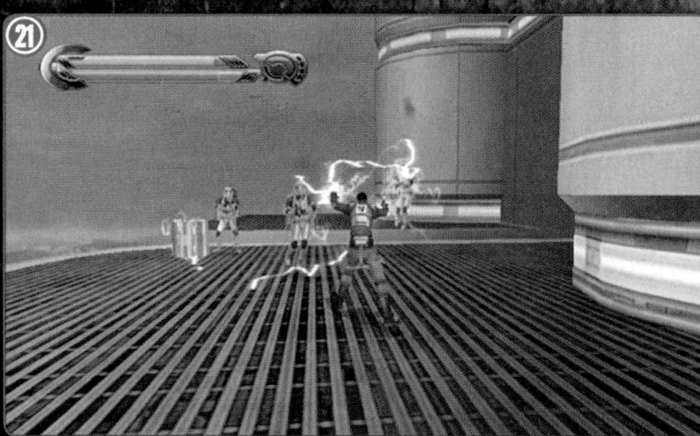

Make a right after exiting and defeat the next few jumptroopers in your way. Use Force Lightning and Saber Throw attacks to bring them down quickly as you navigate the platforms on the outside of the casino.

When you reach the platform with the diamond switch, use a lightning blast to charge it up and ride the small platform to the building's roof.

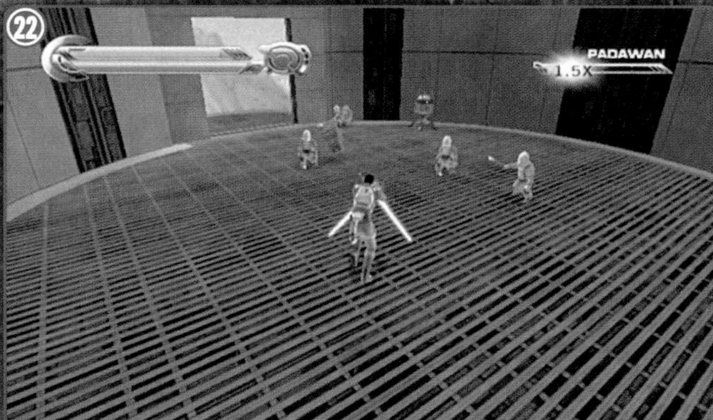

Finally, rush around the roof, battling several Ughnaughts as you go until you reach a transport similar to the one the baron used to escape.

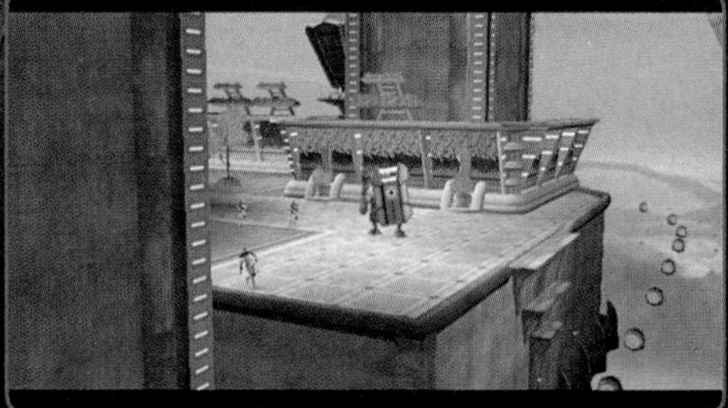

You jump onto the transport and begin to ride it down the sky-track. En route, more of the baron's jumptroopers pull up alongside you and attack. Follow the onscreen commands to strike them down. Continue following the commands onscreen as you near a long bridge in your way and then again when you approach your final destination.

With no other obstacles in your way, you can ride the tram to the other side of the baron's city. Unfortunately, more enemies await you on the other side.

Cato Neimoidia

Having fought past the Baron's guards, the Starkiller clone narrowly escapes a horrible death, high above the Neimoidian planet. The speeding tram goes down in flames and almost takes the clone with it.

Were it not for his heightened abilities and Jedilike reflexes, the troubled clone would have fallen thousands of feet to his death. But he is Starkiller's clone, and Starkiller knew the ways of the Force. That's how the clone was able to make the heroic leap off the tram and onto the western side of Tarko-se City.

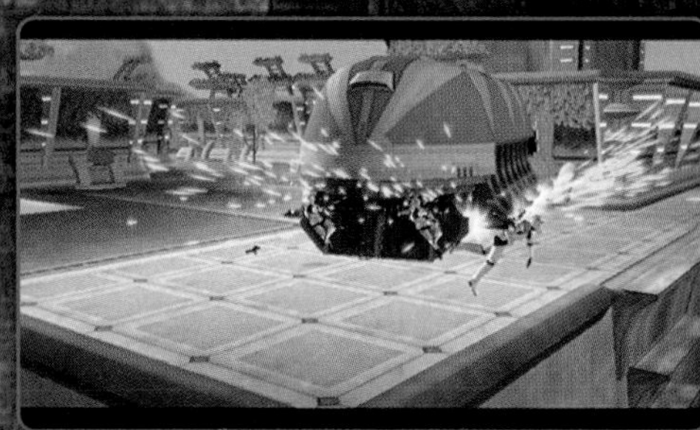

Baron Tarko's Palace

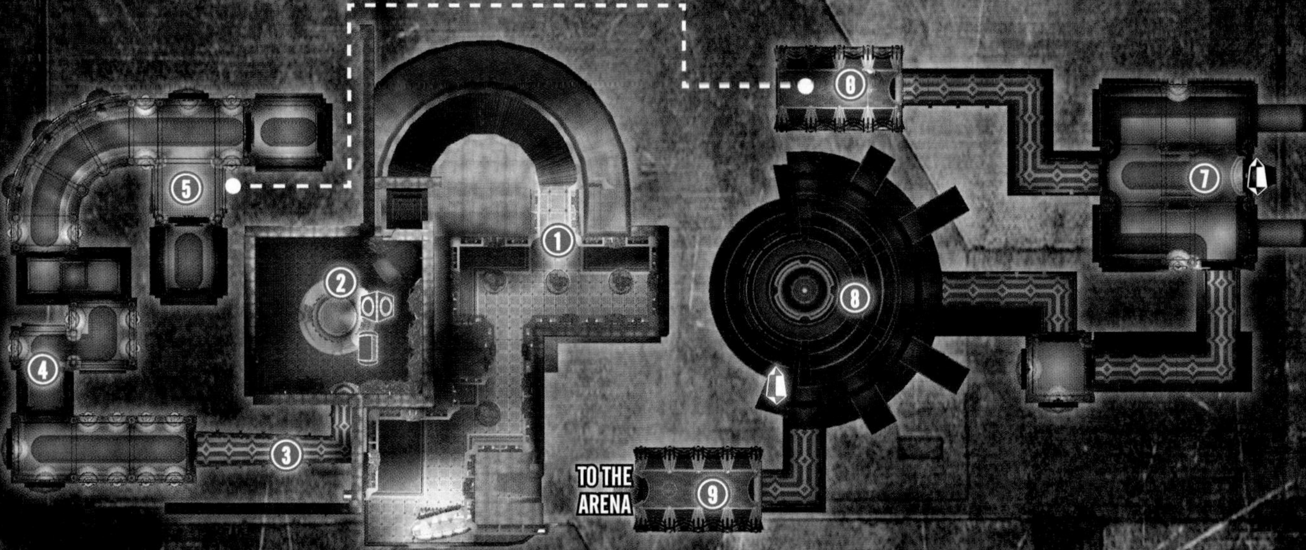

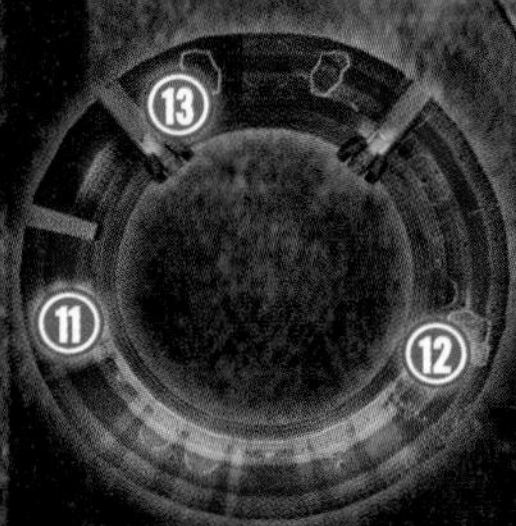

MISSION DETAILS

OBJECTIVE

Cross the city of Tarko-se and reach the baron's arena to free General Rahm Kota.

ENEMIES ENCOUNTERED

- Imperial stormtrooper
- Imperial riot trooper
- Jumptrooper
- Carbonite wardroid
- Ughnaughts
- Arena fighters
- The Gorog

HOLOCRONS FOUND

- 2 holocrons
- 1 Force Energy Bacta Tank
- Kaiburr power crystal
- Kaiburr power crystal (Unleashed Mode)

LEGEND

- Checkpoints (see corresponding images)
- Power Crystal
- Power Crystal (Unleashed Mode)
- Holocron
- Blue Tank
- Rubble Ramp

On the Hunt for the Baron

Immediately upon landing, turn left and storm down the courtyard. Use Force Push blasts to clear the way and demolish the Imperials.

Near the end of the courtyard, you encounter a few riot troopers. Build up your Combo meter and unleash a Lightsaber Special on them. When you take down the riot troopers, the gate at the far end opens, allowing more enemies to rush out.

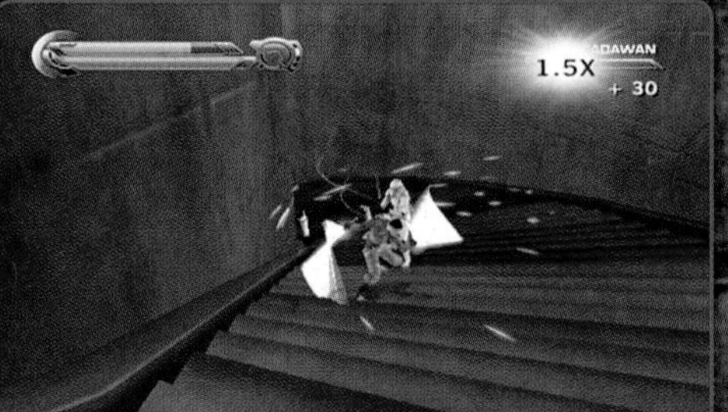

Fight your way down the curved steps and enter a large courtyard with a tall tower at the center.

The tower has two sets of small platforms rotating around it—one at the top and another near the center. Double-jump onto the lower set of platforms as they spin around.

Ride it around the tower until you pass by a small ledge jutting out from the tower's middle. Double-jump dash onto it, then follow the small stationary ledges up and to the right, until you're within leaping distance of the next set of rotating platforms.

HOLOCRON

There is a holocron sitting on one of the platforms high above the ground. After climbing up the center tower, wait for the platform to pass around. Double-jump onto it before it passes you by and grab the holocron.

Double-jump onto one of the top platforms and immediately turn around. Locate the next small ridge jutting out from the tower, then carefully double-jump onto it. Follow the stepped ledges up to the tower's top.

ITEM FOUND

Before leaving the top of the tower, locate the blue Force Energy Bacta Tank atop the nearby pedestal. Double-jump onto it and grab it.

3

Double-jump dash off the center tower and into the nearby hall entrance. Dash down the hall toward the far door and use Force Push to pry it open. A carbonite wardroid and a small complement of Imperial stormtroopers waits on the other side!

Take out the stormtroopers quickly, then rip away the wardroid's shield. Once its shield is gone, zap it with Force Lightning to weaken it. Finish it off with saber combos.

4

Use the Force to lift the door on the right, then rush out and electrocute the enemies in the next hall. Force Push through the next door and rush out to a long curved corridor with more Imperials in it.

Take down the stormtrooper first, then engage the riot troopers that follow. Swat them down with saber strikes. After making short work of them, continue to the corridor's end. When you reach it, both exits get caved in by the Imperials!

HOLOCRON

There's a holocron hiding behind the statue on the left near the hall's end. To grab it, destroy the statue with a Force Push blast, then jump up and grab it.

5

6

Even though the two exits in this hall are blocked, the explosion that created the blockages also cracked the floor. Go stand on the crack in the ground and use Force Repulse to break through and fall down to the lower level.

Destroy the bothersome Ughnaughts upon landing, then use the Force to open the door at the far end. Speed down the winding hall until you reach a large, square room with a fireplace along the far wall.

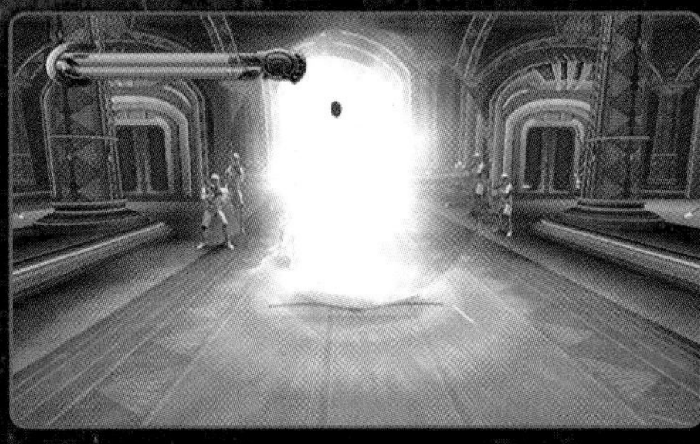

The large room is full of Imperials. Use Force Repulse to blow away the squad as it approaches, then pick them off one at a time with saber combos and Force powers. There are several riot troopers in the room. Leave them for last, since the stormtroopers can pick you apart with their blasters.

If the troopers surround you, string together several saber combos to build up your Combo meter and dish out a ton of damage with Lightsaber Specials.

ITEM FOUND

Once the room is clear, inch closer to the fireplace. There is a fire raging, but hidden in the flames is a Kaiburr power crystal. Jump in, then quickly jump out after you grab it.

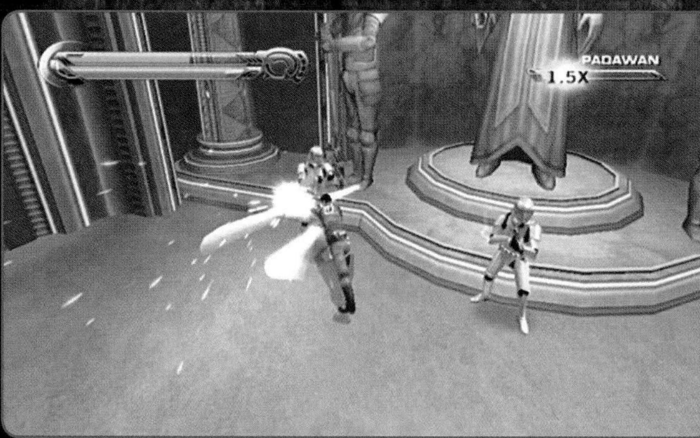

When the door on the right opens, a few more riot troopers rush out. Slice them up, then enter the hall they emerged from. Speed down the hall until you reach a small room with more Imperials. Cut through the stormtrooper commander first, then destroy the weaker soldiers.

Follow the halls to a large circular room where a pair of carbonite wardroids ambushes you. The room has a ledge high along the wall where Imperial stormtroopers take position and rain down blaster fire on you.

Rip away the wardroids' shields, then dash away toward the far right wall. Climb up the ledges until you reach the top ledge, and eliminate the stormtroopers. With the stormtroopers out of the way, jump down and take on the droids.

Hit them with Force Lightning and begin to drain them of their health. If they gang up on you, double-jump into the air and dash away. Take on one wardroid at a time and destroy them both.

JEDI WISDOM

If you take too much damage and need to get away, escape back to the top ledge to recover health. Once your health is full again, drop back down and return to work on the wardroids.

When you destroy the droid, the elevator at the room's end delivers Ughnaughts to the fight. Use Force Repulse to decimate them, then hop on the elevator and ride it down.

With the wardroids out of your hair, a group of riot troopers rushes out of the surrounding rooms. Greet them with several saber strikes and Force power attacks. The room fills with many waves of riot troopers. Fend them off with Force Repulse if they get too close, then pick them apart.

After clearing the room, approach the locked door on the far end. Activate your Force Vision and use it to peer through the door. Slide over the locks, then pass through the door into the next area.

Pass through the hall into a smaller chamber to find another carbonite wardroid with a group of Imperial stormtroopers. The room is much smaller, so take out the stormtroopers first before concentrating on the wardroid and dismantling it.

THE PET

With no one left to oppose you, the baron orders his Neimoidian attendee to send out the Gorog. The Neimoidian is shocked at the request. He insists that the arena's restraints are not ready for the Gorog to be unleashed.

Still, the baron insists. His fury may be the only thing that matches the Gorog's. Meanwhile, down on the arena floor, you join General Rahm Kota, who is very pleased to "see" you....

Just then, the sliding door across the arena opens up, releasing a large, hungry...rancor? You slacken your defensive stance, relieved that the beast that ambles out is a measly rancor. But before you can leap to the attack, a large three-fingered hand rises over the rancor and smashes it completely.

The hand then grabs the rancor and pulls it down into a pit. That is when the rest of the beast hoists itself out of the pit. The Gorog is a massive monster, as big as the arena itself. When it sees you, it lowers its rancor-sized head and roars. You're in for a fight!

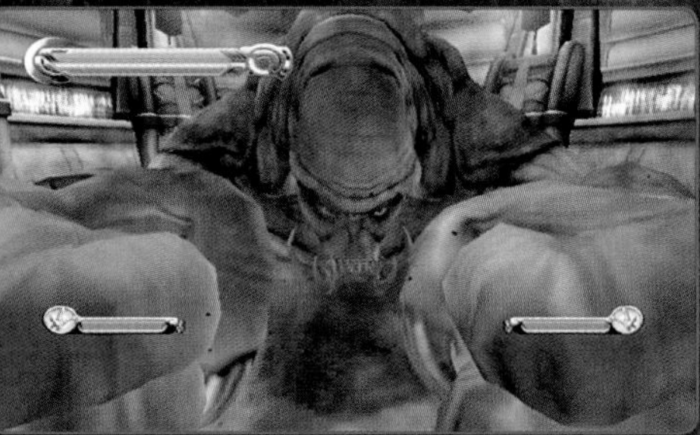

The Gorog is a massive monster. With no way of reaching its face from the ground floor, the only way you can deal damage on the Gorog is to lash out at its hands. As soon as it slams a hand down, double-jump in the air and dash over it as the hand swipes at you.

Dodge the beast's swiping attacks until it slams both hands down. Stand between both hands as they slam down to keep from taking damage, then strike a hand with saber attacks or blast it with Force Lightning.

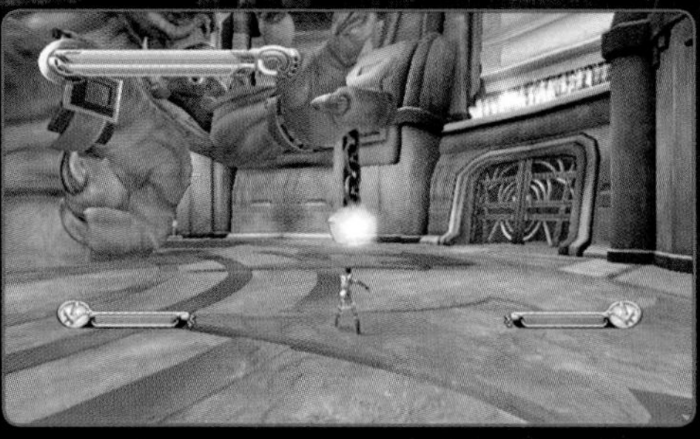

Repeat this process until you've damaged one of the hands enough for the Gorog to lift it in the air. While it's in the air, use Force Grip to shackle the Gorog's hand against the arena wall.

As the Gorog struggles to free its hand, several arena fighters rush out and attack. They're not tough at all, so run them through with your lightsaber and dispatch them quickly.

Eventually, the Gorog attacks again with its free hand. Retaliate and damage the monster's free hand. Repeat the process again until you shackle its second hand against the wall.

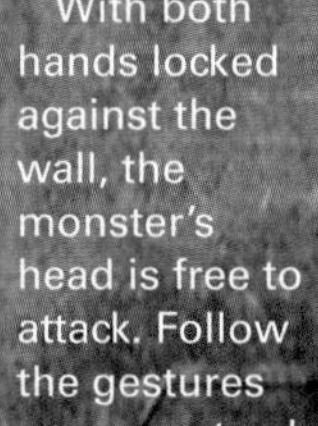

With both hands locked against the wall, the monster's head is free to attack. Follow the gestures onscreen to slam the monster's head into the ground, then drive your saber into its eye!

The pain drives the beast to shake loose from its shackles. While you proceed to the next level in the arena, the monster begins to tear through the structure. Dash down the hall. No sooner do you get a few feet than the Gorog manages to break through the wall and grab you. Execute the gestures onscreen to shake loose, then drop back down into the arena building.

Continue dashing down the hall until you reach a red force field. Destroy the enemies in your way to deactivate the force field. If the Gorog grabs you again, follow the onscreen prompts to shake loose again, then resume your trek down the hall.

12

13

Continue past two more force fields until you reach an area in the structure where the roof crumbles. Dash up the fallen roof segment and take the fight to the Imperials in your way. Speed down the hall, through several more enemies, and up two more fallen roof segments until you reach the next section of the arena.

14

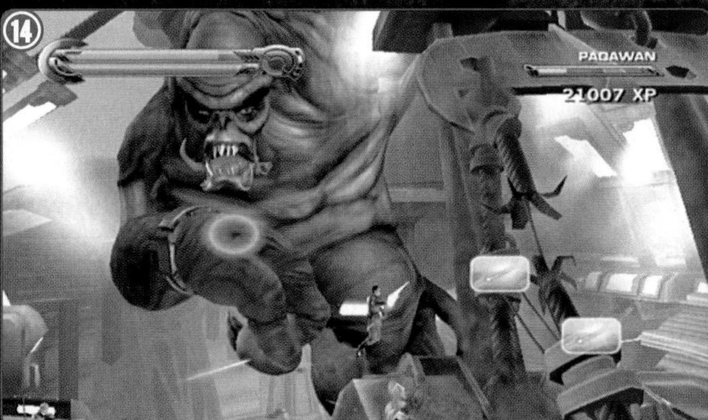

On the next section of the arena, the Gorog confronts you again. Rush down the walkway until you come upon a large support. Dodge the Gorog's attacks and dash through the Imperials in your way. When you reach the support, strike it with your saber, then sever the cables with a Saber Throw.

Since the Gorog is too big to destroy, the only way to defeat it is to destroy the arena. Speed farther down the long corridor and destroy the next two supports in the same fashion.

When you sever the final support, the arena begins to crumble. You reach the baron just in time to join Master Kota in confronting him. Before you can crush the baron, however, the Gorog crashes through, grabs him, and eats him!

The monster's weight forces the entire city to finally give. As it falls, the Gorog grabs Kota in its massive hand. You leap after it and find yourself in a free fall after the monster.

You reach the hand and pry it open, freeing Master Kota. As you and Master Kota free-fall to the planet's surface, you realize that there's no way you can survive this. Luckily, the *Rogue Shadow* is nearby and zooms in just in the nick of time to pluck you from your free fall. You speed away to safety with Master Kota.

Dagobah

Safe in the *Rogue Shadow*, the clone quickly begins to look for Juno. Of all of Starkiller's memories, it is the memories of Juno that drive him. Unfortunately, Master Kota has long since lost communication with her.

With the Rebel fleet scattered across the Outer Rim, he was unable to keep track of her, especially after his capture. Regardless of Juno's location, Master Kota wants the clone to lead the Rebellion.

Starkiller's clone refuses. He may have Starkiller's memories and feelings, but he is not the same person. When he tells Kota that he's nothing more than a clone, the Jedi Master refuses to believe it.

Kota insists that the clone join them and lead the fight, but the Starkiller clone insists that that was Starkiller's destiny, not his; he must find his own way.

He begins his search in Dagobah.

MEANWHILE...

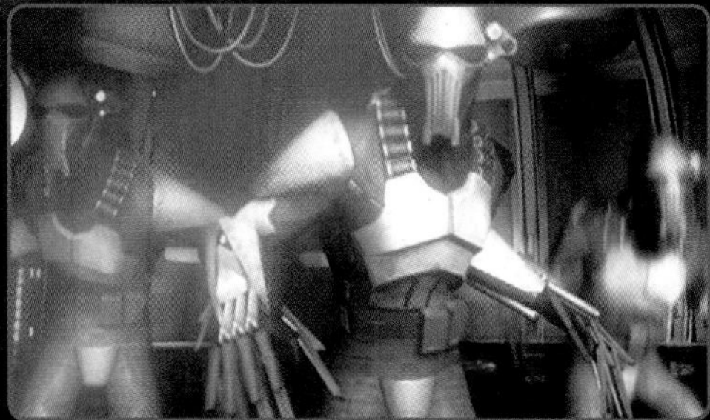

Back on Kamino, the Dark Lord, Vader, meets with the bounty hunter Boba Fett. The two plot to hunt down the rogue clone, but he's had a few days' lead in his escape. The Dark Lord quickly formulates a plan to draw the escapee to him rather than chase him.

Darth Vader grants Boba Fett a squad of super soldiers and instructs him to find and capture Juno Eclipse. Once captured, she will be the perfect bait for the Starkiller clone.

A Watcher

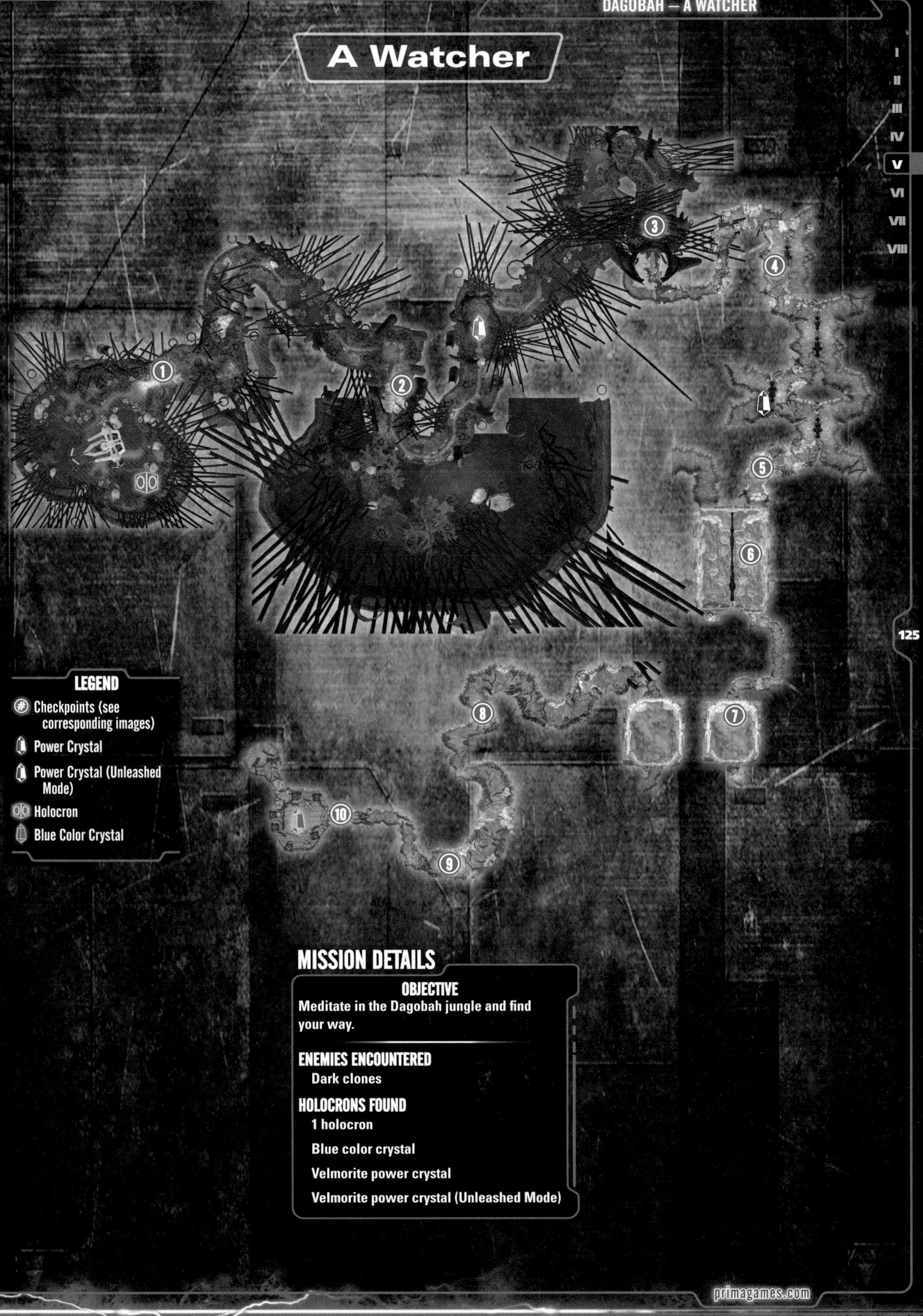

MISSION DETAILS

OBJECTIVE

Meditate in the Dagobah jungle and find your way.

ENEMIES ENCOUNTERED

Dark clones

HOLOCRONS FOUND

1 holocron

Blue color crystal

Velmorite power crystal

Velmorite power crystal (Unleashed Mode)

THE VISION

When you arrive in Dagobah, you find a dark and dank planet. The marshy landscape is perfect for hiding, and yet, for some reason, it seems like the perfect place to find oneself.

HOLOCRON

As soon as you disembark the *Rogue Shadow* in Dagobah, turn right and locate the holocron hiding in the far corner of the landing area.

The path through the Dagobah jungle begins at the rear of the *Rogue Shadow*. Turn around and follow it out of the landing area. Run down the winding path until you come across several piles of rubble. Climb up and continue running down the path.

NEIMOIDIAN NOTES

Shortly after climbing up the second rubble pile, look to the right. In the distance you'll see a small hut. That belongs to Master Yoda!

Follow the winding path until you approach the entrance to the cave.

Approach the cave entrance and meet Master Yoda. As you are about to enter, he greets you with a sly smile. He knows something that you don't; you're about to find a part of yourself that has been lost.

Enter the cave and begin exploring. Drop to the area below. When you do, you see Juno in the distance! Follow her deeper into the cave.

However, before you get far, you come across a long, mirrored surface along the left side of the cave. You can see your reflection, but it's not entirely you. Suddenly, your mirror self leaps into a sprint and runs away. Turn left and head in the direction he ran.

ITEM FOUND

Follow the winding path, past the second mirrored wall, until you come across the third mirrored surface, this one on the right. Look into the wall and you'll see it reflecting the Velmorite power crystal, which isn't in your path. To grab it, go stand in front of the mirrored surface where the crystal is reflected (there's a small light-colored stone where you should stand) and jump up to grab it. As long as your reflection gets it, you will too.

JEDI WISDOM

The Velmorite power crystal is one of the most useful items in the game. It allows you to increase the rate at which your Combo meter builds up. Equip it immediately!

5

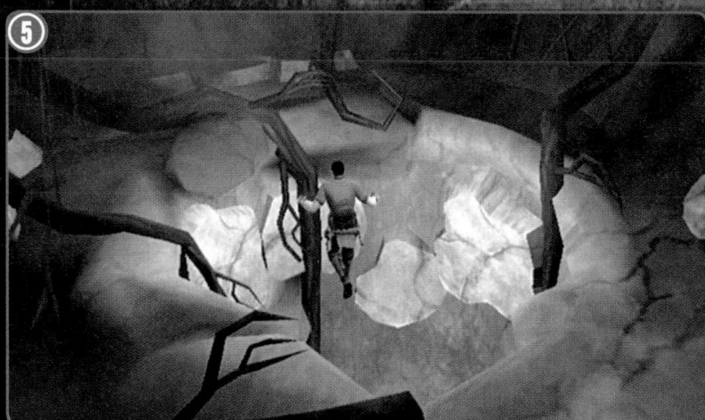

6

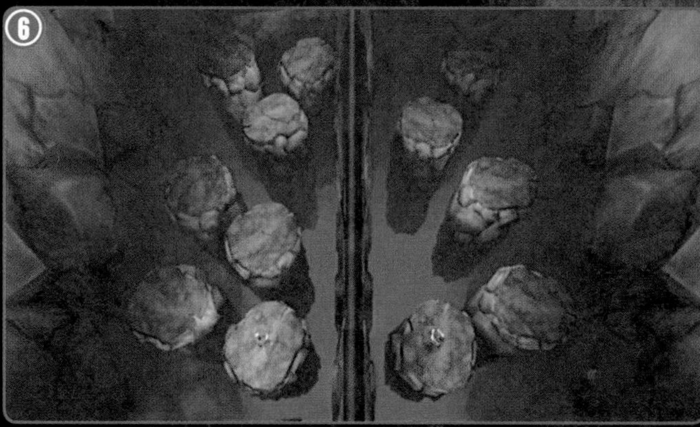

Resume your trek deep into the cave until you come across a small pit. Drop into it. Follow the narrow path deeper until you find a long canyon with several stone platforms reaching across.

The right of this chasm has a mirrored surface reflecting the stone platforms. However, the reflection reveals fewer platforms than are actually in your path. Hop across the canyon using only the platforms reflected in the mirrored surface.

CLONER'S CAUTION

If the platform isn't reflected in the mirrored surface, don't jump onto it! You'll fall to your doom.

After crossing the canyon, continue deeper into the cave until you come upon another small chasm. On the other side is your dark self; he's under attack by Starkiller clones. He uses the Force to rip away your lightsabers, leaving you defenseless, and fends off the zombielike clones.

7

When a pair of zombielike clones attacks you, you have no way of defeating them. That is, of course, until you learn Mind Trick. Use Mind Trick on the next two lightsaber-toting clones and turn them on each other!

8

Go back into the cave the way you came. This time, though, the cave is different. The path leads past several ruptured cloning tanks.

Follow the path. As you do, the dark clone that took your sabers is captured by a vine. The vine squeezes the life out of the dark one, and he releases your sabers. You pick them up and continue. Rather than slash through the vines, however, you sense that they are not malicious and put your sabers away.

With a short wave of your hand, the vines clear a path for you. When you emerge on the other side of the vine-covered path, you are wearing Jedi robes.

Run down the winding path and follow the light at the end. It leads to a cloning tank. As you pound on the tank's glass, you can see Juno and Vader on the other side. They're surrounded by dark clones.

Wait until a pair of clones get close to your tank, then use Mind Trick on them to turn them against Vader. The clones allow Juno to go free, but Vader isn't done. He appears behind you for a brief moment, just before the tank's glass shatters.

ITEM FOUND

The next color crystal appears after the tank shatters. Walk out of the tank and grab it before leaving the cave.

Continue exploring the cave until, in the distance, you see the silhouette of a feminine figure. As the scene comes into focus, you realize that it is Juno. Suddenly, as if a holographic display was suddenly switched on, the area around Juno materializes.

She's in a ship, giving out commands to the rest of the crew. They're under attack! A nearby explosion rocks the control room where she's stationed and she's shot. As she stumbles away from her assailant, the ship begins to fade.

Eventually, she fades too. The vision is over and your purpose is now clear. You must save Juno Eclipse. When you emerge from the darkness, Master Yoda is waiting outside. He insists that you follow this vision. And you agree.

The Rebel Ship *Salvation*

Having found his purpose, the clone reunites with General Kota and heads to the Rebel ship *Salvation*. There, Captain Juno Eclipse commands a portion of the ragtag Rebels.

If the clone's vision was true, then the ship would be under attack. Since there was no sign of attack, then the vision must not have come to pass yet.

The duo docks inside the *Salvation* and quickly begins their trek to the control room aboard a moving platform. As they make their way, General Kota explains that the Rebels are slowly losing heart. Fewer and fewer fighters are willing to do what needs to be done.

But with a Jedi on their side, surely the rest of the Rebel fighters will jump at the chance to bring down the Galactic Empire. When the clone reminds Kota that he's just a clone, Kota still refuses to put stock in that fact. With little else to convince Kota, the clone hands over a data cylinder with coordinates and schematics for the secret cloning facility on Kamino.

An explosion rocks the ship before the daring duo's platform reaches its destination. The assault from the clone's vision has begun!

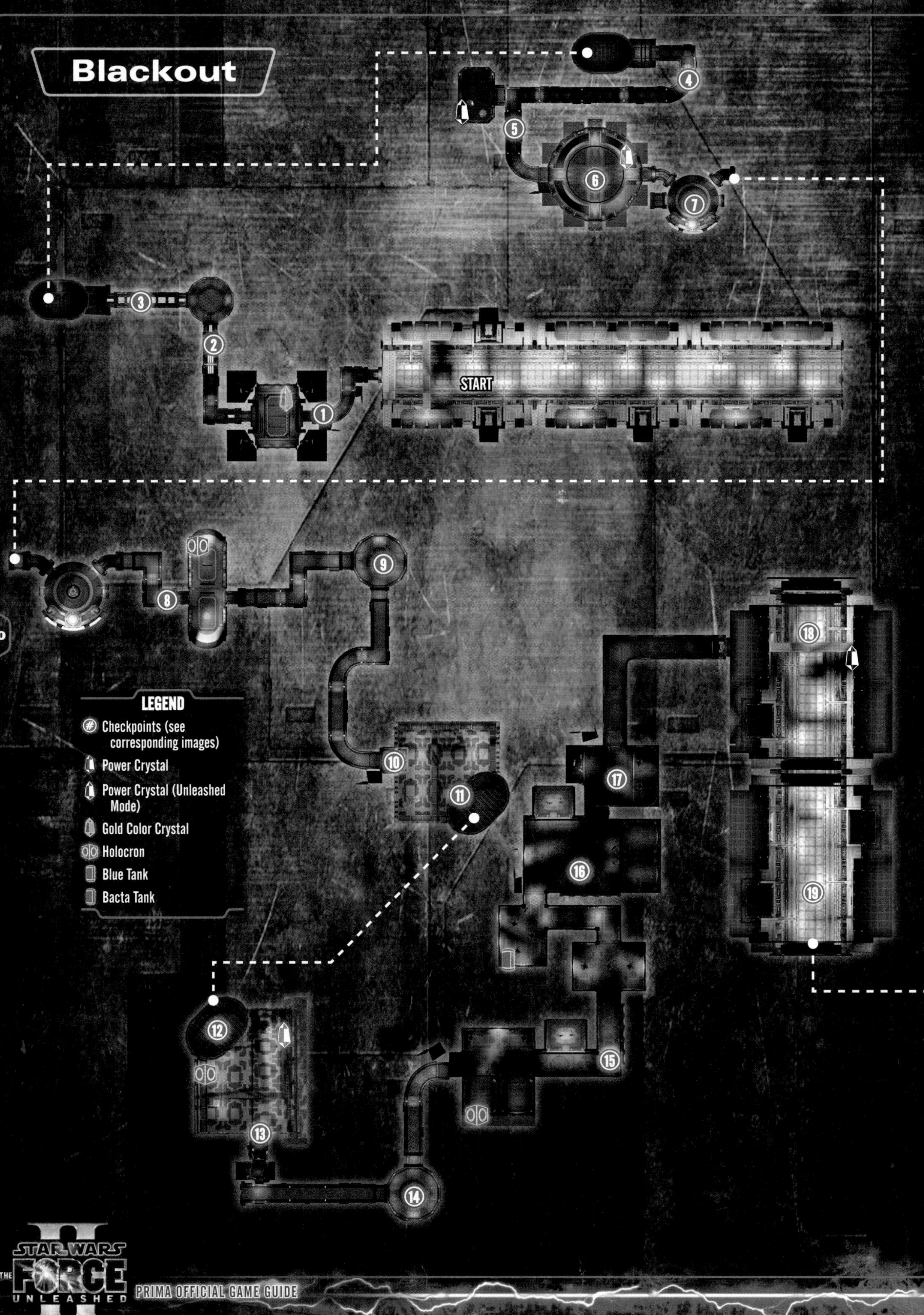
Blackout
START
1
2
3
4
5
6
7
8
9
10
11
12
13
14
15
16
17
18
19
LEGEND
Checkpoints (see corresponding images)
Power Crystal
Power Crystal (Unleashed Mode)
Gold Color Crystal
Holocron
Blue Tank
Bacta Tank

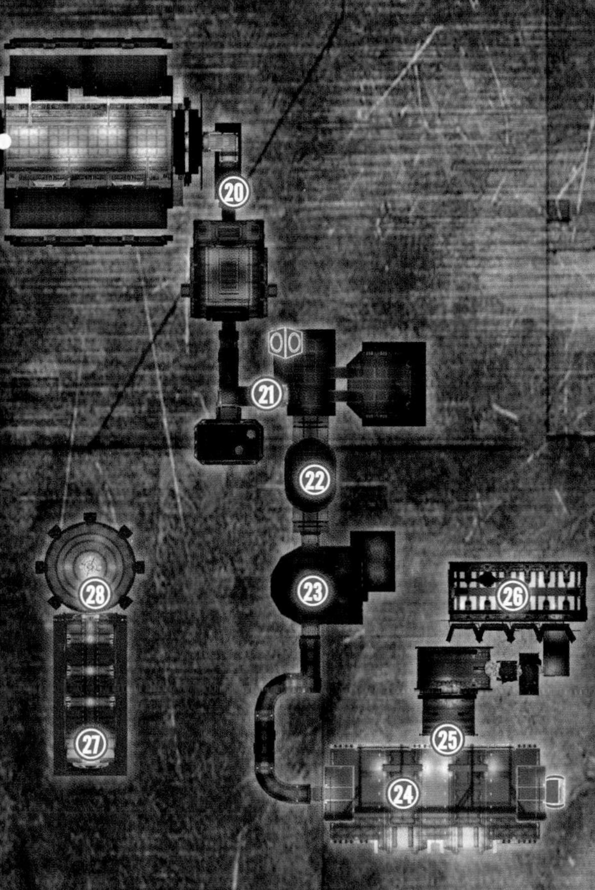

VISIONS FULFILLED

Hop off the platform and sprint to the hall at the far end. Use Force Grip to lift the sealed door, then rush in. There are no enemies nearby, so follow the corridor left as it curves around toward another section of the ship.

Grab the sealed door with the Force and lift it; head into the small, sealed room beyond.

Upon entering the room, you're ambushed by several small terror spider droids. Use a combination of saber combos to build your Combo meter and use Force Repulse to destroy them.

ITEM FOUND

There's a gold color crystal in the near, right corner of this room. Remove the crates stacked in the corner, and grab the crystal before setting off after Juno.

MISSION DETAILS

OBJECTIVE

Fight your way to the ship's control room where Juno Eclipse is stationed.

ENEMIES ENCOUNTERED

- Imperial stormtroopers
- Riot troopers
- Terror spider droid
- Terror trooper
- AT-MP
- Terror walker
- Boba Fett

HOLOCRONS FOUND

- 6 holocrons
- Health Bacta Tank
- Force Energy Bacta Tank
- Gold color crystal
- Sigil power crystal
- Katak power crystal
- Sigil power crystal (Unleashed Mode)
- Katak power crystal (Unleashed Mode)

Force Grip the next door and slide it open. Follow the corridor as it turns right, and you come to another sealed door. Before you can force open the door, clear the short hall of all terror spider droids.

Enter the next room, which is a small circular area, and immediately get to work on destroying the spider droids. String together several saber combos to build your Combo meter, then unleash Lightsaber Specials to clear the room.

Exit through the next door and rush down the hall. Just when you're about to reach the hall's end, the hall behind you caves in, separating you from Kota!

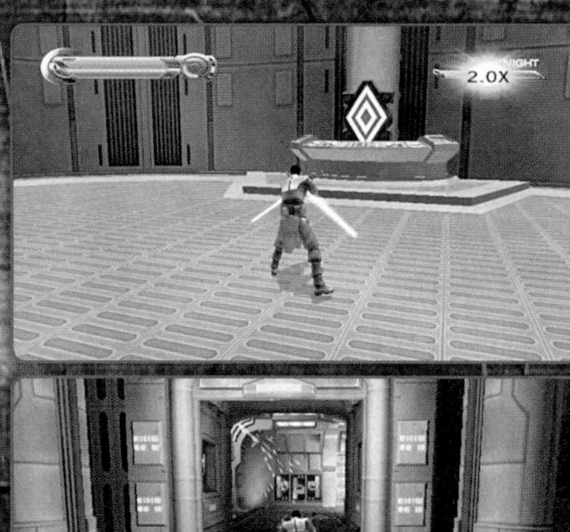

Lift the next door and step onto the elevator. Use Force Repulse to destroy the attacking spider droids, then use a Force Lightning blast to charge the diamond-shaped switch on the right. Ride the elevator to the lower level, then use the Force to open the next door.

Slowly creep out into the hall and sneak up on the Imperial stormtroopers ahead of you. Use Mind Trick to turn them into unwilling allies, then watch them turn on each other rather than fight the Rebels.

Rush out behind your stormtrooper friends and speed down the curving corridor. When the corridor straightens out into a long hall, dash to its end where it splits into two paths.

ITEM FOUND

The path directly ahead leads to a small room with three stormtroopers and a power crystal. Rush in and run your saber through the stormtroopers in the room. With the room clear, explore the far left corner. Tucked behind several crates is the Sigil power crystal. Grab it, then exit the room the way you came.

Turn left at the split in the hall and fight past the stormtroopers in your way. Use the Force to open the doors blocking your path, and enter the large, circular room.

The room has two walkways leading to the top level. Rush up the one on the right and take the fight to the stormtroopers perched above you. When you reach the top level, you find the Rebels fiercely engaged in battle with the Imperials.

Lend the Rebels a hand and cut through the Imperials with your saber. When the riot troopers rush out, Mind Trick them, then join them as they turn on each other. Use Lightsaber Specials to destroy the rest of the troopers and clear the room.

Remove all of the enemies, then enter the command room via the door on the far wall. Upon entering the room, you find your—or rather Starkiller's—holodroid! When you ask it about Juno, it informs you that a bounty hunter has taken her to the hangar bay on Deck 7.

You tell Kota to order the attack on the Kamino cloning facility while you set off after Juno!

THE CHASE

Rush out of the command room via the only open door. Dash down the halls until you see Boba Fett carrying Juno ahead of you. Before you can catch up, though, the door ahead of you closes and you're ambushed by riot troopers. Use saber combos and Force powers to destroy them.

HOLOCRON

Explore the far left corner of this room after entering. There is a holocron here.

Get up close and personal and fry the walker's circuits with Force Lightning. Stay on the move to keep from being blasted to death, and duck for cover behind the crates in the bay to recover health when you take too much damage.

Mix in a few saber combos to cut off major chunks of health from the metal monster, and finish it off. When the room is all clear of enemies, approach the elevator platform.

In the next hall are a pair of riot troopers. Dispatch them quickly and continue down the hall. Follow the winding corridors to a room where a squad of Imperials waits to tear you to shreds.

Build your Combo meter and clear the room with Lightsaber Specials and Force power attacks. Leave the room through the spider-droid-infested hallways, and reach another sealed door at the end. Lift it with the Force and proceed.

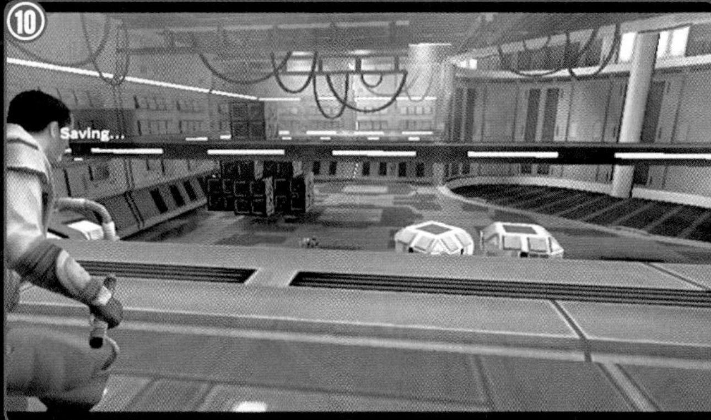

When you reach the first storage bay, you find that it's storing an Imperial AT-MP walker. The walker wastes no time in attacking, so get to cover as soon as you enter!

HOLOCRON

As soon as you enter the bay, make a sharp left. Double-jump dash onto the walkway, running across the left wall, and follow it out to a holocron in the room's far left corner.

The elevator delivers a group of Imperial enemies into the bay. Rush your foes and use Mind Trick on the riot troopers. Allow them to defeat the lesser stormtroopers, then finish off any remaining enemies. With no one left to pester you, charge the diamond switch on the elevator and ride it up.

About halfway up, the elevator stops and a swarm of spider droids attacks. Squish the spiders with Force Repulse and saber combos, then zap the diamond switch again to resume your ascent.

As you near the top of the elevator shaft, Boba Fett speeds away with Juno. He blows a hole in a far wall and flies through, carrying Juno on his shoulder!

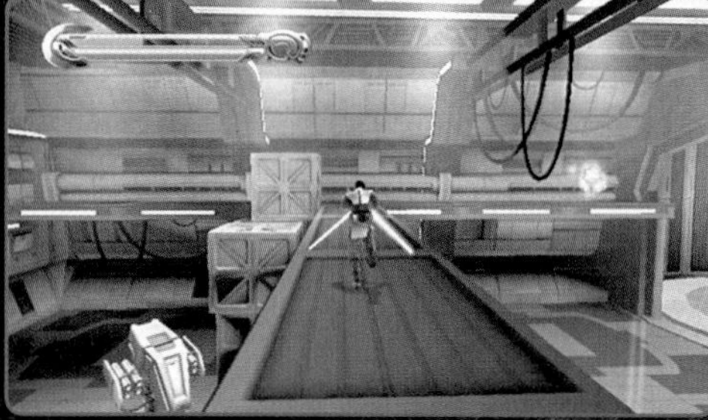

You've reached the top storage bay only to find that this one is inhabited by two AT-MP walkers! As the walkers stomp around the room, several stormtrooper squads scurry into position. Use Mind Trick to turn the stormtroopers on the walkers, then rush the nearest AT-MP and lash out with saber combos.

Wait for your Force energy to refresh, then hit the walker with Force Lightning to dish out even more damage. Use the upper walkways above the room to get a height advantage and attack your enemies from above. Carefully pick them apart with lightning blasts when you're above and use saber combos while on the ground to clear the room of all enemies.

HOLOCRON

There's a holocron in the upper-right corner of the room as you exit the elevator. Use the grippable crate in the far left corner to reach the walkway, then follow the walkway back toward the elevator to find the holocron.

In his escape, Boba Fett blasted a series of holes through the ship. Move the large grippable crate to the right. Place it directly underneath the hole that the bounty hunter created, and use it to jump through.

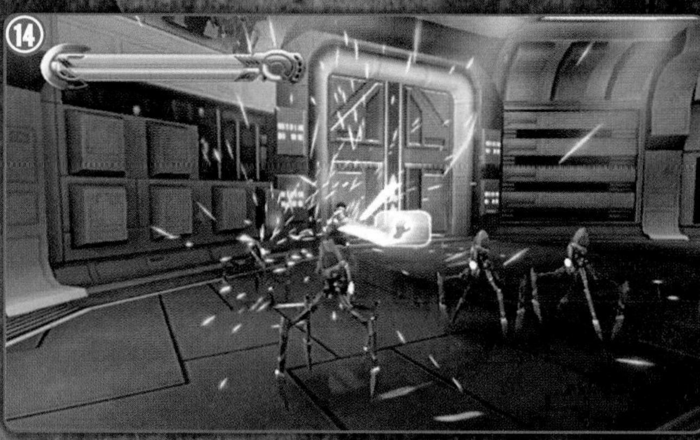

Follow Boba Fett's path of destruction. Use the Force to open the door at the end, then scrap the spider droids that attack.

Open the next door and dash down the hall. Blow open the window with a Force Push blast to blow the attacking spider droids into space, and cut the remaining spiders with your sabers.

HOLOCRON

Enter a large, square room and activate your Force Vision. Look to the far right corner and you'll see that there is a holocron hiding behind another stack of crates. Remove the crates and claim the holocron before continuing across the

With your Force Vision active, you can see the terror troopers even while they're invisible. Use this to your advantage and lay into them with saber combos and Lightsaber Specials. They'll never see it coming!

JEDI WISDOM

Even though you can fight them without your Force Vision, the terror troopers spend more time being invisible than visible. Don't risk it. Rely on Force Vision every time you battle a terror trooper.

room.

Sprint across the room toward the Rebels at the far end. As you get near, the Rebels are savagely destroyed by blaster fire coming from the hall on the left. Turn left and enter the next large room.

Take out the spider droids in the next chamber, then engage the riot troopers in the attached hallway. Mind Trick the first, and help him defeat the other two. In the next section, veer left and immediately decimate the stormtroopers that attack.

ITEM FOUND

There's a red Health Bacta Tank in this room's far left corner. Grab it before turning right into the next hall.

Once again, you manage to catch up to Boba Fett just as he narrowly escapes into a chamber ahead of you. However, before you can bust through, you're ambushed by several terror troopers. Immediately activate your Force Vision to locate the sneaky scoundrels.

Follow Boba Fett through the door. You'll encounter more terror troopers there. Once again, rely on the Force to reveal the enemies' location and tear through the terror troopers.

Force open the next door and go through. Crush the terror spider droids in the hall and make your way into the hangar bay. Boba Fett is one step ahead of you and manages to escape with Juno through the hangar bay doors.

Below you are several more Imperial enemies to contend with, including two AT-MPs and a group of terror troopers.

ITEM FOUND

Before jumping down to the area below, make a sharp left and follow the catwalk around toward the hangar bay doors. Double-jump over the small gap and grab the Katak power crystal in the corner.

18

Jump to the area below and activate your Force Vision. Locate the terror troopers first and take them out quickly. If you allow them to live, they'll interrupt your fight with the walkers and knock you to your feet, allowing the walkers to shred you with blaster fire.

Lure the terror troopers behind the transport platform near the center of the bay and fight them one-on-one, outside the walker's firing radius. With the troopers gone, allow your Force Energy to replenish, then zap them with Force Lightning to deplete their health. Duck behind the transport platform to recover energy and resume the fight once you've got enough Force Energy.

After you destroy both walkers, hop on the transport platform and power it up with Force Lightning to send it speeding after the bounty hunter!

19

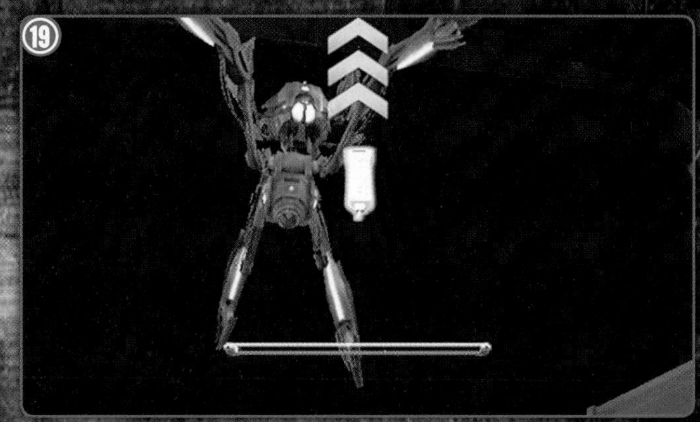

As you rush along, a giant terror walker joins the chase! Follow the onscreen commands to shoo away the massive metal monster and its mini metal minions!

HUNTING THE HUNTER

20

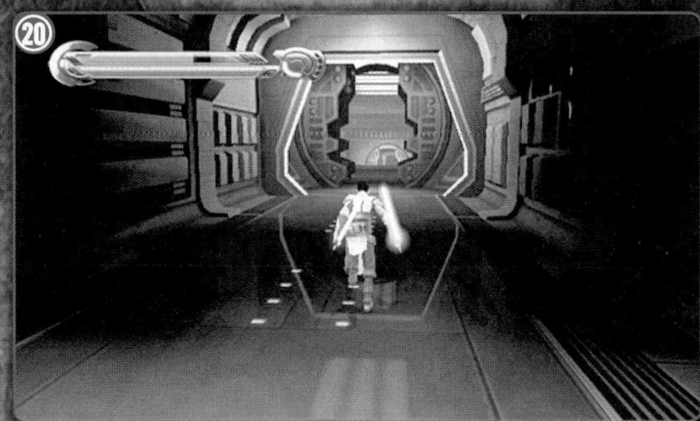

Upon arriving at the far end of the *Salvation*'s transport conduit, sprint through the door there. Follow the corridor until you reach a large room with a stormtrooper squad waiting below you.

Jump down into the room and rush the stormtroopers at the far end. Dispatch the Imperials, then leave the room via the hall at the far end.

21

Dash down the hall. When you catch up to Boba Fett, follow the onscreen commands to dodge his missile attacks. After missing with the first two missiles, Boba Fett launches a third missile behind you. The explosion blows a hole in the wall and creates a powerful vacuum that almost sucks you out to space while he gets away.

Follow the onscreen prompts and pull yourself up the hall and away from the hole in the wall.

HOLOCRON

In the next chamber of the ship is another holocron. Remove the crates near the right side of the large lock puzzle to find it.

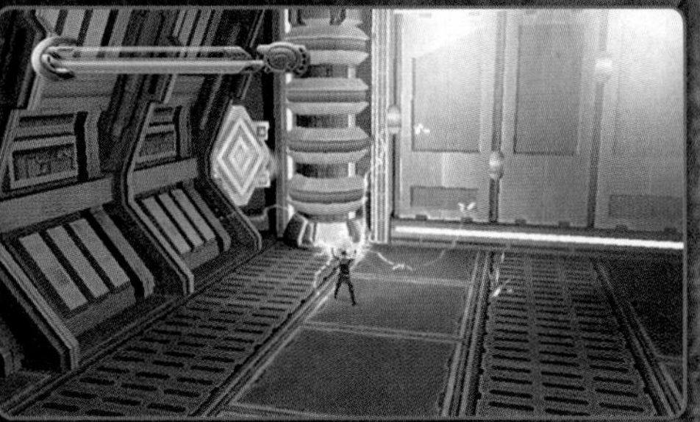

Approach the large, locked puzzle on the room's opposite side and activate Force Vision. Use Force Grip to move the lock mechanisms into the bright white spots that are in the puzzle's locking circuit. With all four mechanisms in place, the circuit is closed. With all four lock mechanisms in place, charge the diamond switch on the left with Force Lightning and activate the circuit. This opens the door behind you on the left.

Exit via the newly opened door and set out on the elevator platform. When you step on it, the platform gives way and begins to fall! Destroy the spider droids that attack on the way down.

Enter the next room and use Force Vision to locate the terror troopers there. Put down the sneaky Imperial soldiers with Lightsaber Specials. After destroying the terror troopers, the far left wall explodes, and an AT-MP comes stomping out. Fry the walker's circuits and destroy it quickly.

HOLOCRON

After the AT-MP busts out of the left wall, examine the room from which it emerged. There's a holocron inside, just next to the room's right wall.

Leave the room through the next hall and fight past more stormtroopers. Rush out to the hangar bay where you catch up to Boba Fett as he attempts to flee in the *Slave I*! Follow the onscreen commands to hurl a nearby Y-wing at his ship and knock it off-kilter.

When that doesn't work, try following the commands onscreen to Force Grip it and pull it back into the hangar bay. Even though you're able to swat away attacking stormtroopers, the terror walker finally catches up with you and knocks you down, allowing the *Slave I* to get away.

When you come back to, you find that the bounty hunter has gotten away with Juno. You're overcome with rage when you realize you failed; this allows you to tap into your Force Rage ability!

Do as the onscreen prompt suggests and activate Force Rage. Target the four stormtroopers nearby and instantly obliterate them. Continue building your Force Rage and using it to dispatch the enemies in the room, clearing the hangar bay.

ITEM FOUND

After clearing the room, double-jump up to the ledge on the hangar bay's far right end. Examine the little niche to find a blue Energy Bacta Tank.

With the room clear, approach the large burned hole left behind by the terror walker and go after it! Pass through the next few smoldering holes left by the giant spider and use saber combos and Force Rage attacks to destroy all enemies in your path.

When you find the hangar bay section with a hole in the ground, jump into it to continue your pursuit.

BATTLE WITHIN

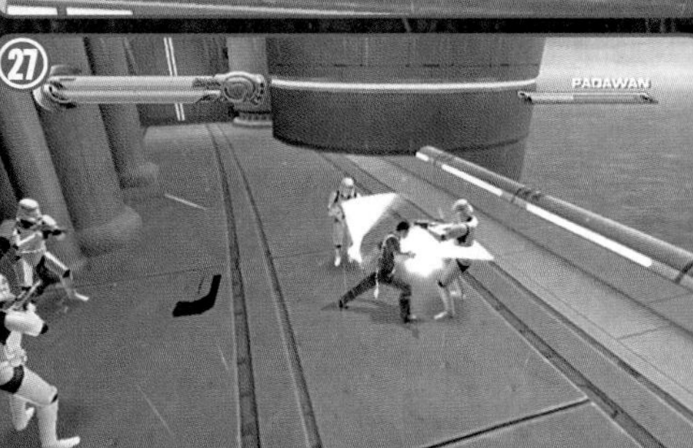

You catch up to the terror walker just as it finishes dislodging several rotating rings around a long firing chamber in the *Salvation*. At the chamber's far end, the walker desperately tries to burn a hole into the next area.

Run up to the first ring and use Force Grip to rotate it back into place. This obviously gets the terror walker's attention, and it begins to fire at you. Dodge the incoming missiles and get back to work rotating the ring.

CLONER'S CAUTION

Don't rotate the rings while the missiles are incoming. The longer you grip the rings, the less time you'll have to dodge the missiles. Let go as soon as the walker fires at you, use lightning on the rings when the missiles are en route. This will create a shield on the ring that will protect you from incoming projectiles.

After getting the ring rotating again, rush to the next one. Once again, dodge the missiles and shift the ring until it begins rotating on its own. Speed down the long hall and destroy the spider droids in your way.

Continue down the hall, rotating rings, dodging missiles, and destroying spider droids as you go until you reach the terror walker.

With all the rings back in rotation, the firing beam comes back online and blasts the walker into the next room.

Once you're in the next room with the terror walker, the supersized spider droid activates its protective shields. At the center of the room is a rotating sphere with part of its shell missing. On the opposite side of the sphere is a diamond switch.

Wait for the rotating sphere to spin around so that the missing section faces the terror walker and the diamond switch faces you. When it does, hit the switch with Force Lightning to blast the walker with a focused electric beam and deactivate its shield. Rush the fallen walker while it's vulnerable, and tear it apart with saber combos.

CLONER'S CAUTION

Be careful of the spider droids and the walker's missile attacks while you wait to line up the rotating sphere. Stay swift of foot and bust through the attacking spider droids to keep from getting knocked down and missing your chance to zap the terror walker.

Repeat this process enough times to bring the walker down. Follow the onscreen commands to dodge the clunker's attacks and rip out its shield generator. When you do, the beam at the center of the room begins to destabilize.

You have three minutes to finish off the terror walker, so rush the enemy's legs and lash out at them with your lightsaber. Dodge the walker's laser attacks and stabbing attempts with its legs, and keep the pressure on the monster by striking at its legs. Jump over the monster's green shock-wave attack and activate Force Rage as soon as you can. Target its legs and chop it down!

Repeat this process and destroy the walker before time runs out.

The Rebel Ship *Salvation*

The *Salvation* jumps to light speed as the Rebels initiate their attack on the Kaminoan cloning facility. When they reach Kamino, the rest of the Rebel fleet is engaged in heavy battle with Imperial forces!

Massive Star Destroyers float high above the battle while TIE fighters and Y-wings trade blaster shots. Inside the *Salvation*, the clone prepares to make his way back onto the planet's surface to find Juno.

Springing the Trap

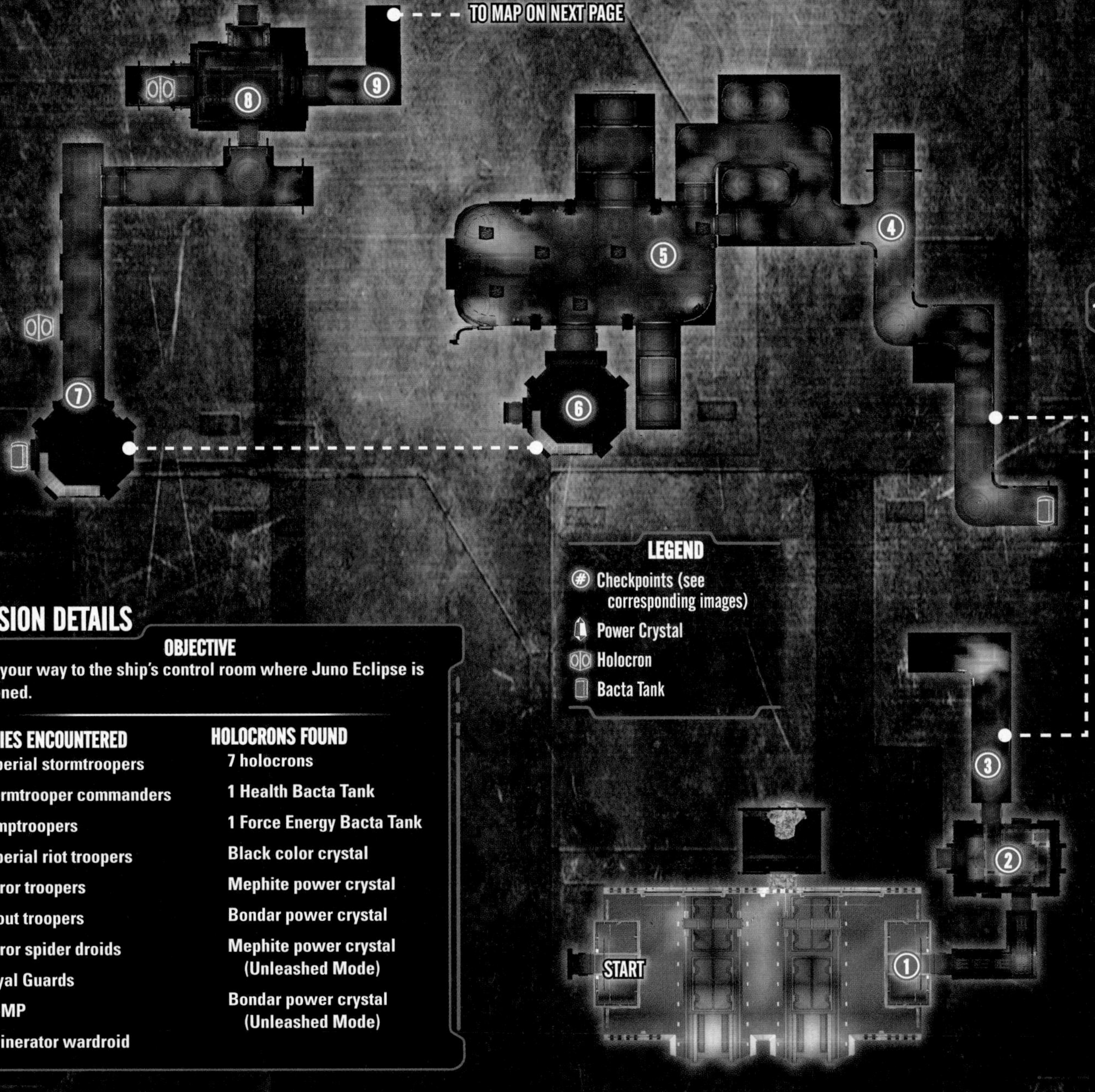

TO MAP ON NEXT PAGE

START

LEGEND
- # Checkpoints (see corresponding images)
- Power Crystal
- Holocron
- Bacta Tank

MISSION DETAILS

OBJECTIVE

Fight your way to the ship's control room where Juno Eclipse is stationed.

ENEMIES ENCOUNTERED
- Imperial stormtroopers
- Stormtrooper commanders
- Jumptroopers
- Imperial riot troopers
- Terror troopers
- Scout troopers
- Terror spider droids
- Royal Guards
- AT-MP
- Incinerator wardroid

HOLOCRONS FOUND
- 7 holocrons
- 1 Health Bacta Tank
- 1 Force Energy Bacta Tank
- Black color crystal
- Mephite power crystal
- Bondar power crystal
- Mephite power crystal (Unleashed Mode)
- Bondar power crystal (Unleashed Mode)

Additional maps on the following page...

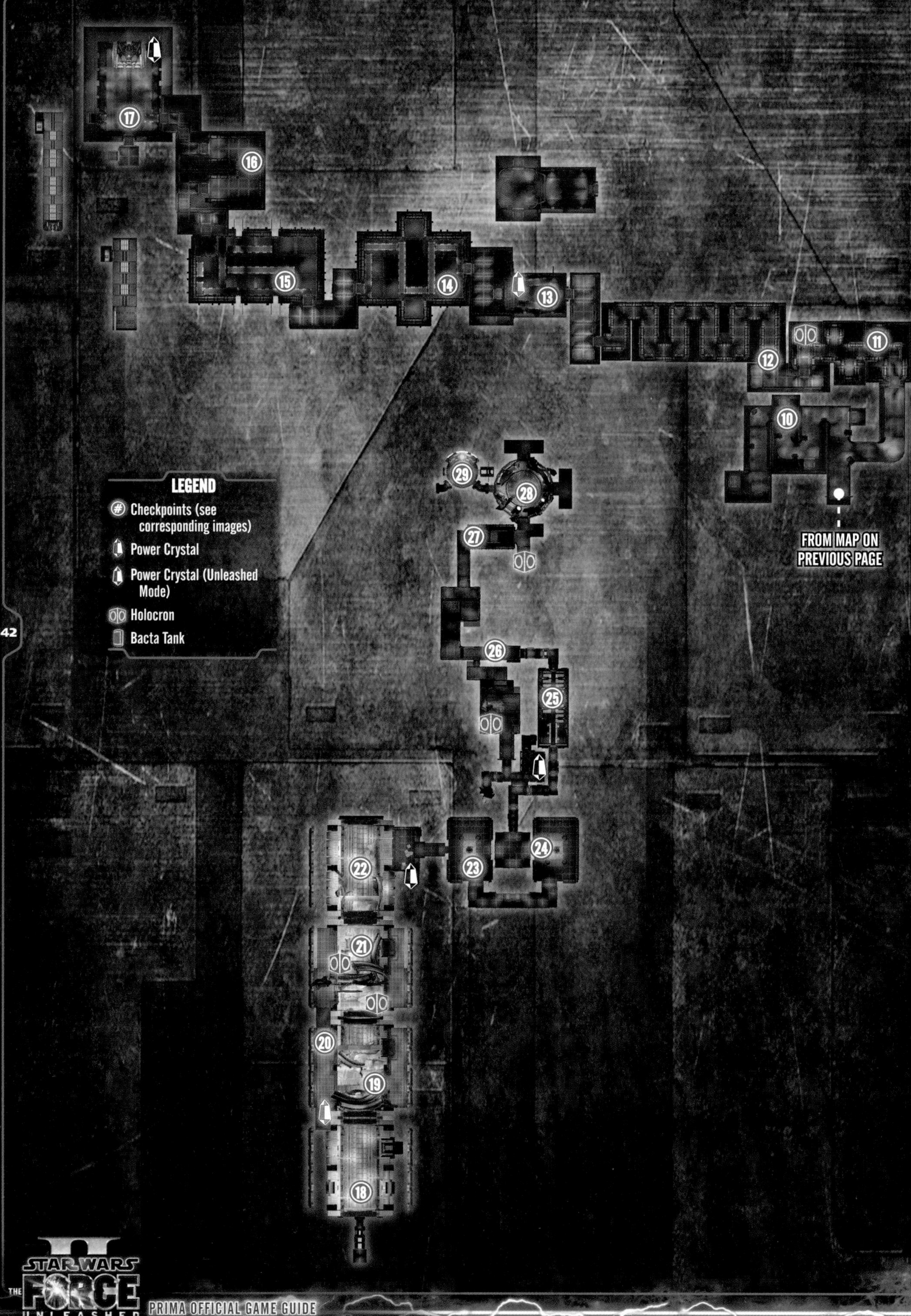
LEGEND
Checkpoints (see corresponding images)
Power Crystal
Power Crystal (Unleashed Mode)
Holocron
Bacta Tank
FROM MAP ON PREVIOUS PAGE
10
11
12
13
14
15
16
17
18
19
20
21
22
23
24
25
26
27
28
29

ATTACK ON KAMINO

Before you can leave the hangar bay, more Imperials come rushing in and attack. Mind Trick the riot troopers first and let them loose on the weaker stormtroopers. Strike down the other riot troopers, then rush the AT-MP.

Blast the walker with a surge of Force Lightning and follow it up with saber combos. Bring down the walker, then sweep the hangar for any remaining Imperial soldiers.

JEDI WISDOM

If you get surrounded by enemies here, use Force Rage to slice through many enemies with ease, including the AT-MP!

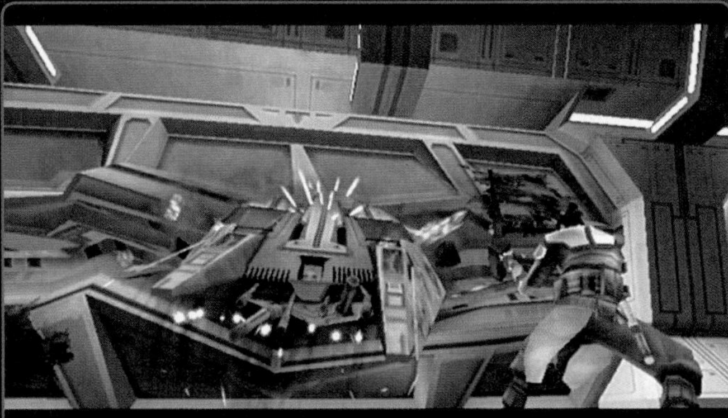

The hangar bay is clear, but the battle still rages on outside the *Salvation*. Follow the onscreen commands when a transport ship attempts to land in the bay. You close the hangar bay doors just in time to slice the transport ship in two.

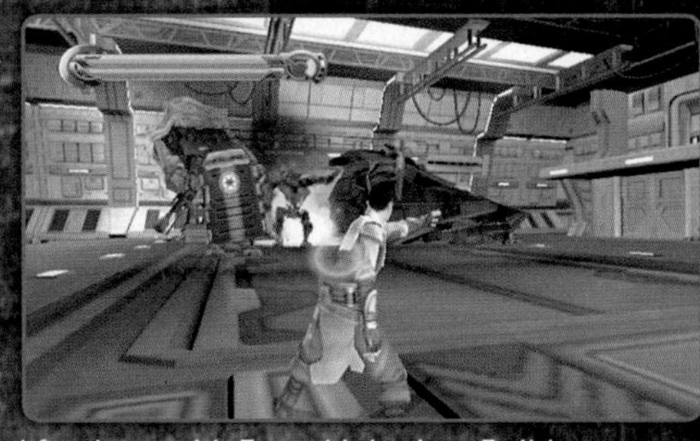

Wait for two large incinerator wardroids to come out, and rip away their shields. Turn right and Mind Trick the stormtroopers near the wall, then return to the wardroids and fry them with Force Lightning. Build up your Force Rage meter and unleash your rage on the wardroids.

① 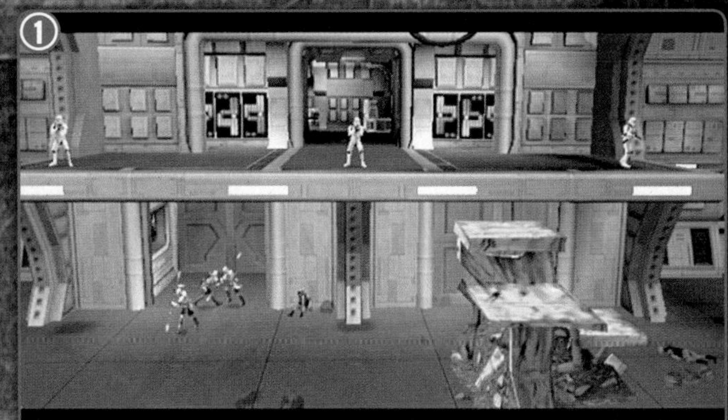

After you destroy the wardroids, a group of Imperials rushes out of the hangar bay's right side. Take out the stormtroopers first, then rush the riot troopers on ground level.

② 

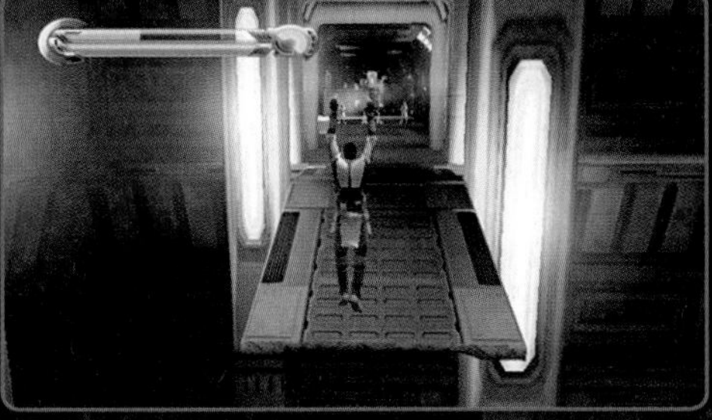

Exit the hangar bay via the newly opened door, high on the wall's right side, and follow the hall to a small room where you encounter some terror troopers. Build up your Combo meter to Unleashed rank and let loose the Lightsaber Special.

Climb up the walkway that winds to the top of the room. Leap over the breaks in the walkway as they explode, then double-jump into the hallway ahead of you.

When you reach the hallway, the AT-MP firing on you from across the hall is crushed by a piece of falling ceiling. However, the coast isn't clear. A swarm of terror spider droids comes rushing out. Greet them with your Force powers and crush them before going up the fallen section of ceiling.

ITEM FOUND

After you go up the incline, stop and turn around. Jump over the hole in the ground and follow the hallway left to a dead end. In the far right corner of the dead end is a Health Bacta Tank!

After climbing up the fallen ceiling, take the corridor up and around. The hall turns left just as more stormtroopers rush out of a nearby room. Bully them with Force powers and follow the hall to another cave-in.

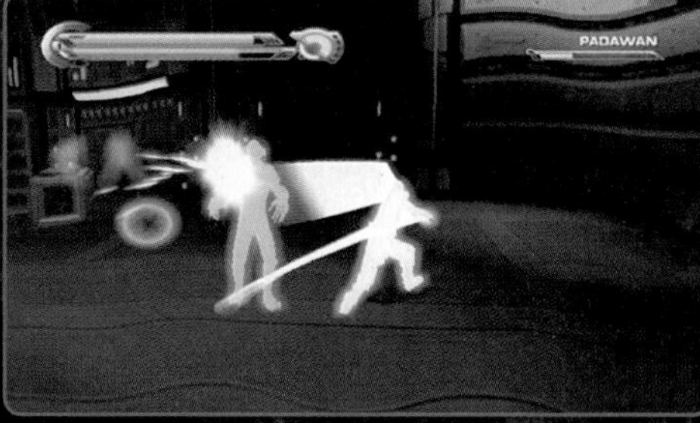

Activate your Force Vision and locate the terror troopers that hide in the hall. Counter their attacks to build up your Combo and Force Rage meters, then wipe the floor clean with them.

Use the Force to open the sealed door at the hall's end, then run into the large room with several flame jets in it. A door slides open on the room's opposite side, revealing an incinerator wardroid and its stormtrooper comrades. Dispatch them easily with Lightsaber Specials and Force Rage.

A second wardroid and a group of Imperials rush out of the door on the right. Do away with this batch of enemies just as you did the first.

CLONER'S CAUTION

Watch out for the flame jets as you fight the enemies in this room. You'll take damage if you touch them!

The room's far left end leads to an elevator. Hop on after destroying your foes, and use Force Lightning to charge the diamond switch and turn the elevator on.

The elevator stops before you reach your destination. Climb up the walkway on the left and follow it to a wall panel high above the elevator floor. Use Saber Throw to dislodge the panel and turn it into a platform; then jump onto it.

ITEM FOUND

Climb all the way up the elevator shaft—past the exit—using these makeshift platforms. When you reach the top, look across the shaft to find a blue Force Energy Bacta Tank hiding in a small niche. Double-jump dash across to land on the ledge leading to the niche and grab it.

Climb up the platforms lining the elevator shaft until you reach the entrance to another hallway. When you enter the hall, the left side is bombarded with landing pods! Riot troopers and Imperial stormtroopers fill the hall, ready to attack. Rush out and greet them with saber combos and Lightsaber Specials. You can also use Mind Trick on the riot troopers and let them do the dirty work for you.

HOLOCRON

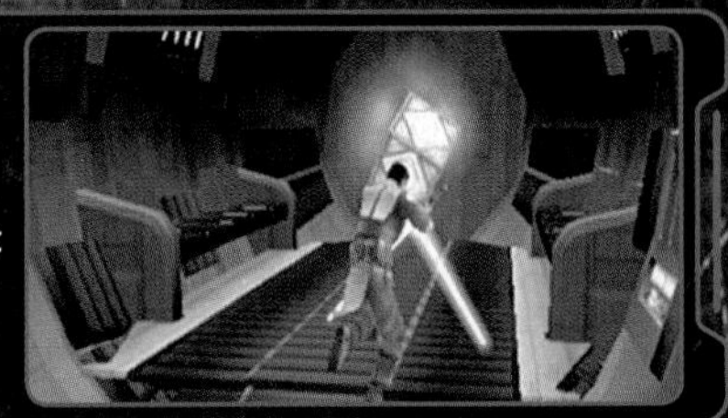

After fending off several waves of enemies, sneak into the landing pod nearest the entrance to this hall. It houses a holocron!

Hold position in this hall as you defeat all of the landing parties. After dealing with the last landing party, make a right at the hall's far end.

Follow the hall to a sealed door on the left. Use Force Push to blow it open, then pass through. An incinerator wardroid rushes in from the opposite side. Dash toward it and quickly tear away its shield before getting to work on it with Force powers and saber combos. While you get to work on the mechanical foe, use Mind Trick on the riot troopers so they can lend a hand.

Double-jump onto the walkways overhead. Use the Force to shift the crates into place and climb up the tall room toward the entrance to another hall high above you.

HOLOCRON

Before you jump into the exit hallway, look across the exit. There is a small compartment holding a holocron. Double-jump dash into it, grab it, then hop back down.

The floor gives way as soon as you reach the hall, and you free-fall deep into the next section of the ship!

BREAKING APART

Dash past the flame jets firing down the hall, and cut through the Imperials in your way. You're ambushed by stormtroopers and riot troopers, so proceed through the hall only when you have full health.

Fight past all your enemies, down the long, winding hall. The hall leads to another long, winding corridor—this one with lasers firing down each bend in the hall.

Wait for the laser to stop firing, then dash across the hall into a small niche on the other side. Stop there and wait for the laser to fire again, then exit once it stops. Carefully navigate the corridor this way, stopping between laser blasts until you reach the end of the first laser section.

HOLOCRON

Just after reaching the end of the first laser section, turn around and look past the laser beam. On the laser's right side is a small area with a holocron in it. Dash across the laser again to grab it before moving along.

Resume your trek across the firing tubes and destroy the spider droids in the way. Once again, wait for the lasers to stop firing and dash across the long halls to the area in between the laser halls. Carefully make your way out of the snaking laser hall.

Turn right at the end and pass through the door on the left wall. A group of riot troopers escorts an incinerator wardroid out of the far end. Hurl the nearby explosive tanks at the attacking troopers, then bring down the wardroid.

Go up the walkway on either side of this room, and cut down the Imperials above you. Turn left into the next room, and fight past another stormtrooper squad.

The next room is in flames! The only way to get across is to carefully navigate a rickety walkway that gives way as soon as you step on it. Edge out of the doorway and double-jump dash from the door to the walkway's left corner. As soon as you land on the walkway, dash around the bend and double-jump dash over the gaps to its end.

CLONER'S CAUTION

Be quick while navigating the walkway. If you hesitate for even a second, the walkway will give way and send you falling into the fire.

Fight through another swarm of spider droids and approach the next burning room. Step onto the walkway's edge and double-jump across the room, temporarily landing on the center span of the walkway. Just before it gives way, double-jump dash right again to the far span of the walkway.

Follow the walkway left to the connecting walkway, and run across it back to the room's other side. Double-jump onto the incline ramp, and run up to a rising platform full of stormtroopers.

After taking out the stormtroopers, ride the platform all the way up. Step out into the next corridor and venture deeper into the ship. Activate your Force Vision when you encounter terror troopers and take them down with Force Rage.

Drop into the next room and begin building up your Force Rage meter with the spider droids that attack you. As soon as your Force Rage is full, use it on the four spider droids sucking the energy out of the generator on the room's far end.

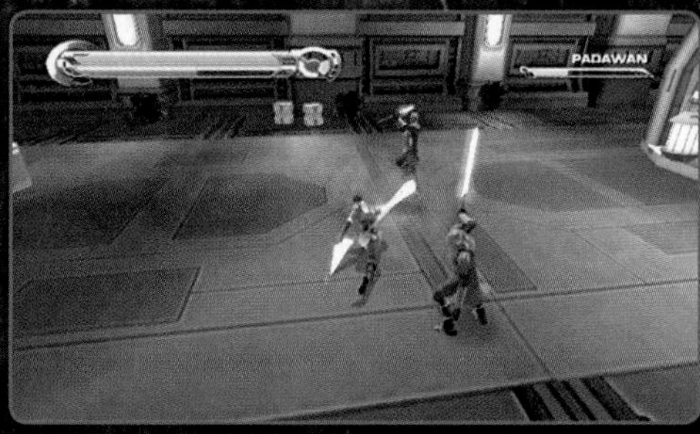

Three Royal Guards come rushing out of the far hallway after you remove the spider droids. They're resistant to Force power attacks, so rely heavily on your saber skills, Lightsaber Specials, and Force Rage. Fend off the following waves of Royal Guards until they're all wiped out.

ITEM FOUND

After fending off the waves of Royal Guards, Force Push open the door on the far right of the generator to reveal the Mephite power crystal.

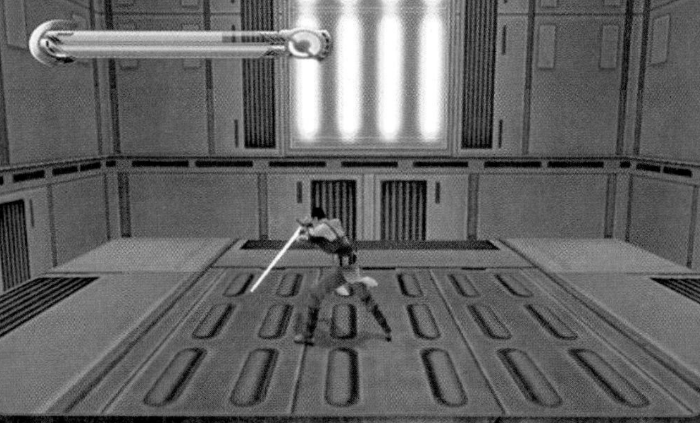

Exit the room via the elevator on the right.

HOLDING IT TOGETHER

Leave the elevator and enter the transport conduit. Approach the transport platform nearby and hop on. Use Force Lightning to charge the diamond switch and activate the platform.

The platform doesn't get very far. In fact, the next section of the conduit is utterly destroyed. Hop off the platform and pass through the small passageway on the far left.

The wall explodes ahead of you as Royal Guards and storm-troopers rush out. Mind Trick the stormtroopers and take your lightsaber to the guards.

Double-jump up the rubble and crush the stormtroopers waiting on the rafters above you. Make a right at the top of the rafters, and climb up the next fallen walkway.

An explosion rocks the area's far end, and Imperials come pouring out. They're led by an AT-MP walker. Don't waste any time running your blade through the stormtroopers nearby.

Make a left and dash across the walkway toward the walker. Double-jump over its missiles to avoid taking damage, then Force Push through the next few stormtroopers.

20

When you reach the AT-MP, build up your Force Rage meter and unleash your fury on the walker and its puny stormtrooper friends.

Go through the hole the AT-MP burst out of, and turn right down the passageway. Leap over the incoming missiles from the next AT-MP. Before you can reach it, the walkway gives way again and you fall to the lower level.

HOLOCRON

After the walkway gives out, make a right and walk over the catwalk's edge. You'll drop into a small area with a holocron in it. Grab it, then jump over the rubble to climb out of the area you're in.

21

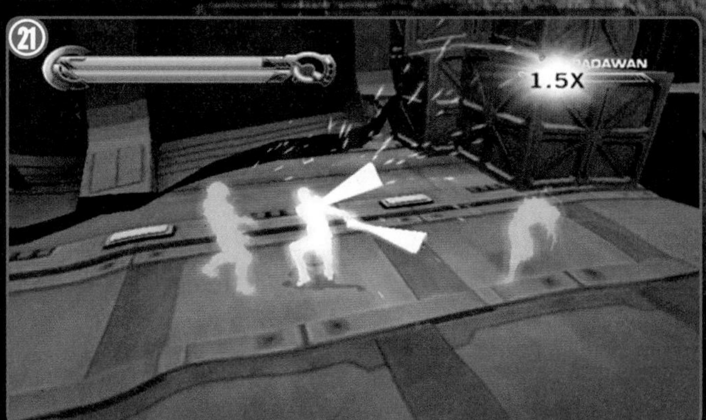

Pass through the hole in the rubble and enter the next section of the massive passageway. Activate Force Vision and locate the terror troopers in the room. Attack them with saber combos to build up your Force Rage meter and wipe them out!

HOLOCRON

There's a holocron in the far corner of this room's upper level. Climb up the stacked crates, then turn left and double-jump dash onto the walkway to find it.

22

Use Force Grip to slide the large door open and venture into the next section. Double-jump over the rubble and climb up. Double-jump dash out into the room's center and come down on the enemies below with a downward slash attack. Eliminate the enemies nearby, then turn left and climb up the rubble to the top walkway.

ITEM FOUND

Don't exit the room just yet. After climbing to the top, make a right and examine the small room behind the crates. The Bondar power crystal is in this room.

23

Step on the elevator and ride it to the next area. Get off and enter the room where four incinerator wardroids are torching the pillars. Dash around the room, tearing off the wardroids' shields; then build up your Force Rage meter with saber strikes. Either take them down with Force Rage or fry their circuits with Force Lightning.

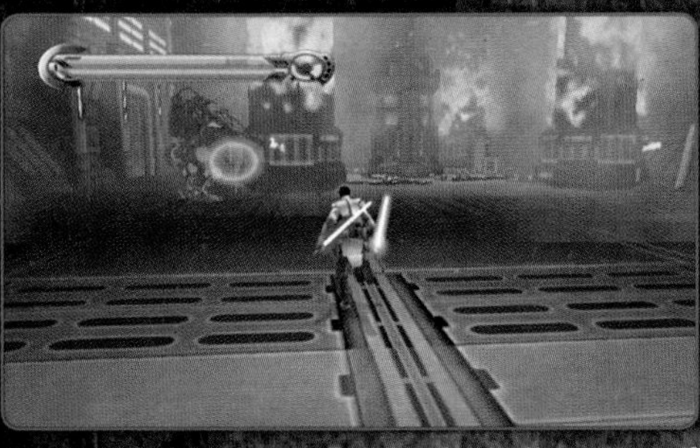

Destroy the wardroids, then turn toward the center tower with the diamond switches. Hit the switches with Force Lightning, and the other pillars in the room will cool down. Follow the hallway out of the room to another room with four more pillars...and four more wardroids. Take them out just as you did the previous four, then cool down pillars by activating the central tower.

JEDI WISDOM

You have three minutes to cool down the pillars in each room, so destroy the wardroids quickly, preferably with Force Rage.

24 Force Push the door in this room and go through.

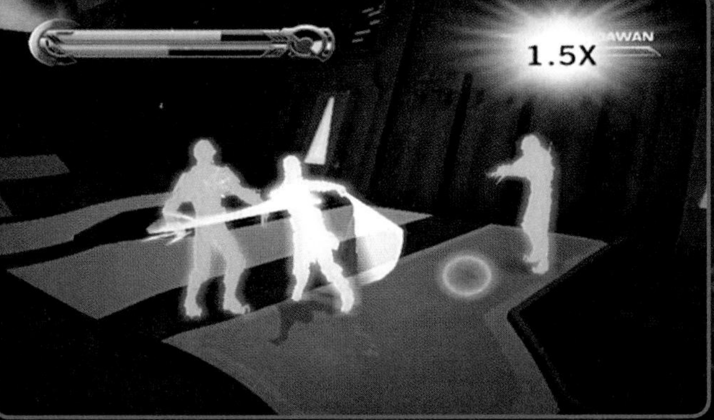

Speed down the hall to the next large room. It stretches out below you, and a fire rages on at the far end. Go down the ramp onto the room's floor and approach the far door. The door quickly closes before you can go through, so turn around and head back toward the room's entrance.

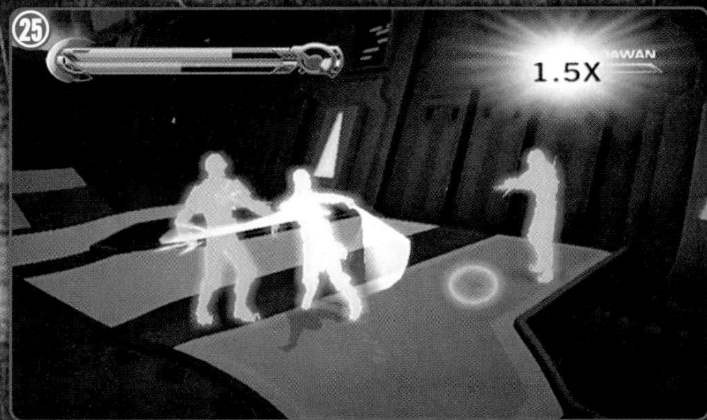

Before you can reach the next door, it explodes in flames! Turn back around and activate Force Vision to spy the terror troopers in the room with you. Slice them up, but stay near the center of the room to keep from falling through the glass as it shatters. When you defeat the terror troopers, the far door slides open and more enemies attack.

Leave the room via the next hall. As you speed down the hall, the ground gives away again and you fall into the corridor below you. Force Push through the next hall and follow them deeper into the ship.

HOLOCRON

As soon as the floor gives way, use Force Push on the blue-lit wall panel on the left. Follow it into a large room with a stack of crates bathed in a green light. Pass the crates and make a right into a small niche where the next holocron is sitting.

ITEM FOUND

Also in this secret area is a black color crystal. Climb up the stack of crates to an area high above the ground. Defeat the Royal Guards that attack, then use Force Grip to lift the door at the far end. Make a left in the next room and locate the black color crystal down the hall.

Just before you enter the next series of corridors, a small group of stormtroopers runs straight into a flame jet! Watch out for the flame jets in the hall as you traverse the dangerous halls.

HOLOCRON

After passing through the flame-jet halls, turn right and blow open the sealed door. There's a holocron behind it!

Enter the large circular room behind you, and use Force Repulse to shatter the glass beneath you. You fall down into the next level of the ship, where you find Master Kota engaged in combat with a Royal Guard.

The room quickly fills up with more and more Royal Guards. Stand in the center of the room and fend off the attackers. Build up your Combo and Force Rage meters, then use high-rank Lightsaber Specials and Force Rage to destroy all enemies.

After defeating the first few waves of Royal Guards, a pod crashes into the top of the room. It delivers even more Royal Guards. Strike them down until the door leading out opens.

Exit the room and return with Kota to the command room. You send off Kota and the combat training droid to evacuate the ship while you find a way to lead the ship down to the Kaminoan surface.

The *Salvation* begins to penetrate the Kaminoan atmosphere. Follow the onscreen commands to swat the flying debris out of the way before it knocks you over, then plug the hole in the command room with the center console. Finally, do as the gestures on the screen suggest to guide the ship down to the oceanic planet.

Return to Kamino

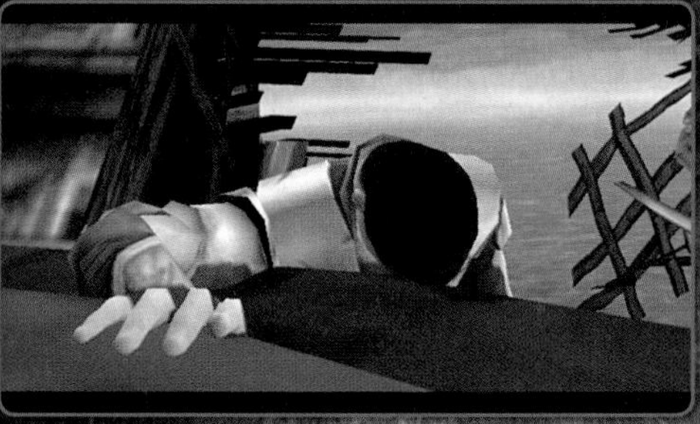

The clone drives the *Salvation* straight into the cloning facility on the oceanic planet of Kamino. As the ship explodes, the clone manages to escape the brunt of the impact. When the dust settles, the ship is utterly demolished and the cloning facility is in ruins.

Out of the rubble rises the clone's hand as he begins to hoist himself up out of the mess. When he pulls himself up, he's got only one thing on his mind: Juno Eclipse.

Homecoming

LEGEND

- # Checkpoints (see corresponding images)
- Power Crystal
- Power Crystal (Unleashed Mode)
- Purple Color Crystal
- Holocron
- Bacta Tank
- Blue Tank

MISSION DETAILS

OBJECTIVE

Return to Kamino and locate Juno Eclipse.

ENEMIES ENCOUNTERED

- Imperial stormtroopers
- Jumptroopers
- Royal Guards
- AT-MP
- Incinerator wardroid
- TIE fighters
- Terror troopers
- Dark clones
- Darth Vader

HOLOCRONS FOUND

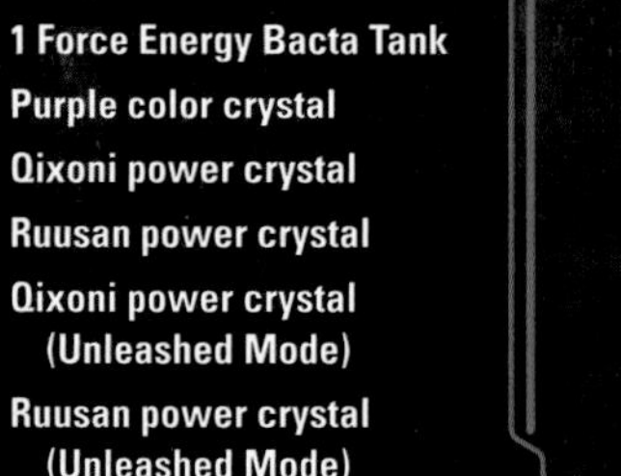

- 8 holocrons
- 1 Health Bacta Tank
- 1 Force Energy Bacta Tank
- Purple color crystal
- Qixoni power crystal
- Ruusan power crystal
- Qixoni power crystal (Unleashed Mode)
- Ruusan power crystal (Unleashed Mode)

24
23
22
15
21
14
16
20
17
18
19
28
27
26
25
31
32
29
30
33
34
36
35

ROUGH LANDING

Set out of the crash site and follow the series of ledges on the left as they wind around the ruined facility.

ITEM FOUND

When you reach the crackling wires on the ground, turn around and look behind you. There's a Qixoni power crystal sitting on a ledge across a short chasm. Double-jump dash out to grab it.

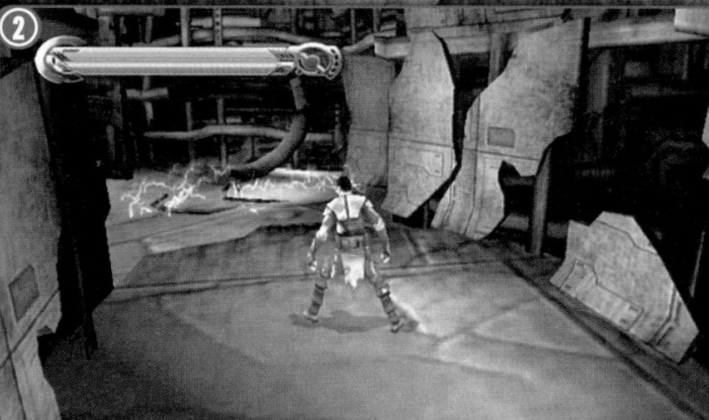

Leap over the crackling electrical wire to avoid taking damage, and trek deeper into the ruins. Carefully creep out onto the bridgelike walkway and follow it down and around. As soon as you set foot on the walkway, it begins to give way, so rush to its end.

Climb up the rubble and follow it around to a locked wall panel. Use Saber Throw to turn the wall panel into a platform and hop onto it. Double-jump off the platform onto the nearby ledge.

HOLOCRON

From the ledge, look left. Just off in the distance is holocron sitting on a small ledge. Double-jump dash out to grab it.

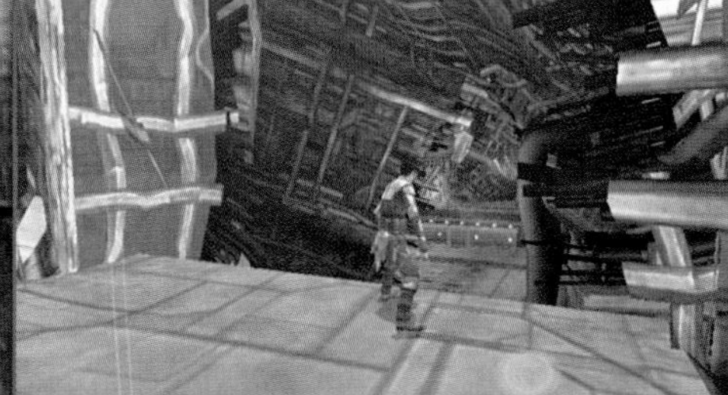

Make a left on the ledge and follow it down into another ruined part of the facility.

HOLOCRON

After dropping down from the ledge, turn left and face the wall. There's a small chamber hidden behind a large piece of rubble. A holocron is hiding inside the room—use Force Vision to see it. Sneak past the rubble into the room and grab it before resuming your journey to rescue Juno.

Make a right at the dead end and speed into the facility. An AT-MP and a pair of stormtroopers come marching out of the room's far side. Rush them and fry the entire lot of enemies.

With the room clear, step on the elevator and ride it down, deeper into the cloning facility. Get off the elevator and follow the hallway out to a hangar bay.

ITEM FOUND

As soon as you enter the hangar bay, run into the small transport ship. There's a Force Energy Bacta Tank inside of it.

The hangar bay has several stormtroopers and a pair of incinerator wardroids on the far right. When you enter, they don't pay you any attention. Sneak up behind them and use Mind Trick to turn the stormtroopers on each other.

When the group of enemies turns around and attacks, focus on the wardroids. Build up your Force Rage and unleash it on them after tearing away their shields. If you can't take down the wardroids quickly with Force Rage, then strafe around the hangar, using the transport ship as a protective barrier while you fry them with Force Lightning.

Turn on the Royal Guards after destroying the wardroids, and run them through with your lightsabers. Build up your Force Rage meter and use your rage to destroy the remaining Royal Guards and the AT-MP that attacks from the hangar's far end.

Activate your Force Vision and approach the locked door at the hangar's far end. Use your vision to see through the lock, and slide the locking mechanisms across the door panels to unlock them.

Exit the hangar and reunite with Master Kota. As he and his men prepare to attack the rest of the cloning facility, the wise Jedi points out your final destination. You'll need to reach the top of the cloning building in order to reach Juno.

You inch out to the edge of the landing platform and use the Force to lift a large hunk of the *Salvation* and bridge the gap between your platform and the building where Juno is being held. Follow the commands as they appear onscreen to dispatch the attacking TIE fighters and safely bridge the gap. Once the ship is in place, you leap across it as you begin your approach on Vader's cloning facility.

Speed down the long path ahead and follow it right, then left. After the second turn, the path sprawls far ahead of you. Dash up the long path and wait for the TIE fighters to zoom by overhead.

7

They'll fire at you as they pass by, so either jump over the blasts or hide behind one of the center supports to shield yourself from the attack.

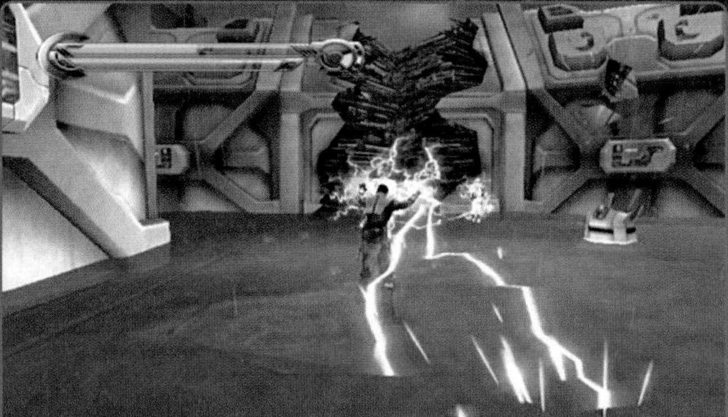

8

Make a right at the end of the long path, and electrocute the jumptroopers in your way. Hop onto the stepped platforms on the left, then drop down to the area below.

HOLOCRON

After dropping into the next area, explore the left side of the tall tower. Hidden behind some stacked crates is another holocron. Use the Force to remove the crates, then grab the holocron before continuing on your journey.

Fight past several more jumptroopers and continue down the long corridor. You'll come across another large drop in your path.

ITEM FOUND

Stop before you jump down into the next area, and examine the small nook on the left of the drop. There's a stack of crates there hiding the Ruusan power crystal. Pick it up, then return to the drop in the path and hop down.

9

Jump down into the next area and use Force Lightning to zap the jumptroopers out of the sky. Rush the grounded troopers while their wings are clipped, and either Force Push them over the edge or cut them up with your lightsaber.

10

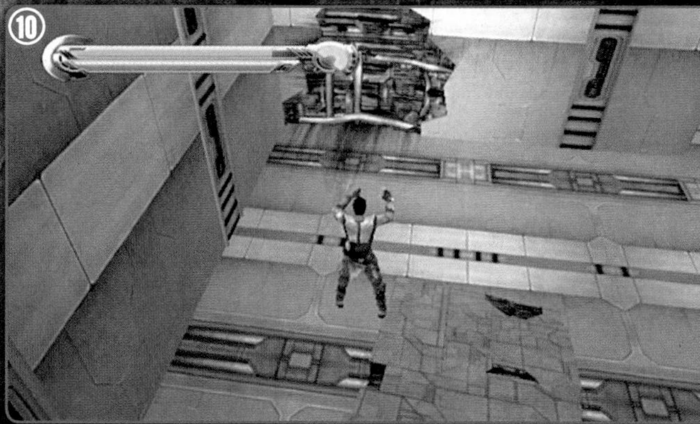

Fight past the troopers in your way and turn left at the dead end. Jump down into the next area.

ITEM FOUND

After dropping down, immediately turn left and locate the stack of crates. Remove them and grab the red Health Bacta Tank tucked away in the corner.

11

Make a right at the next section, and set off across a path made of debris. Jump from chunk to chunk, until you reach a large square piece of debris. Stand at the center and wait for a group of jumptroopers to approach. Knock them out of the sky with Force Lightning or Saber Throws, then finish them off while they're on the platform with you.

Continue navigating the debris pathway until you come across a section of the walkway that you must bring down with a Saber Throw. Dash across the walkway after it falls into place and make a right.

Follow the path until you reach a series of debris chunks. You must move them into place using Force Grip.

HOLOCRON

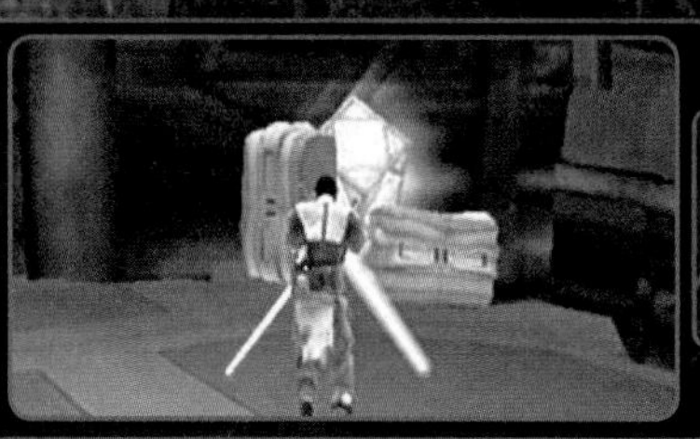

After moving two debris platforms into place, make a sharp left and fry the jumptroopers guarding the area. Examine the corner of the area; behind a stack of crates is a holocron.

12

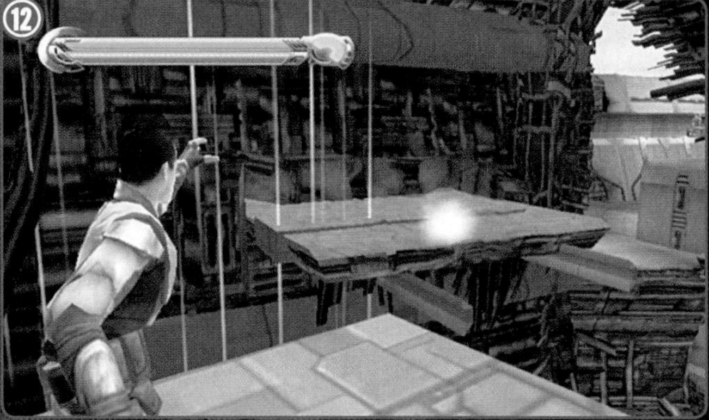

Near the end of the long chasm, stop and use the Force again to slide the platform on the left out of its niche and into place in front of you. Dash across the newly placed walkway and double-jump dash across the final few debris platforms.

Make a right at the path's end, and follow it to a long walkway with an AT-MP on it. Rush the walker and double-jump dash over the missiles. Get close enough to fry it, then unleash Force Lightning on it and bring it down with saber combos.

13

As you fight the walker, you build your Force Rage meter. Wait for the onslaught of Imperials from across the walkway, and use your Force Rage to take them all out at once. If you miss any, strike them down, then use your Force powers to clear the way before crossing.

THE CAPACITATOR CORE

The next area leads to a large, wide-open space with a series of tall spires. Attached to those spires are small circular platforms leading all the way up. In order to reach Vader and Juno, you'll need to climb up the tall, towerlike room.

Turn left at the first connecting walkway, and wait for the purple electrical rings to stop firing on the next platform. When they stop, rush out and double-jump dash onto the ring overhead.

Turn right and, once again, wait for the electrical rings to disappear before jumping across the next platform.

HOLOCRON

The fifth circular platform has a connecting walkway to a sixth platform. Cross the walkway and go around to the platform's other side to find a holocron.

Follow the platforms out of the first section and into a small connecting corridor. Drop to the lower level of the corridor, and follow it out to another section of the facility.

This time, the section is split up into two long, curved walkways: one above you and another one on the lower level. Head onto the first lower walkway and take out all of the enemies.

Double-jump dash onto the nearby circular platform and turn right. Wait for the electric rings on the next platform to stop, then use it to reach the higher walkway. Quickly destroy the Imperial stormtroopers in your way, then follow the walkway left.

Once again, pass through the connecting corridor and enter the next area with several more circular platforms. Make a sharp right and locate the pair of platforms connected by a single walkway. Double-jump dash onto them and turn left.

Wait for the electrical rings on the next series of platforms to stop firing, then quickly double-jump dash across the three of them.

HOLOCRON

When you reach the exit platform, turn around and use Force Vision to locate the holocron hiding behind a distant pillar. Double-jump dash across the two pillars behind you and grab it before returning to the exit.

Exit this section of the facility through another connecting corridor.

Rush into the next section, and follow the curved walkway out. Use Force Lightning to zap the jumptroopers overhead, then hop across the nearby walkways to reach the walkway overhead.

HOLOCRON

Before exiting this section, turn right on the long, curved walkway and follow it to its end. You'll find another holocron hiding behind more crates.

Exit the area through the connecting walkway and venture back out to the rainy Kaminoan landscape.

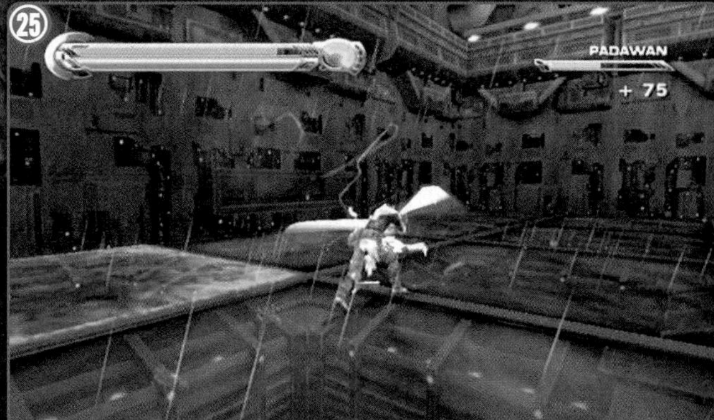

The next area has a large spire at the center and is patrolled by jumptroopers. Scorch the troopers and knock them out of the sky. Once they're on the ground, use saber combos to finish them off and build your Force Rage and Combo meters.

CLONER'S CAUTION

As you fight the enemies in this area, watch out for the electrical panels that light up on the ground. If you set foot on them, you'll take a nasty shock!

Destroy the jump-troopers that attack, then look to the right. Two small slits in the left and right walls open up, revealing several blaster turrets. They waste no time in opening fire on you, so rush them and use Force Push blasts to crush them quickly.

Once the room is clear of all threats, approach the center pillar and use Force Grip to lift its upper section and stop the electrical current running throughout the room.

With the electrical current gone, the far door slides open. Pass through the door and eliminate the terror troopers stalking you.

Speed through the corridors to a small elevator, and ride it out to a landing area. Rush out of the elevator as a transport ship departs, and take the fight to the stormtroopers waiting outside. Eliminate the commanders first, then cut down the lowly stormtroopers.

Fend off the waves of Royal Guards as they attack by immediately using your Force Rage. You slice them up with ease. Sweep the surrounding area and eliminate the fresh batch of stormtroopers that comes out. When another group of Royal Guards rushes out, once again build your Force Rage and Combo meters to put a swift end to them.

ITEM FOUND

There is a purple color crystal along the right wall of this area. Remove the stack of crates along the wall and grab it before proceeding.

With the Royal Guards defeated, other enemies rush into the small arena. Activate your Force Vision to locate the terror troopers and run your lightsabers through them.

Fight your way across the room and destroy every last enemy. When you do, the far door will slide open. Go through and follow the corridor to its end.

DESTINED ASCENT

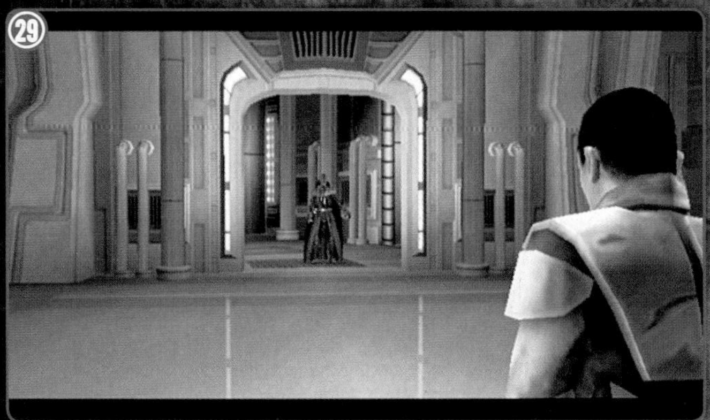

The halls are empty. Dash through the empty hall as it wends to a medium-sized room. There you encounter the Dark Lord, Vader. He insists that you bow to him and finally give in to the dark side.

But before you can refuse, you're ambushed by two dark clones wielding lightsabers! Follow the onscreen prompts to fend off the dark ones and strike them down.

Follow the hall to a larger room housing cloning tanks. Vader threatens you once again before unleashing a group of dark clones on you. Blast the clones with a Force Push attack, then move from clone to clone as you string together your combos.

After clearing the room of enemies, leave it and storm down the next hallway. Follow the hall to an elevator; ride it up into another section of the facility.

Once again, battle Vader's clones upon entering the next chamber. By now you should be able to unleash Force Rage or quickly string together several combos to fill your Combo meter to maximum rank. Do so and put a much-deserved end to the dark clones.

HOLOCRON

The final holocron in the game is hiding behind the near left tank as you enter the room. Clear the room of all enemies first, then explore the nook between the tank and the left wall to find it.

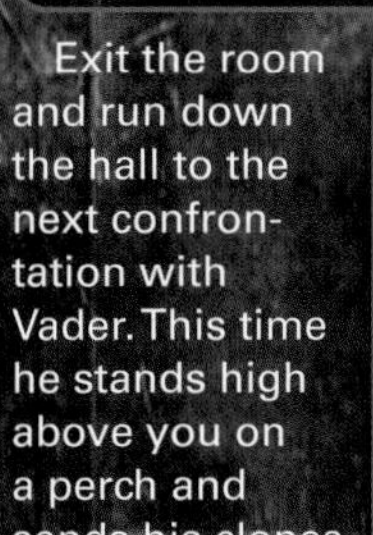

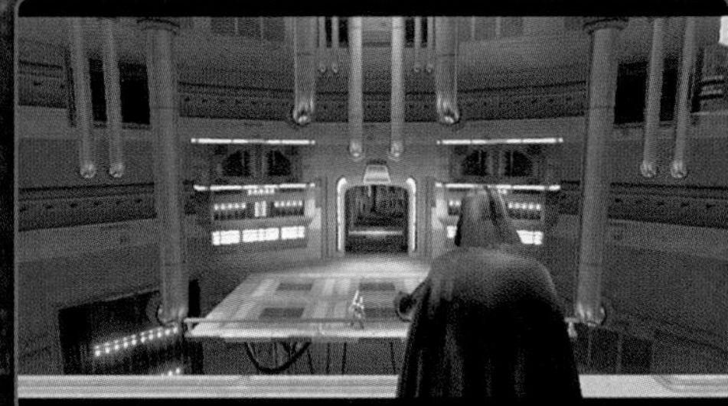

Exit the room and run down the hall to the next confrontation with Vader. This time he stands high above you on a perch and sends his clones down to attack. Deal with them as they attack. If they surround you, use Force Repulse to knock them back; then use combos, Force Rage, and Lightsaber Specials to endure the clones' attacks.

When the coast is clear, turn toward the ledge where Vader greeted you as you entered, and use Force Grip to bring it down. Jump onto the newly made ledge and walk up.

Cross the walkway and step onto the elevator on the other side. The elevator slowly rises as several waves of clones drop in and attack. Keep to the center of the platform and fend off the clones as they strike. Endure the slow ascent until you reach the top.

CLONER'S CAUTION

Warning! The following section contains spoilers. If you don't mind spoilers, read on.

Vader Boss Battle

When you reach the top, you find that Darth Vader is waiting for you. Engage the Dark Lord in saber combat and follow the commands on the screen to gain the upper hand. He encourages you to indulge in your rage.

Before you can reply, his men escort Juno out onto your battleground. When he draws her in with the Force, your focus wavers and he seizes the opportunity. He grips you with the Force as well and takes you up to a platform high above you.

He tosses you like a rag doll, and with Juno in his grip, he offers you a choice. Either bow before him or let Juno die. He holds her in the air to display her to you while you make your choice.

You drop your lightsabers and fall to your knees, vowing to do his bidding. Vader slams Juno down onto the ground. In a rage, you pick up your lightsabers and leap between Vader and Juno!

Vader is highly skilled in manipulating the Force. His knowledge of the dark side is enough to render most of your Force attacks useless. Instead, focus on lightsaber combat, using combos to drive Vader back.

Wait for Vader to throw his lightsaber at you and block it. Dash toward the defenseless Dark Lord and lash out at him with fierce lightsaber combos!

If Vader grabs you with the Force and attempts to choke you, follow the onscreen gestures to shake loose, then retaliate with saber combos. Continue blocking the Dark Lord's Saber Throw attack and striking while he's defenseless until he takes too much damage.

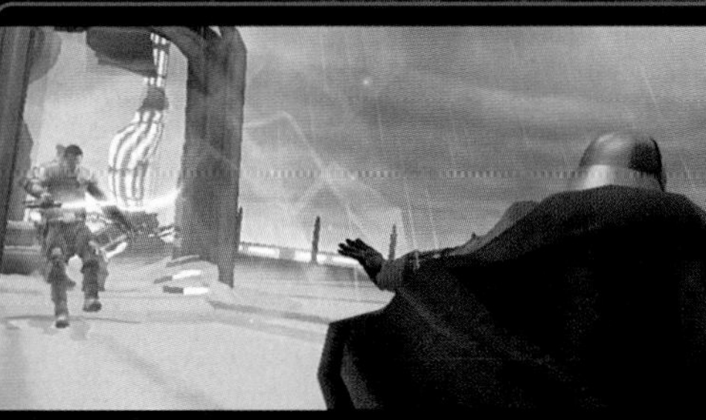

Lord Vader drops to one knee and violently pushes you away with a Force Push blast! The blast sends you flying through the structure at the center of the area.

When you get up, a group of dark clones comes charging at you. Mind Trick the first few, then turn on the remaining clones and eliminate them. Meanwhile, the Mind Tricked clones can take the fight to Vader and each other.

Rush Vader while he's distracted, and help your clone comrades strike the Dark Lord down. Wait for another wave of clones to attack, then repeat the same process as before.

Eventually Vader uses Force Grip to hurl a clone at you. He misses you, and the clone crashes though the center structure, revealing a large ball of electricity at the top. Re-engage the Dark Lord in saber combat and build up your Force Rage meter.

Fend off the clones, and use your Force Rage to strike a savage blow to Vader and his minions. When the Dark Lord is ready to fall, he grips you in a last-ditch effort to subdue you.

He slowly moves you toward the electrical current. Follow the commands onscreen just as he's about to push you into the electrical current, and turn the tables on him!

With Vader at your feet, you must make a choice: Strike him down and avenge Juno's death or allow him to live so that the Rebel Alliance can interrogate him. The choice is yours....

NEIMOIDIAN NOTES

Since there is no gameplay after you make this choice, we will not continue and reveal either ending. Instead, we leave it up to you to find out.

EXTRAS

The following section is dedicated to the challenges you unlock in the Xbox 360 and PS3 game, and the multiplayer mode you unlock in the Wii version of the game.

Challenges

As you play through the single-player campaign, you will unlock 10 challenges. These vary from mastering combat techniques to navigating complex landscapes in a limited amount of time. Each challenge has four ranks you can achieve: Bronze, Silver, Gold, and Platinum. Depending on how well you perform, you can unlock any of four rewards: cinematics, costumes, experience points, and saber crystals. Use the following strategies to complete each challenge. However, to truly master a challenge and attain a Platinum rank, pay special attention to the tips from the masters at LucasArts.

Developer Tips and Tricks

The following are tried-and-true tips and expert strategy from the best and brightest at LucasArts. In order to master every challenge, you must first master everything from saber combat and defensive techniques to speed and agility training. Keep the following in mind if you want to score Platinum ranks across all challenges!

GENERAL TIPS

These two tips are a great starting point before attempting to complete all challenges with Platinum rank.

Have all powers at Rank 3. Lightning, Push, Mind Trick, and Repulse are the most important.

Collect all saber crystals; use two Focus crystals on levels where Force powers are the dominant moves needed.

SPEED TIPS

The following tips are for challenges that prize speed over saber skill. These "race courses," such as the Deadly Path Trial and Retrieval Trial, require players to shave as much time as possible in order to attain Platinum rank.

Dash as much as possible. Dash will "cancel" out just about everything; for example, if you're jumping, using a dash will interrupt the jump and cause you to quickly move forward without having to wait until you reach the top of the jump. This is also true of combo attacks; you do not need to wait to finish the string of combo animations before performing other actions. Pressing the Dash button while you're attacking will immediately halt the combo and take you to whatever action you'd like next.

When needing to jump between platforms, use a quick dash to reach the edge of the platform you're currently on in order to jump off its edge immediately.

Dashing off an edge will allow you to perform another dash midair. However, using this technique will not allow you to double-jump. The second dash replaces the first jump, and any jump after that will be your last unless you reach another platform.

Avoid using double-jumps when they aren't necessary. Double-jumping can add approximately one extra second to the overall time it takes to double-jump and land on a platform. Instead, use only single-jumps when a double is not needed.

NEIMOIDIAN NOTES

All medals unlock experience points. The following tables will list what the medals will unlock aside from experience points.

CHALLENGE 1: THE COMBAT TRIAL

Rank	Requirement	Reward
Platinum	01:05 or more	—
Gold	00:55–01:04	Fury Saber Crystal
Silver	00:45–00:54	--
Bronze	00:00–00:44	Cinematic

The trick to mastering this challenge is to anticipate the next combo before it begins. With each successful combo you execute, you will extend the timer by a few seconds. The goal is to execute all 26 combos so quickly and fluidly that you extend the timer past 1:05 by the time you finish the last combo. Practice the combos before starting, and begin the next combo as soon as it appears on the screen.

Study the following table and master the combos in the order they appear in the table; it's the same order as they appear in the Combat Trial.

THE MASTERS AT LUCASARTS SAY...

You must be Saber Rank 3 before attempting to attain Platinum rank.

All combos must be performed flawlessly. If you mess up on any combo, restart the challenge.

You successfully gain completion once you've pressed the required buttons, so it isn't necessary to wait until Starkiller has finished his animation. As long as all the button prompts show that you've successfully performed a combo, then time is added and the "combos remaining counter" is decreased.

THE MASTERS AT LUCASARTS SAY... (continued)

Using Force Dash to cancel out of Starkiller's animation will help achieve a time above 1:07, though it is not required for 1:05.

You can execute all combos that come after aerial combos as soon as Starkiller lands on the ground.

Combo	Xbox 360	PS3
Lightsaber Combo 2	X, X, X	■, ■, ■
Leaping Slash 3	A, X, X, X	×, ■, ■, ■
Saber Blast	X, B	■, ●
Lightning Strike	X, Y	■, ▲
Saber Sling	X, X, B	■, ■, ●
Saber Smash 1	X, X, Y	■, ■, ▲
Saber Slam 1	X, X, X, B	■, ■, ■, ●
Saber Smash 2	X, X, X, Y	■, ■, ■, ▲
Aerial Ambush 1	X, X, X, B (hold)	■, ■, ■, ● (hold)
Aerial Ambush Flurry 1	X, X, X, B (hold), X, X, X	■, ■, ■, ● (hold), ■, ■, ■
Aerial Blast 2	X, X, X, B (hold), X, B	■, ■, ■, ● (hold), ■, ●
Aerial Shock 2	X, X, X, B (hold), X, Y	■, ■, ■, ● (hold), ■, ▲
Aerial Assault 3	X, X, X, B (hold), X, X, B	■, ■, ■, ● (hold), ■, ■, ●
Aerial Assault 4	X, X, X, B (hold), X, X, Y	■, ■, ■, ● (hold), ■, ■, ▲
Lightsaber Combo 4	X, X, X, X, X	■, ■, ■, ■, ■
Saber Slam 2	X, X, X, X, B	■, ■, ■, ■, ●
Saber Smash 3	X, X, X, X, Y	■, ■, ■, ■, ▲
Aerial Ambush 2	X, X, X, X, B (hold)	■, ■, ■, ■, ● (hold)
Aerial Ambush Flurry 2	X, X, X, X, B (hold), X, X, X	■, ■, ■, ■, ● (hold), ■, ■, ■
Aerial Ambush Flurry 3	X, X, X, X, B (hold), X, B	■, ■, ■, ■, ● (hold), ■, ●
Aerial Ambush Flurry 4	X, X, X, X, B (hold), X, Y	■, ■, ■, ■, ● (hold), ■, ▲
Aerial Ambush Flurry 5	X, X, X, X, B (hold), X, X, B	■, ■, ■, ■, ● (hold), ■, ■, ●
Aerial Ambush Flurry 6	X, X, X, X, B (hold), X, X, Y	■, ■, ■, ■, ● (hold), ■, ■, ▲
Lightsaber Combo 5	X, X, (pause), X, X	■, ■ (pause), ■, ■
Lightsaber Combo 6	X, X, X (pause), X, X, X	■, ■, ■ (pause), ■, ■, ■
Lightsaber Combo 7	X, X, X, X (pause), X, X, X, X	■, ■, ■, ■ (pause), ■, ■, ■, ■

CHALLENGE 2: KAMINO DRILLGROUNDS TRIAL

Rank	Requirement	Reward
Platinum	04:00 or over	—
Gold	03:00–03:59	Protection Saber Crystal
Silver	02:00–02:59	—
Bronze	01:30–01:59	Cinematic

This challenge requires you to endure past the time requirement before 20 stormtroopers dash from the surrounding portals to the exits. Scattered throughout the drillgrounds are dozens of explosive canisters. Use the quick-turn camera to scour the area around you, and spot the stormtroopers as they emerge from the portals. When they do, use your Force powers to eliminate them before they reach the exits.

JEDI WISDOM

Use the explosive canisters to destroy big batches of enemies quickly.

THE MASTERS AT LUCASARTS SAY...

Upgrade to Rank 2 or, preferably, Rank 3 of Force Lightning before starting.

Since enemies stagger into the arena between their two entrances, you'll need to be at an entrance when a group spawns. This means that you'll be running between the two entrances as fast as possible. Once the enemies have run through the blue force field you're currently waiting at, press the Lightning button twice. If you angle yourself properly toward the enemies, you can stun up to five stormtroopers at once. Two quick taps of the Lightning button can kill them quickly. After you dispatch one group, run to the entrance of the next group as fast as you can and repeat.

CHALLENGE 3: DEADLY PATH TRIAL

Rank	Requirement	Reward
Platinum	Less than 00:18	—
Gold	00:23–00:19	Corrosion Saber Crystal
Silver	00:43–00:24	Kota costume
Bronze	01:00–00:44	Cinematic

The Deadly Path Trial requires you to travel across several floating platforms in a short amount of time. To do so, you must skip over every other platform, beginning with the first one. Double-jump dash from platform to platform, spending little to no time on the platforms when you touch down. Try to maintain a straight line across the long chasm until you reach the exit.

THE MASTERS AT LUCASARTS SAY...

Use Dashing Blast constantly (Force Dash + Force Push).

At the start of the challenge, you can jump over the second floating platform and Dash Blast to the third one, allowing you to skip the second one. This can save you nearly two seconds.

CHALLENGE 4: DEFLECTION TRIAL

Rank	Requirement	Reward
Platinum	06:00 or over	—
Gold	04:00–05:59	Life Drain Saber Crystal
Silver	02:00–03:59	Rebel Soldier costume
Bronze	01:00–01:59	Cinematic

In the Deflection Trial, you're tasked with deflecting volleys of incoming missiles from AT-MPs and thermal detonators from AT-STs on a platform opposite your own. If they blast you off the platform or destroy you, the challenge is over. Use Force Grip to throw incoming missiles back at the AT-MPs, then dash away from the other incoming missiles as your Force Energy replenishes. When AT-STs begin to appear with the AT-MPs, use the AT-MPs' missiles against the larger walkers and take it out first. Maximize the amount of time the walkers remain on the opposite platform, and eliminate all but one for every wave. When only one walker remains, allow it to live longer by simply tossing its projectiles away. When another one joins it, destroy the first. Repeat this process until you've achieved your desired rank.

THE MASTERS AT LUCASARTS SAY...

Use Block to deflect missiles.

Missiles can be blocked with one tap of the Block button, but only when they are coming at you in quick succession. You can also block them by pressing the Block button at the right time when each missile arrives; however, using one Block is easier when available, especially if five missiles are headed your way. In some cases, when five or more missiles are arriving in quick succession, only two or three taps of the Block button are necessary to deflect all of the missiles.

Force Grip is very useful. You can grip missiles from a distance and throw them quickly, and you can also aim toward other units, like the AT-ST. Use this when your health is low so that you can quickly kill enemies to regain some life.

CHALLENGE 5: RETRIEVAL TRIAL

Rank	Requirement	Reward
Platinum	00:40 or less	—
Gold	00:41–00:50	Focus Saber Crystal
Silver	00:51–01:10	—
Bronze	01:11–01:40	Cinematic

This challenge is particularly tricky. Like the Deadly Path Trial, you must traverse a series of platforms toward your goal. In this challenge, though, you must travel over the platforms as they circle around in midair, retrieve a holocron, then backtrack to the starting area. To get through this challenge quickly, double-jump dash across the platforms as they circle around. Save time by leaping from the platforms as they circle toward each other.

The path across the platforms turns right, then left as you reach the holocron. To get across the platform course quickly, double-jump dash onto the first set of platforms as they rotate to the right. As soon as you land, double-jump dash to the stationary pillar on the right. The next set of platforms should be floating left as you land; double-jump dash across the next floating platform as it floats left, and land on the next pillar. This time, double-jump dash across the next two sets of platforms, bypassing the stationary pillar, then finally make a final double-jump dash onto the pillar with the holocron. To return, follow the rotating platforms back to the beginning, bypassing the first and second stationary pillars.

THE MASTERS AT LUCASARTS SAY...

Check out the "Speed" tips in this chapter for basic strategy.

Keep in mind that there is always a platform to jump to if you move quickly; you should never have to wait for a rotating platform to stop.

CHALLENGE 6: DOMINATION TRIAL

Rank	Requirement	Reward
Platinum	00:55	—
Gold	00:56–01:30	Regeneration Saber Crystal
Silver	01:31–02:00	Neimoidian costume
Bronze	02:01–03:00	Cinematic

The Domination Trial is a very unique challenge. In this contest, you must defend a small green circle at the center of a circular platform. Attached are three walkways that enemies use to attack you and infiltrate the green circle. As long as the green circle is free of enemies, the timer to the screen's left counts down. If an enemy steps into the circle and turns it red, the timer stops counting down until the foe is removed from the circle. The timer begins at 55 seconds, so in order to score Platinum rank, you must not allow a single enemy to step into the circle the entire time.

Upgrade your Force Repulse to maximum before starting this challenge, and equip both Focus crystals. Stand near the center of the circle and use Repulse attacks to repel the attackers before they set foot in the circle.

THE MASTERS AT LUCASARTS SAY...

Mind Tricking enemies when they are near their spawn point will sometimes cause them to fight enemies as they spawn near the outer edges. Be careful, though, since a Mind Tricked enemy may direct himself to an enemy who is near the center circle

Rely heavily on Force Repulse and Force Push to keep enemies away.

Focus saber crystals are extremely useful, as they allow you to consume less Force Energy with increased Force Power usage.

CHALLENGE 7: TERROR TRIAL

Rank	Requirement	Reward
Platinum	01:15	—
Gold	01:30	Wisdom Saber Crystal
Silver	01:40	Terror Trooper Costume
Bronze	02:00	Cinematic

In this challenge, you're locked in a small, cramped room as five waves of terror spider droids and terror troopers attack you. Use Force Repulse to fend off the terror spider droids, then Mind Trick the terror troopers to stun them. While they are stunned, attack them with saber combos and take them out. If they fall to the ground, stab them to finish them off quickly.

THE MASTERS AT LUCASARTS SAY...

Use three blasts of Force Repulse during the first wave to clear out all the spider droids; there is one in the center as soon as the level begins, one about four feet to the left of your starting position, and another about four feet to the right of your starting position.

Wait for terror troopers to teleport to your position, and quickly fry them with Force Lightning. As they are stunned, charge Force Repulse and release it on them.

CHALLENGE 8: THE CLONING SPIRE TRIAL

Rank	Requirement	Reward
Platinum	00:35 or less	—
Gold	00:25–00:34	Incineration Saber Crystal
Silver	00:15–00:24	Saber Guard Costume
Bronze	00:00–00:14	Cinematic

Like the Combat Trial, your goal is to continuously increase the time limit until the trial is over. To increase the time limit, destroy the rising and falling clone tanks on each platform. Watch the tanks as they pop up out of the platforms, then dash toward each one and slash it just as it pops out. The tanks rise and fall in a counterclockwise or clockwise pattern, so follow the edge of the platforms and destroy the tanks one by one.

Don't cut across the center of the platform; you'll only waste time. Instead, maintain one steady, circular path around the edge as you shatter the tanks.

THE MASTERS AT LUCASARTS SAY...

Saber Throw is necessary to attain Platinum rank. Timing this properly can destroy up to five tanks at once.

CHALLENGE 9: SCOUT TROOPER TRIAL

Rank	Requirement	Reward
Platinum	00:30 or less	—
Gold	01:00–00:31	Disintegration Saber Crystal
Silver	01:30–01:01	—
Bronze	03:00–01:31	Cinematic

To complete this challenge, you must speed down a long path that is watched over by scout troopers, and collect five holocrons along the way. The troopers immediately hone in on you, tracking you with their rifles and firing as soon as they've got a positive lock on you. As soon as you pick up a holocron, the scout troopers disappear. Also on the path are bright blue areas on the floor. Whenever you stand on these, a small protective barrier pops out of the ground.

As soon as you begin, dash out of the starting area and make a beeline for the first holocron. Bypass the barrier spot on the right, and dash straight at the holocron. You'll barely reach it before the scout troopers fire at you. On the next section, dash straight to the barrier area and let the scout troopers fire into the short wall before setting out after the next holocron. In the third area, use the boulders as protection from the troopers. On the final area, use Force Push blasts to knock away the scout troopers as you approach them before reaching the final holocron.

THE MASTERS AT LUCASARTS SAY...

Always Dash Blast throughout the entire trial.

Run to the goal in as direct a path as possible; there are some gaps between sections that you can jump over, which means it is not necessary to follow the direct path for a Platinum medal.

CHALLENGE 10: GAUNTLET TRIAL

Rank	Requirement	Reward
Platinum	03:30	—
Gold	03:00–03:29	Shock Saber Crystal
Silver	02:30–02:59	Sith Acolyte Costume
Bronze	00:00–02:29	Cinematic

The final challenge is split up into four small battle arenas. Before the blue force field to the next area is removed, you must first defeat the batch of enemies in the area you're in. The first area houses a carbonite war droid and a group of riot troopers. Tear away the droid's shield and Mind Trick the troopers to turn

on each other and the droid. You can also allow the war droid to freeze the troopers, then shatter them. The next area has a group of jumptroopers and a terror giant. Fry the jumptroopers, then focus on the giant.

Wave three has scout troopers and an incinerator droid. Eliminate the scout troopers first, then bring down the war droid. Use Force Lightning attacks and Force Grip to hurl its fireballs back at it. The final wave has Sith acolytes and terror troopers. Turn the troopers with Mind Trick and help them slice through the Sith acolytes.

THE MASTERS AT LUCASARTS SAY...

GATE 1

1. **Rip off the carbonite war droid's shield.**
2. **Jump into the air and use a charged Saber Throw on the carbonite war droid; repeat until you destroy it.**
3. **Use Force Grip and Force Lightning grenade to take out the other enemies.**

GATE 2

1. **Mind Trick the jumptroopers.**
2. **Double-jump over the terror giant's body and use a charged Saber Throw against him. Position the Saber Throw so that you're floating above the enemy.**
3. **Repeat**

GATE 3

1. **Kill all the scout troopers first.**
2. **Rip off the incinerator war droid's shield.**
3. **Use charged Saber Throws to destroy it.**

GATE 4

1. **Mind Trick the terror troopers when possible.**
2. **If possible, stun the terror troopers if you can't Mind Trick them.**
3. **Try to take out the Sith acolytes immediately; their long-range attacks can be devastating, especially if you're busy dealing with terror troopers.**

Collector's Edition Trials

The following three trials are available only if you purchased the Collector's Edition of *Star Wars: The Force Unleashed II.*

CORE DESTRUCTION TRIAL

Rank	Requirement	Reward
Platinum	01:05 or more	—
Gold	00:45–01:04	—
Silver	00:30–00:44	—
Bronze	00:00–00:29	—

This challenging trial takes place in the same arena where you battled the terror walker. You must lift four pylons out of the ground near the center generator to complete the trial. Unfortunately, the swarms of terror spider droids and other enemies will do everything they can to keep you from doing this. As you lift pylons out of the ground, more and more enemies will spawn. You'll face spider droids, Sith acolytes, riot troopers, terror troopers, and even a terror walker! The key to this trial is speed. The quicker you move from pylon to pylon, the more time you'll rack up for a better score.

Use spider droids to replenish your health, and keep a close eye on your Force Energy. Mind Trick riot troopers so that they can defend you—or at least leave you alone—while you lift the pylons out of the ground. When the terror walker spawns, try to lure it away from the final pylon, then dash back to the pylon and lift it out of the ground.

JEDI WISDOM

Don't worry if the terror spider droids try to swipe at you while you're lifting the pylons. Their swipe attacks can't interrupt you. However, their leaping "hug" attacks will cause you to drop the pylon instantly.

THE MASTERS AT LUCASARTS SAY...

Use Repulse often.

Avoid killing enemies besides the spider droids; your goal is to move quickly between pylons and lift them as soon as possible.

Allow terror troopers to teleport to your location when you are standing near a pylon. After they arrive, quickly stun them with Force Lightning. As they are stunned, they act as a temporary shield against enemy attacks.

Position yourself so that a pylon is between you and a Sith acolyte. Otherwise, they will continue to use their long-range attacks and prevent you from lifting the pylon out of the ground.

TOWER OF DEATH TRIAL

Rank	Requirement	Reward
Platinum	01:30 or more	—
Gold	01:15–01:29	—
Silver	00:30–01:14	—
Bronze	00:00–00:29	—

Like the Gauntlet Trial, you must destroy several waves of enemies in this challenge. However, this time you must defeat the waves of enemies on a series of rising concentric rings. After defeating the enemies on the first ring, the next ring will lower, delivering more enemies. This continues until you reach the final batch of enemies. On the first few rings, use Force Grip to hurl foes across the gap to the opposite side of the ring and destroy their comrades. Use Force Throw, Repulse, and Push to quickly knock enemies off the rings.

If you have Repulse maxed out to Level 3, you can instantly disintegrate foes with a single Repulse blast! When you reach the final level, use Mind Trick to distract the riot troopers, and bounce the AT-MPs' grenades back at them.

THE MASTERS AT LUCASARTS SAY...

Use Grip and Saber Throw on the first three rings to quickly dispatch enemies.

On the fourth ring, jump above the group of melee fighters and use a Charge Repulse; this will destroy all of the them.

On the top level, stand near the platform's edge so that you're a good distance away from the AT-MPs. Use the walkers' missiles against them from a distance by bouncing them back at the mechanical menaces. You can also use Lightning Grenade on the AT-MPs by using the melee fighters as your grenades.

JEDI WISDOM

You can grab an enemy or item with the Force, then zap them to charge them, effectively turning them into a charged grenade. Once charged, they can be tossed.

THE TRIAL OF AGILITY

Rank	Requirement	Reward
Platinum	00:10 or less	—
Gold	00:11–00:12	—
Silver	00:13–00:15	—
Bronze	00:16--00:30	—

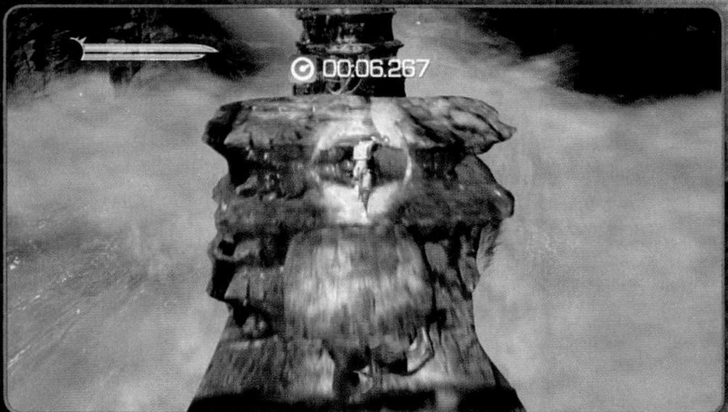

This trial is very similar to the Retrieval Trial and the Deadly Path Trial. In this trial, however, you must navigate a long, straight row of platforms in as short a time as possible. Refrain from using double-jump, and stick solely to Dashing Blast to speed past the platforms as quickly as possible. If you miss a platform, restart the entire trial for a better time.

THE MASTERS AT LUCASARTS SAY...

- Use Dashing Blast constantly (Dash + Push).
- At the start of the challenge, you can jump over the second floating platform and Dash Blast to the third one, allowing you to skip the second one. This can save you about two seconds.
- Refer to the Speed tips above to achieve your desired time.

MULTIPLAYER MODE (WII ONLY)

The following section covers the multiplayer mode in the Wii version of the game. Since every fight is different, this section will provide tips and tricks for each battle arena and general strategy for each duelist.

Basics

ATTRIBUTE RATINGS

Each of the following fighters is rated on a scale of one to three in Power, Speed, and Hit Points. Power is a combatant's ability to deal damage—the higher the rating, the more damage they inflict with each strike. Speed measures how quickly a fighter moves around the battle arena, while Hit Points indicates how much damage a fighter takes with each attack.

SPECIAL ATTACKS AND FORCE POWERS

Each fighter also has two special types of attacks—special attacks and Force powers. Force powers require blue Force Energy tanks to execute, while special attacks are simply assaults that are more powerful than standard attacks; they don't require anything to execute.

JEDI WISDOM

The longer you charge a Force power, the most powerful its effects will be. However, you can only charge your Force Power if you have at least one of three Force Energy tanks.

Duelists

STARKILLER

Power	Speed	Hit Points	Special Attack	Force Power
Level 2	Level 2	Level 2	Saber Throw	Force Lightning

Starkiller is a good, all-around fighter. With midlevel ratings across all three attributes, he'll always be able to hold his own in nearly any fight. His Saber Throw makes him a great long-range combatant, while Force Lightning is the perfect tool for stunning speedy foes.

DARTH VADER

Power	Speed	Hit Points	Special Attack	Force Power
Level 3	Level 1	Level 3	Heavy Attack	Force Choke

With a lethal Power rating of three and a Hit Point rating to match, Vader is a tough fighter to take on. Not only can he dish out major damage, but he can take it as well. When charged to its maximum, Force Choke can become a one-hit kill on many rivals. The only downside to Vader is his slow speed and short-range special attack. Speedier enemies can employ hit-and-run tactics and whittle down the powerful Dark Lord.

MARIS BROOD

Power	Speed	Hit Points	Special Attack	Force Power
Level 2	Level 3	Level 2	Saber Throw	Force Repulse

Maris Brood, once an apprentice to the much-respected Shaak Ti, has always been torn between the light and the dark side. Despite her inner turmoil, she's managed to become a formidable warrior skilled in the ways of the Force. She uses her excellent speed to complement her better-than-average Power and Hit Points. Use her Saber Throw to keep enemies at a distance, and use her speed to rush in and attack. Her Force Repulse is also helpful in keeping more powerful enemies at bay or knocking foes off platforms.

171

Starkiller

Darth Vader

Maris Brood

ASAJJ VENTRESS

Power	Speed	Hit Points	Special Attack	Force Power
Level 3	Level 1	Level 2	Saber Throw	Sith Confusion

Asajj Ventress is a deadly warrior. Her impressive Power makes her very deadly with her lightsabers. Coupled with her midlevel Hit Points, Ventress can stand toe-to-toe with many powerful adversaries. Like Vader, however, she's slow and susceptible to hit-and-run tactics. Luckily, her ability to mete out damage will make foes think twice about getting in close. If enemies choose to keep a distance, Ventress can still lash out with Saber Throw.

Ventress is also the only combatant with the Sith Confusion power. When used, it causes the targeted fighter's Wii Remote to act unpredictably. Use this ability against highly skilled fighters to give yourself an edge; attack while the affected enemy is scrambling around!

RAHM KOTA

Power	Speed	Hit Points	Special Attack	Force Power
Level 2	Level 1	Level 3	Spin Attack	Force Push

Having defeated everything that Baron Tako had to throw at him, Kota takes his Jedi skills into the multiplayer arenas. Master Kota may be blind, but he's tough as nails. As evidenced by his superb Hit Point rating, Kota can take a beating better than most. With powerful skills like Spin Attack and Force Push, Kota can keep foes at bay or shove them off the arena floor.

BOBA FETT

Power	Speed	Hit Points	Special Attack	Force Power
Level 1	Level 2	Level 1	Thermal Detonator	Missile Barrage

Boba Fett's weapon of choice is the EE-3 Carbine Rifle. That makes Boba Fett the perfect long-range fighter. Use his blaster pistol to fire on enemies from across the arena, and hurl Thermal Detonators when they attempt to get close. Perhaps no other attack is as dangerous as Boba Fett's Missile Barrage. When it is charged to full, Boba can rain missiles on enemies anywhere in the arena, causing near-instant death.

Unlike other fighters, Boba Fett is the only one who can hover in midair rather than double-jump. Hold the Jump button while in the air to hover temporarily.

TERROR TROOPER

Power	Speed	Hit Points	Special Attack	Force Power
Level 2	Level 3	Level 1	Heavy Attack	Cloaked Fury

When it comes to hit-and-run tactics, no other enemy is better suited for it than the terror trooper. Its phenomenal Speed and great Power ratings make it perfect for attacking enemies when they least expect it and retreating to safety before they can retaliate. The only downside is the trooper's weak Hit Point rating. Luckily, the trooper is well equipped to minimize damage. Its Cloaked Fury power allows it to retreat when necessary and avoid enemy aggression, while its Heavy Attack can damage foes that get too close.

PROXY

Power	Speed	Hit Points	Special Attack	Force Power
Level 1	Level 1	Level 1	Shape Change	Self-Destruct

PROXY is, by far, the weakest warrior in the game, but he is also the most versatile. Initially, the Level 1 ratings across the board reveal little reason for PROXY to be atop the list of fighters. However, upon closer inspection, you see that PROXY is a skilled fighter's best friend. PROXYs' Shape Change ability allows him to transform into any of the above-mentioned fighters. Not only will he take their appearance, but he'll also gain their special attacks and Force powers for a limited time. PROXY is the perfect fighter for players who can excel using multiple characters.

Battle Arenas

MUSTAFAR INDUSTRIAL COMPLEX

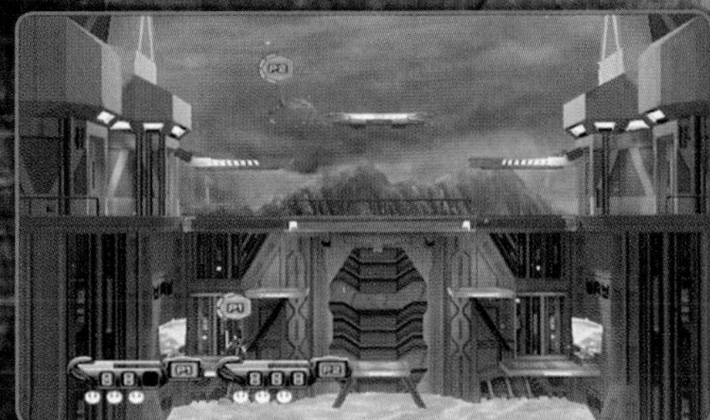

In this arena, you battle within one of the smelting plants of a former Separatist industrial complex, where various minerals are harvested from the deadly lava.

This is the largest battle arena. It extends high up the complex as the lava below slowly fills up. Though there are plenty of platforms to fight on and climb up, all it takes is a nudge to send enemies falling into the lava below.

JABBA'S SAIL BARGE

The infamous gangster Jabba the Hutt has arranged a battle royale for his amusement above the arid sands of Tatooine.

Jabba's Sail Barge is a dangerous place for a fight. Not only does it consist of a barge and four rickety platforms, but Jabba's place of business is constantly under attack! Rivals zoom by and fire on the barge, blasting the rickety platforms to pieces. If you're anywhere near the targeted platform, you'll take damage too.

JEDI WISDOM

Even though the bottom level of the barge looks solid, you can actually cross through it via a secret hall.

DEATH STAR BEAM TUNNEL

Utilize a variety of service catwalks and moving repulsorlifts at your peril within the Empire's planet-sized secret weapon: This battle station is operational!

This is one of the most dangerous spots for a fight. Not only is the arena small, but it also has a large firing tube right in the middle of it. The tube, in fact, is the size of nearly the entire room. If you're foolish enough to be standing in front of the tube when it fires, it'll obliterate you along with the platforms in the center of the room.

KAMINO OUTPOST

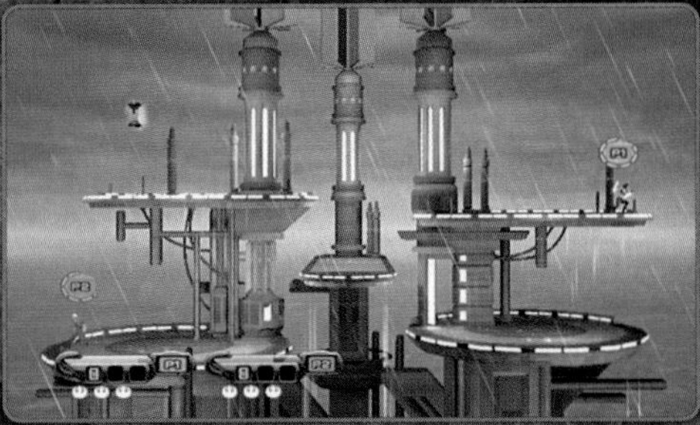

Make death-defying leaps from platform to platform on an isolated ocean outpost high above the raging seas of the storm-swept world of Kamino.

The towers of the Kamino Outpost are a great place to battle. The tiered platforms make for a great fighting arena, but the electrical currents that run across the top three platforms raise the stakes. Players can use these electrical currents to stun their prey before shoving them off the platforms.

TARKO-SE ARENA

This arena is the famed attraction of the pleasure planet Cato Neimoidia. Hundreds come to witness gladiatorial combat at its finest and most bloody.

You and your opponents are not the only combatants in the Tarko-se Arena; you must also contend with the massive Gorog shackled to the center of the arena. As you fight, the Gorog will lift its shackled hands and slam them down with no concern as to who might be under them when they come down. Fighters foolish enough to stand at the center of the arena also risk being eaten by the monster!

SALVATION HANGAR

Here you fight inside the hangar of the assault frigate Mk. 1 *Salvation* as it fights against the Imperial Navy.

This is the smallest battle arena. It also lacks environmental hazards, making it the best arena for combat purists. Fighters who want to prove their mettle with nothing more than a lightsaber, their hands, and Force powers need look no further.

UNLOCKABLES

This chapter covers all of the unlockables found in *Star Wars: The Force Unleashed II*. It will detail everything from achievements and trophies found in the Xbox 360 and PS3 versions of the game to the multiplayer unlockables of the Wii version!

Achievements and Trophies

While most of the achievements and trophies can be unlocked throughout a normal playthrough of the game, some will require you to accomplish specific tasks to unlock. To unlock them all, read the "Tips" section of the table for expert strategy!

Icon	Achievement	Description	Gamer Points	Trophy	Tips
	Escape from Kamino	Escape Kamino in Vader's TIE Advanced fighter.	20	Bronze	Unlocked during critical path playthrough.
	The Nemesis in Flames	Destroy the gunship.	20	Bronze	Unlocked during critical path playthrough.
	Bring Down the Giant	Defeat the Gorog.	20	Bronze	Unlocked during critical path playthrough.
	The Exter-minator	Defeat the terror walker.	20	Bronze	Unlocked during critical path playthrough.
	Crack the Sky	Destroy the Star Destroyer.	20	Bronze	Unlocked during critical path playthrough.
	Meeting of the Jedi	Reunite with Kota.	20	Bronze	Unlocked during critical path playthrough.
	Betrayed by Rage	Complete the game and choose the dark side ending.	20	Bronze	After beating the game, replay the last level to unlock both dark side and light side achievements
	Padawan	Complete the game on Easy difficulty.	50	Bronze	Defeat the game on Easy difficulty.
	Jedi Master	Complete the game on Hard difficulty.	50	Gold	Defeat the game on Hard difficulty.
	A Measure of Mercy	Complete the game and choose the light side ending.	20	Bronze	After beating the game, replay the last level to unlock both the dark side and light side achievements
	Jedi Knight	Complete the game on Medium difficulty.	50	Bronze	Defeat the game on Medium difficulty.
	Jedi Grand Master	Complete the game on Unleashed difficulty.	50	Gold	Defeat the game on Unleashed difficulty. Unlock the Unleashed difficulty setting by beating Hard difficulty first.
	Amplified	Kill 10 enemies with the lightning towers.	10	Bronze	While on your second visit to Kamino (The Return), use Force Grip to throw enemies into the lightning towers.
	Kamfetti	Kill five stormtroopers with the big fans on Kamino.	10	Silver	While on your first visit to Kamino (The Escape), use Force Grip to throw five enemies into the fans.
	Imperial Painball	Throw 10 enemies into the Kamino Plaza generators.	10	Bronze	While on your first visit to Kamino (The Escape) use Force Grip or Force Push to hurl 10 enemies into the small, red generators.
	Droid Rage	Control the terror walker and destroy all the terror biodroids.	10	Bronze	After taking control of the terror walker, use its lasers and stomp attacks to destroy the terror biodroids.
	Strike!	Kill three enemies with a single "bowling" ball.	10	Bronze	Unlock this during your visit to Baron Tarko's casino.
	Shattered	Shatter 10 enemies frozen in carbonite.	10	Bronze	Lure a carbonite war droid toward Imperial troopers while it's firing its carbonite cannon. Once the enemies are frozen, shatter them with Force Push or lightsaber attacks.
	Break the Bank	Smash up to 10 game machines.	10	Bronze	Smash these machines while in Baron Tarko's casino.
	Valet	Use Vader's TIE Advanced fighter to destroy the AT-MP.	10	Bronze	After arriving on Cato Neimoidia for the first time, use Force Grip to throw the TIE Advanced fighter at the attacking AT-MP.
	Stay On Target...	Get to the falling Gorog without crashing into any debris.	10	Bronze	Clear a path toward the falling Gorog using Force Push. Dodge the incoming debris and use Force Dash to reach the Gorog quicker.
	Master of Disaster	Break all of the coolant tanks aboard the Salvation.	10	Bronze	While on your first visit to the Salvation, destroy all of the coolant tanks. Don't forget to break the three coolant tanks in the side room with the holocron.
	Stakross Medal of Excellence	Destroy all lightning pylons on the Kamino dive.	10	Bronze	Immediately after leaving Vader in the opening, use Force Push to destroy the electric pylons on the way down. Don't worry about your Force Energy; you have an unlimited supply.
	Jedi Bomb Squad	Remove all of the terror spider bombs on the Salvation.	10	Bronze	After acquiring the second holocron from the small side room on the Salvation, use Force Repulse to destroy all of the red terror spider bombs in the room.

Icon	Achievement	Description	Gamer Points	Trophy	Tips
	"No match for a good blaster at your side, kid"	Kill 20 enemies using the turbolasers on the Kamino Drill Grounds.	10	Bronze	While in the Kamino Drill Grounds, lure 20 enemies into the red targeting reticle of the turboblasters overhead just before they fire. This will most likely require two visits to the Kamino Drill Grounds, so you may need to replay "The Escape" twice.
	Top of the World	Reach the top of the spire without falling once.	10	Bronze	Tread carefully while climbing the spire. There is no need to rush through this section.
	Champion	Complete all challenges with at least a Gold medal in each.	30	Gold	Skip to the Challenges section of this book for tips.
	Rookie	Complete all the challenges with at least a Bronze medal in each.	30	Bronze	Skip to the Challenges section of this book for tips.
	Challenger	Complete one challenge and receive at least a Bronze medal.	10	Bronze	Skip to the Challenges section of this book for tips.
	Hat Trick	Get a Gold medal on any three challenges.	30	Silver	Skip to the Challenges section of this book for tips.
	Platinum	Get a Platinum medal on any challenge.	30	Silver	Skip to the Challenges section of this book for tips.
	Competitor	Get a Silver medal on any five challenges.	20	Silver	Skip to the Challenges section of this book for tips.
	Unleashed	Activate Force Fury 10 times.	10	Bronze	Simply unlock Force Fury 10 times. This will unlock across multiple playthroughs.
	Enjoy the Trip See You Next Fall	Cause 50 enemies to fall to their deaths.	10	Bronzo	Use Mind Trick, Force Push, and Force Grip to send enemies falling to their demise.
	Maxed Out	Upgrade all powers to Rank 3.	30	Bronze	This requires multiple playthroughs to unlock.
	Use the Force, Luke	Complete any level using only Force powers.	20	Bronze	This is more easily unlocked after upgrading several Force powers. Once you do, replay the first level and use only Force powers to beat the level. Do not use your lightsaber.
	Lucky Streak	Defeat 300 consecutive enemies without dying.	20	Bronze	If you don't unlock this on your first playthrough—it should unlock by the midpoint of the second level—then replay the game on Easy difficulty after upgrading several Force powers.
	Sky Killer	Destroy 15 TIE fighters.	20	Bronze	Use Force Grip to destroy TIE fighters on Kamino and Cato Neimoidia.
	Arachnophobia	Destroy 200 terror spider droids	20	Bronze	Be very thorough as you progress through the Salvation on your first visit. Upgrade Force Repulse and use it to destroy terror spider droids.
	It Burns!	Disintegrate 15 enemies by throwing them into red force fields.	20	Bronze	This can be easily unlocked on the Kamino drillgrounds during The Escape. Use Force Grip and Force Push to throw enemies into the red force fields.
	Pied Piper	Entice 10 enemies to leap to their deaths with Mind Trick.	20	Bronze	Use Mind Trick as much as possible while on Kamino and Cato Neimoidia. Remember to do this while on high platforms so enemies will throw themselves over the edge.
	Holocron Hunter	Find every holocron.	40	Bronze	Use the maps and holocron sidebars described in the walkthrough to locate every holocron.
	Poor Bob	Force Grip a trooper, impale him with a lightsaber, zap him with Force Lightning, then throw him into an explosive object.	10	Bronze	This can be unlocked during The Escape from Kamino. Do this before upgrading your Force powers too much. Use Force Grip to lift the enemy into the air, then press the Attack button to impale him, and press the Force Lightning button to zap him before tossing him into an explosive object.
	Return to Sender	Kill AT-MPs by gripping their own missiles and throwing them back at them.	20	Bronze	Unlock this on Cato Neimoidia during your first encounter with an AT-MP. Use Force Grip to grab an incoming missile, then throw it back at the walker.
	Up, Up, and Away	Overload 20 jumptrooper jet packs.	20	Bronze	Use Force Lightning to fry 20 jumptrooper packs.
	Passive Aggressive	Parry and counter 10 melee attacks.	20	Bronze	Block just as an enemy is about to attack you in melee combat to parry the attack. Do this 10 times to unlock this Achievement/Trophy.
	Awww Yeah...	Perform every combat move in the game.	30	Silver	Execute all of the moves listed in the "Becoming Starkiller" chapter of this book.
	To the Face!	Reflect 20 missiles back at AT-MPs.	20	Bronze	If this doesn't unlock during the single-player campaign, use the Deflection Trial to finish it off.
	Specialist	Upgrade one Force power to Rank 3.	10	Bronze	This unlocks as soon as you upgrade one Force power. It can be unlocked during the first level.
	Fully Charged	Use an entire bar of Force power on a Lightning attack.	10	Bronze	Lock on to an enemy, preferably a war droid, and unleash an entire bar of Force Energy while blasting it with Lightning. If you're interrupted while attacking, allow your Force Energy to replenish, then try again.
	N/A	Earn all other trophies.	N/A	Platinum	This PS3-only Trophy unlocks only after acquiring all other above-listed trophies.

Challenge Unlockables

Nearly every challenge medal, from Bronze to Platinum, unlocks something special. See below to find out what!

Challenge	Bronze	Silver	Gold	Platinum
The Combat Trial	Experience points, cinematic awarded	Experience points	Experience points, Fury saber crystal awarded	Experience points
Kamino Drillgrounds Trial	Experience points, cinematic awarded	Experience points	Experience points, Protection saber crystal awarded	Experience points
Deadly Path Trial	Experience points, cinematic awarded	Experience points, Kota Costume awarded	Experience points, Corrosion saber crystal awarded	Experience points
Deflection Trial	Experience points, cinematic awarded	Experience points, Rebel Soldier Costume awarded	Experience points, Life Drain saber crystal awarded	Experience points
Retrieval Trial	Experience points, cinematic awarded	Experience points	Experience points, Focus saber crystal awarded	Experience points
Domination Trial	Experience points, cinematic awarded	Experience points, Neimoidian Costume awarded	Experience points, Regeneration saber crystal awarded	Experience points
Terror Trial	Experience points, cinematic awarded	Experience points, Terror Trooper Costume awarded	Experience points, Wisdom saber crystal awarded	Experience points
The Cloning Spire Trial	Experience points, cinematic awarded	Experience points, Saber Guard Costume awarded	Experience points, Incineration saber crystal awarded	Experience points
Scout Trooper Trial	Experience points, cinematic awarded	Experience points	Experience points, Disintegration saber crystal awarded	Experience points
Gauntlet Trial	Experience points, cinematic awarded	Experience points, Sith Acolyte Costume awarded	Experience points, Shock saber crystal awarded	Experience points
Core Destruction Trial	Experience points	Experience points	Experience points	Experience points
Tower of Death Trial	Experience points	Experience points	Experience points	Experience points
The Trial of Agility	Experience points	Experience points	Experience points	Experience points

Wii Multiplayer Unlockables

The only way to access new arenas and characters for multiplayer is to unlock them. See the following table to find out how to unlock everything in multiplayer!

JEDI WISDOM

After unlocking a cheat, access it by pausing the game and selecting "Cheats."

Unlockable	Description	Requirement
Kamino Outpost multiplayer arena	Fight on the Kamino Outpost in multiplayer	Unlocks when crossing lightning-switch-triggered bridge at end of Kamino: The Escape
Tarko-se multiplayer arena	Fight in Tarko-se arena in multiplayer	Unlocks upon reaching the Gorog
Salvation hangar multiplayer arena	Fight on the Salvation hangar in multiplayer	Unlocks upon reaching the terror walker boss
Rahm Kota multiplayer character	Fight as Rahm Kota in multiplayer	Unlocks upon reaching Dagobah
Boba Fett multiplayer character	Fight as Boba Fett in multiplayer	Unlocks upon reaching the Salvation: Hunting the Hunter
Terror trooper multiplayer character	Fight as a terror trooper in multiplayer	Unlocks upon reaching Into the Fray: Springing the Trap
PROXY multiplayer character	Fight as PROXY in multiplayer	Unlocks upon reaching the Darth Vader boss fight
Invulnerability cheat	Take no damage from attacks	Unlocks after collecting all holocrons
Unlimited Force cheat	Unlimited Force Energy	Unlocks after upgrading all Force Powers to maximum rank
Overwhelming Power cheat	Do incredible damage with each hit	Unlocks after upgrading all Force Powers to maximum rank
Insane difficulty	Take incredible damage from each hit	Unlocks after completing all levels on Unleashed difficulty

UNLOCKABLE NOTES

Costumes unlock at the end of each stage of the game.

The final stage has two unlocks after Darth Vader: one for the light side and one for the dark side.

If you're having a hard time locating all of the holocrons, Force tanks, bacta tanks, and crystals, refer to the level details page in-game (Pause menu) for a list of how many are in each level. These are different for Normal versus Unleashed difficultly. Of course, you can always use the walkthrough to locate all of the collectibles across all levels.

To get a 100 percent playthrough, you must get everything listed in the level description.

To get a 200 percent playthrough, you must beat each level and collect all the new collectibles for Unleashed difficulty, max out all Force powers and have both costumes from the light and dark side endings.